RMAN . IGOR ANDERSEN . BENI ARAPI . VAN AREND . GINA ARIAS . ANGELO ⬛URIN
CHAD BENNETT . **STEVE BENZ** . OLIVERA BERCE . ELKE BERGER ⬛⬛⬛⬛ELL
. MAURA BROUILLETTE . MATT BROWNELL . PHILLIP BR⬛⬛⬛⬛⬛⬛⬛⬛NT
CALLEVA . JOHN CAMPBELL . ANGEL CANTU . NICK CAP⬛⬛⬛⬛⬛⬛
DAVID CLOUGH . RICK COLAVECCHIO . TRESKA COLE . **JOHN C**⬛⬛⬛⬛ **CORNEIL**
⬛NO . **STU DAWSON** . **MARK DAWSON** . MICHAEL DAY . TIM ⬛EACON . **NEIL DEAN**
⬛NER . BILL DOYLE . **RIC DUMONT** . CHRISTINE DUNN . TRACY DUPONT . DAN DWYER
⬛R . STEPHANIE EVANS . KATHARINE FAVRET . TRACY FINLAYSON . JUSTIN FINNICUM
⬛OX . **NANCY FREEDMAN** . ANTONIO FURUKAWA . NICOLE GAENZLER . **DICK GALEHOUSE**
⬛US GORGATI . KEN GOULDING . TERRI GRAY-PEARCE . JIM GRESALFI . **MICHAEL GROVE**
⬛ESSICA HARRINGTON . TERRY HARRIS . **NANCY HARROD** . MARIA-ANNA HATZILIADES
⬛LD . LORI HESSAMFAR . **JOE HIBBARD** . **DAVE HIRZEL** . LIZ HIXSON . CHRIS HODGES
⬛ CHUNSHENG HUANG . JIANXIANG HUANG . ALEX HUSSEY . LAURA INCATASCIATO
⬛SHUSAK JANPATHOMPONG . SUNEETH JOHN . TRACEY JOHNSON . YU-JU KAO
⬛ KENNEY . TAEYEON KIM . TALA KLINCK . ELIZABETH KOSTOJOHN . WILLA KUH
⬛ DIANE LANDRY . **OWEN LANG** . MATT LANGAN . CHANG-KEUN LEE . LESLIE LEE
⬛SPRINGMAN LEE . PONTUS LINDBERG . CHRISTIANA LINERA . HANNAH LOOMIS
⬛ARSHALL . DAVID MARTIN . BILL MASSEY . ANIA MATTESON . TRAVIS MAZERALL
⬛ MCDONOUGH . FONTAINE MCFADDEN . **ALISTAIR MCINTOSH** . MATT MCKOUEN
⬛IDGLEY . REBECCA MIHELICH . **JAMES MINER** . JOSE MIRANDA . AL MININCLERI
⬛MOSES . NEDA MOVAGHAR . CAROL MOYLES . FRANCESCO MOZZATI . PAT MULLANEY
⬛MURA . PABLO NISTAL . GRACE NUGROHO . SCOTT ODOM . TAKAKO OJI . **DON OLSON**
⬛O . OSWALDO PALENCIA . CRYSTAL PALLESCHI . EUNJIN PARK . PHILIP PARSONS
⬛THEVEE . MICHELE PHELAN . **DENNIS PIEPRZ** . ADDIE PIERCE-MCMANAMON
⬛ SIMON RAINE . KATIE RAYMOND . ANNA REAVES . MARK REAVES . ROBYN REED
⬛TEVE ROSCOE . SUSANNAH ROSS . LUCILA ROSSO . CHRIS ROUSSEAU . ANN SALAS
⬛ SARAGA . ELIZABETH SARGENT . SASAKI 2008 . TREY SASSER . BRAD SAUNDERS
⬛AN . KELLY SCHOONMAKER . **TAD SHULTZ** . LARRY SCHWIRIAN . KAREN SERAFIN
⬛ETLER . LAURA SHIFLEY . KENT SHING . **SCOTT SMITH** . SUSIE SMITH . JOEL SMITH
⬛TEVENS . **TIM STEVENS** . **JIM SUKEFORTH** . DAN SULLIVAN . GAUTAM SUNDARAM
⬛CHARD TEPP . PHILIP THIBAUDEAU . NITZA THIEN . JEN THORNTON . ROBERT TITUS
⬛SON . LILLY VAZQUEZ . REBECCA VERNER . REETIKA VIJAY . ROBERTO VIOLA OCHOA
⬛MAN . **ALAN WARD** . DEBBIE WEST . STEVE WILSON . CATHERINE WINFIELD
⬛ ZEMPEL . DOU ZHANG . XIAOYANG ZHAO . BRIAN ZIEMBA . KATHRYN ZMRZLIK

sasaki intersection and convergence

edited by oscar riera ojeda   foreword by susan szenasy

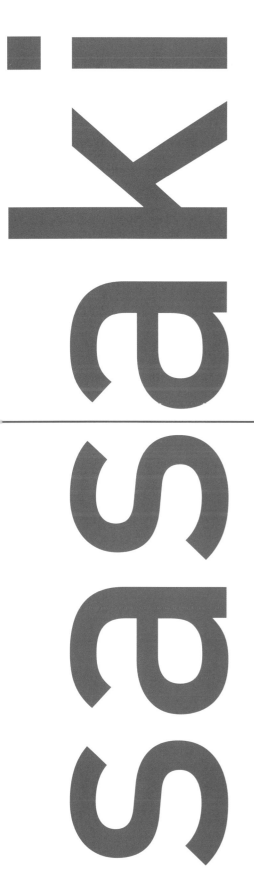

sasaki

intersection
AND convergence

ORO *editions*

Contents

007 Acknowledgements

008 Foreword by Susan Szenasy

010 Introduction

016 Spaces and Learning

134 Regenerative Cities

226 New Social Realities

322 SasakiGREEN

342 Sasaki Strategies

346 Selected Awards Since 2000

350 Project Credits

356 Book Credits

Spaces and Learning

018 Utah State Performance Hall
028 NTNU Strategy Plan
032 Monitor New York
036 Monitor San Francisco
038 University of Balamand
048 Potomac School Master Plan and Landscape
050 Wildcat Activity Center
054 Cal Poly Residential Suites
060 Henry C. Lee Institute of Forensic Science
062 Sacred Heart University
068 The Commons
078 Miller Nichols Library and Interactive Learning Center
082 Segundo Commons
086 West Campus Lands
090 St. Edward's Landscape
094 Glen Mor Student Apartments
098 Graduate School of Management
104 Grumbacher Sports and Fitness Center
108 Stony Brook Recreation Center
110 Arizona Student Recreation Center Expansion
112 UC Santa Barbara Recreation Center Expansion
118 Valparaiso Student Union
122 Purdue West Lafayette Master Plan
124 Residential and Student Life on Rose Hill Campus
128 Joseph Edward Gallo Recreation and Wellness Center

Regenerative Cities

136 Charleston Waterfront Park
144 Penn Connects: A Vision for the Future
152 Dallas Area Rapid Transitway
156 Charlotte Light Rail Transit
158 798 Arts District Vision Plan
162 Drexel Recreation Center
166 East Baltimore Neighborhood Plan
170 Detroit Civic Center Riverfront Promenade
172 The Wilmington Waterfront
182 Auraria Higher Education Center Campus Plan
186 Central Indianapolis Waterfront
194 Loyola Intercollegiate Athletic Complex
198 Providence 2020
204 Savannah East Riverfront Public Spaces
208 601 Congress Street Roof Garden
210 Harbor Point
214 Cincinnati Riverfront Park
218 Southworks

New Social Realities

228 2008 Beijing Olympic Green
236 Addison Circle Park
240 Agilent Technologies
244 Innovista Master Plan
252 RPI Stadium and Athletic Events Center
256 Thu Thiem New Urban District
262 Koeppel Community Sports Center
266 Caohai North Shore, Daguan Park Regeneration
270 Lashihai Conceptual Master Plan
274 The Village at Centennial Square
278 Philips Solid-State Lighting Solutions
280 Grand Resort Lagonissi
286 Lulu Island Vision Plan
292 Continuum
298 Hongxing Oceanfront Community
306 Sasaki Associates Offices
310 Student Resource Building

SasakiGREEN

324 Green Principles
326 Green Organization
328 Green Practice
330 GreenLAB
332 GreenRED
334 GreenDAY/Green NEWS

Acknowledgements

The kind of design Sasaki Associates practices—across multiple disciplines in the United States and the far corners of the world—would not be possible without our exceptionally engaged, passionate and visionary clients. To them we offer our sincere gratitude and wish for many future collaborations.

We owe an equally immeasurable debt to the many talented Sasaki employees, present and past, both within our various design disciplines and in other facets of the firm's practice.

We realize that design today requires the collaboration of many specialists, and so we thank the many consulting firms with which we have had the privilege to work.

A special thanks to Susan S. Szenasy, editor-in-chief of *Metropolis*, for being a believer in the firm and for writing the foreword to this book.

Walking the Green Walk

by Susan S. Szenasy

The rain is pouring in downtown Boston as our car heads for the Sasaki offices in Watertown where the firm's annual GreenDAY convocation is about to begin. Dennis Pieprz, principal, is driving. He informs me that a tent has been set up in the parking lot behind the offices to house nearly 300 people, including members of the Watertown office and others from Sasaki's San Francisco office, as well as some outside experts and clients. This multifaceted group will take part in discussing environment-related issues throughout the day. A handful of workshops has been organized—each centered on an existing project, each focused on the project's unique problems and needs. The design teams will work with expert advisors who have been invited to share their knowledge on everything from water to sunlight. And later that day, the whole firm will get involved in discussing each group's proposal.

We talk about the possibility of flooding in this low-lying spot near the Charles River. As we turn into the parking lot, I spy a large tent as well as some experiments embedded into the tarmac showing how various brands of pervious pavers behave under the local conditions. On this day in May 2006 I'm about to deliver the keynote to kick off GreenDAY.

The rain abates and people file into the tent—men and women of all stages of youth and maturity and many ethnicities. The day begins and I launch into my presentation which concentrates on the next generation of design ideas, as they manifest themselves in sustainable products, planning, buildings, interiors, and materials. Half way into my talk I feel water from the drenched pavement seep up my trouser legs. Afterwards, a lively discussion ensues, led by the various specialists from the many practice groups that make up the firm: architects, planners, urban designers, landscape architects, civil engineers, and interior and graphic designers. The conversation is clearly interdisciplinary; everyone seems at ease in voicing an opinion.

In this free-flowing idea exchange, I gather that the Sasaki designer is a committed collaborator, on easy terms with his or her fellow employees and appreciative of the value that outside specialists bring to the table. With the complexity and scale of many Sasaki projects, it's clear that every voice is essential to problem solving on a grand scale. For instance, there are lake- and waterfront developments from Chicago to Charleston. These involve everything from working with local environmental legislation to dredging healthy mud from one spot and moving it to the site where it will support the necessary vegetation. Then there is the pioneering work like the numerous LEED®-ND (Leadership in Energy and Environmental Design—Neighborhood Development) projects to test the limits of the U.S. Green Buildings Council's latest rating system. These mileposts are significant entries in the firm's portfolio.

GreenDAY is part of Sasaki's comprehensive in-house educational program which extends from the big picture to the minute detail. It is supported by a lively newsletter, GreenNEWS, which shares the firm's vision with all its employees—interior designers can learn about what makes a college campus green, planners find out how LEED®-CI (Commercial Interiors) enhances office workers' lives, and everyone celebrates the most committed biker in the firm. Also reported in the newsletter are the findings of Sasaki Green Laboratory, be these experiments with building or landscaping products in the parking lot or attempts to use non-toxic cleaning solvents for the office.

After my time in the big tent, I tour the office and watch people gather with their team leaders and consultants, in preparation for an afternoon of exploring the sustainability features of the project assigned to each group. As they run to join their colleagues, many stop to say a quick hello and to express their appreciation for my adding to their conversations.

I come away inspired by their passion and commitment to make the world a better place. The projects I have seen pay close attention to the natural and cultural environments they occupy, be they in Beijing or Santa Barbara. It is clear to me that the green story coming out of Sasaki is real, earnest, and informed.

As I settle in the Prius that takes me to the airport—Sasaki uses a green car service owned by a local man—I remember what it means to walk the green walk; there needs to be a commitment that embraces all of one's activities. When I ask the driver to tell me about his transport business, he speaks of the growing demand for hybrid cars in Boston and his own thriving car service, and then he points out that the graphics on the dashboard make transparent his vehicle's energy consumption. And so the dialogue we started in the tent continues.

Susan S. Szenasy is Editor in Chief of *Metropolis*, the award-winning magazine of architecture, culture, and design, a position she has held since 1986. She is recognized as a preeminent authority on sustainability and design. She was a long-time professor at New York's Parsons School of Design and is a visiting lecturer at universities across the U.S. Susan has authored several books including *The Home and Light*, and sits on numerous design boards and councils. Her recent awards include the 2007 Civitas August Heckscher Award for Community Service and Excellence and the 2008 Medallion of Honor by the Society of American Registered Architects/New York Council (SARA/NY). She holds an MA in Modern European History from Rutgers University, and lives in New York's East Village in a small loft, where she moved in 2001 to reduce her ecological footprint.

Intersection and Convergence: A New Context for Design

While many great design firms revolve around a single personality or a dominant aesthetic, Sasaki's distinctiveness derives from collaboration. In the wide-open, informal spaces of Sasaki's offices outside Boston—an agglomeration of rambling old mill buildings along the Charles River—sharing trumps privacy, informality upstages hierarchy, teaching is preferred to directing. The voices of experts in one discipline are welcome in another. In San Francisco, Sasaki's West Coast office perpetuates the same values.

The approach has been successful. After half a century, Sasaki has been able to concentrate its practice on projects that speak to a commitment to solid principles and enduring social values. Sasaki's careful attention to the public realm, whether it be in the planning and design of cities or the creation of better settings for higher education—integrating architecture, landscape, and planning—has won over 450 design awards. In the private sector, the firm's work has equally always stood for an integrated and substantive approach.

The informality, lack of hierarchy, and collective energy at Sasaki are not a recent by-product of contemporary culture. The values of an older and influential design firm are persistent, and contagious. In the early 1950's, while chair of Landscape Architecture at Harvard, Hideo Sasaki established in his fledgling firm a way of working across disciplines, integrating the multiple aspects of design that exemplified the best of American mid-century Modernism. The integration led to designs that were fresh, elegant, harmonious, and spirited. They had the clarity of Aaron Copland's music, and won an immediate appreciation that much of the American Modernist movement had to struggle for. As a manifestation of democratic values, the firm's work demonstrated that a collaborative, supportive, integrative, and invariably curious approach to work could produce dramatically successful results.

The impact of Sasaki Associates on design practice today is global. While Hideo Sasaki's vision of collaborative and interdisciplinary design was unique a half-century ago, today it has permeated much of the design profession, so that it is almost commonplace. Since 1953, close to 3,000 people from more than thirty-seven countries have worked at Sasaki Associates. They have taken the Sasaki vision of collaboration among disciplines with them, and like any good idea, it has achieved acceptance around the world—though it is unevenly practiced. Today, the concept of integrated design has joined a strong current that now runs through the public and private sectors, in business, education, medicine, and elsewhere, where the virtue of making connections across disciplines is constantly extolled—to the point of being a cliché, perhaps honored more than understood.

Like any good idea that has gained general acceptance, the concept of integrated design carries similar risks to the worst excesses of any design movement. What was challenging, witty, stimulating, provocative, even healthily disorienting in the design process, becomes a comfortable set of clichés, appealing to nostalgia, sentimentality, and predictable formulae. Sasaki has avoided this trap, perhaps largely because of a constant influx of new blood (often recent graduates from the world's top schools) but also because of its loose, flat hierarchy and its distributed ownership structure. Debate is constant, and unavoidable.

In the Crit Room at the top of the stairs in Sasaki's Watertown, Massachusetts, office, thirty to forty designers and planners gather every Monday morning to hear a colleague present a project. The project typically draws together a range of disciplines. Sometimes the presenter is just out of graduate school, presenting a thesis project. Sometimes a team is presenting progress on a multi-million dollar contract. Discussion follows, with muttered dissent mingling with enthusiastic applause, and persists through the office over coffee, lunch, e-mail, and instant messaging, and in chance conversations as staff members pass by a colleague's space on the way to a work session. Dialogue and learning are the lifeblood of the practice. Every day, almost everyone is learning something new, or forms a new association.

As the day progresses, questions about projects surface, opinions are sought, solutions are tested. The range of experience and expertise is huge. An education planner critiques the interpretation of program in an architectural project. An architect questions the materials and massing that will give life and form to a planner's diagram. Engineers question the feasibility of a landscape architect's poetic vision. Landscape architects remind architects of the complexities and unique characteristics of a site. Interior designers and environmental graphics experts suggest a fresh perspective. In this richness of interaction, the presence of professionals from thirty-seven countries, speaking close to thirty languages, makes itself felt. In place of an assumption of consensus, there is sensitivity to divergent opinion and an expectation of cultural variation.

While the continuum of an integrated practice is a major theme of this monograph, another theme is that the human brain has been rewired in the last twenty years, by technology and globalism. We think differently and we work differently. Our clients also think and work differently, and consequently have different expectations of the firm. We are less rigidly methodical, more intuitive; we leap from analysis to synthesis and back again. Our work is non-linear—rigorous, then impressionistic, then rigorous again. The Web has taught us that single-mindedness is not necessarily a virtue. We can incorporate a multitude of influences on our thought, barely captured in our peripheral vision. When we say blithely that design is more than design, we mean that successful design is a vigorous synthesis of a full spectrum of human concerns—aesthetic, cultural, economic, social, environmental. We have struggled to understand how technology can enrich our practice, rather than dumb it down and anesthetize it, and how it can support new approaches to problem identification and problem solving. We have worked to understand how we can best incorporate a range of new information at each stage of planning and design, and move the concept of an integrated practice to a new level, responsive to new demands. We have embraced the notion of sustainable design as a holistic approach that goes beyond environmental issues to include social, economic and aesthetic commitments.

While a monograph celebrating a dynamic and integrated design practice that has expanded the notion of integration would naturally resist organization and sequence, we have grouped projects under four main headings. These highlight the dramatic cultural shifts that our integrated practice has responded to more recently. Inevitably, many projects would sit comfortably under more than one of these headings, and this truth emphasizes the drive to adapt to new demands on integration.

The first heading, "Spaces and Learning," captures a major focus of our current practice: higher education. More than half of the firm's work is in this area, spanning the full range of disciplines. Universities and colleges aspire to integrate "mission and place" perhaps more than any other type of institution, and consequently draw most heavily on integrated planning and design. With the growing reality that learning is lifelong, and happens everywhere—and the observation that cities and campuses are becoming in many ways indistinguishable, with intertwined economies—new approaches to architecture, urban and campus planning are emerging, and new building types are evolving. Not only is the approach to design integrated and more multifaceted, but the problems that design and planning must address can no longer be segmented. Libraries are more like student centers; recreation centers are more like areas of learning and socializing.

Our second theme, "Regenerative Cities," responds to the growing impulse to recover and reinvent our concept of cities. Sasaki's recent practice has drawn on urban design, landscape architecture, planning, and architecture across a broad range of issues.

The urge to heal and re-create American cities devastated by urban renewal in the sixties and seventies, by suburban migration, and by the move away from an industrial economy, has led, for example, to transformative revitalization of abandoned industrial waterfronts. On the Pacific Rim, massive movement of peoples from rural isolation to mushrooming cities has created enormous challenges of preserving social and environmental quality, while accommodating rapid growth. In the Persian Gulf, sudden and unprecedented wealth creates tension between durable urban design supported by environmental awareness, and pressures for rapid expansion.

The third theme, "New Social Realities," can be seen at every scale. Globalism has shaped Sasaki's practice dramatically in the last two decades. We have designed a university committed to transparency and dialogue in the Middle East; we have planned the Beijing Olympics site, transforming Beijing; and we have established a new heart for Ho Chi Minh City. In the United States, we increasingly struggle to mitigate the effects of growing inequality through improvement of the public realm. In our architecture, we work to respond to the design challenges generated by technology and the erosion of hierarchy.

Finally, "Sustainability" is a theme deeply ingrained in the culture of Sasaki. The fragile and finite nature of the earth's resources shapes every decision the firm makes, from employee benefits and office locations, to corporate travel policy. This, too, is a legacy —Hideo Sasaki was an environmental pioneer in the firm's early work by insisting upon non-invasive interventions along fragile coastal areas, as well as the repair and regeneration of damaged ecosystems, particularly along the Carolina coast. Increasingly, every project is seen as an exercise in multifaceted sustainability—social, economic, and environmental—and this commitment draws deeply and necessarily on the collaborative environment sustained over the last half-century.

architectur
planning+u
strategic
landscape a
interior
eco-techno
graphic des

e

rban design
planning
architecture
design
logies
ign

spaces
and learning

Sasaki's concept of Spaces and Learning both encompasses and extends beyond the walls of academia. A learning space can be redefined, such as the new library at Morgan State University in Baltimore. At this traditionally African-American university, the new learning center is designed to accommodate a collaborative style of study while sharing a rich collection of African and African-American artwork with surrounding neighborhoods. Less obviously, a learning space can also be a corporate office on the East Coast that de-emphasizes hierarchy, while placing a premium on interaction among all levels of the organization. Thousands of miles away, on a stunning site overlooking the Mediterranean Sea, the landscape and architecture of the University of Balamand in Lebanon are put in service of the most urgent learning of all—understanding among the various ethnic and religious groups of the region.

Utah State University, Logan, Utah

The creation of a new School for the Arts at Utah State University was emblematic of the desire of individual faculty members and administrators to create a vibrant, multi-disciplinary environment where cross-fertilization of ideas and learning could be greatly enhanced. In this same spirit, Sasaki provided interdisciplinary services to the university comprising urban design, architecture, and landscape architecture to make the USU Arts Campus a reality.

The plan envisioned renovations, additions, and new buildings articulated around new and existing plazas and courtyards. The first implemented building, the Manon Caine Russell/ Kathryn Caine Wanless Performance Hall, followed the plan for the Arts District and is flanked by an entry plaza located at the district's gateway. The building combines the high acoustical qualities associated with world-class music venues and music instruction spaces for students.

An orthogonal concrete shell with eighteen-inch-thick concrete walls encloses the main performance space, whose height, shape, and materials were carefully considered for optimum sound qualities. A contrasting zinc panel-coated entrance pavilion has origami-like folded volumes that suggest a melding of the man-made and the natural—precise architectural geometry that also recalls primordial tectonic forces that formed the surrounding Bear River Mountains. By day, triangular skylights angle light into interior spaces; at night, the pavilion faces the outdoor piazza and is dramatically lit, highlighting playful splayed columns in a pattern suggesting musical notes. To lend a sense of procession and ritual consistent with the university's heavy commitment to arts education, Sasaki conceived an entry precinct with an alée of native trees and a series of pea-stone fields that lead from one of the main campus portals into the new piazza.

top left Bear River Mountains

above and right entrance pavilion

As part of a master plan anticipating strong university growth in the next decade, a process articulating a vision for a cross-disciplinary arts district was forged by Sasaki. This vision created strong interior connections between departments, as well as vibrant meeting places at the café, galleries, and open media studios that would allow for the essential exchange of ideas between departments, professors, students, and the public.

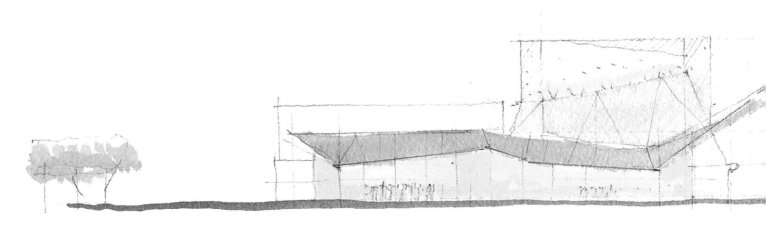

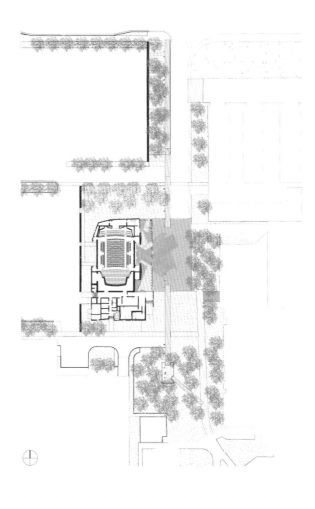

above first floor and site

below arts district masterplan

bottom left pavilion sketch

left and following spreads pavilion exterior and interior views

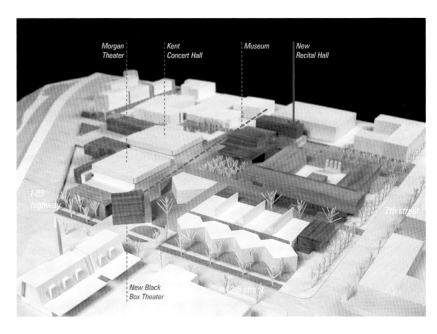

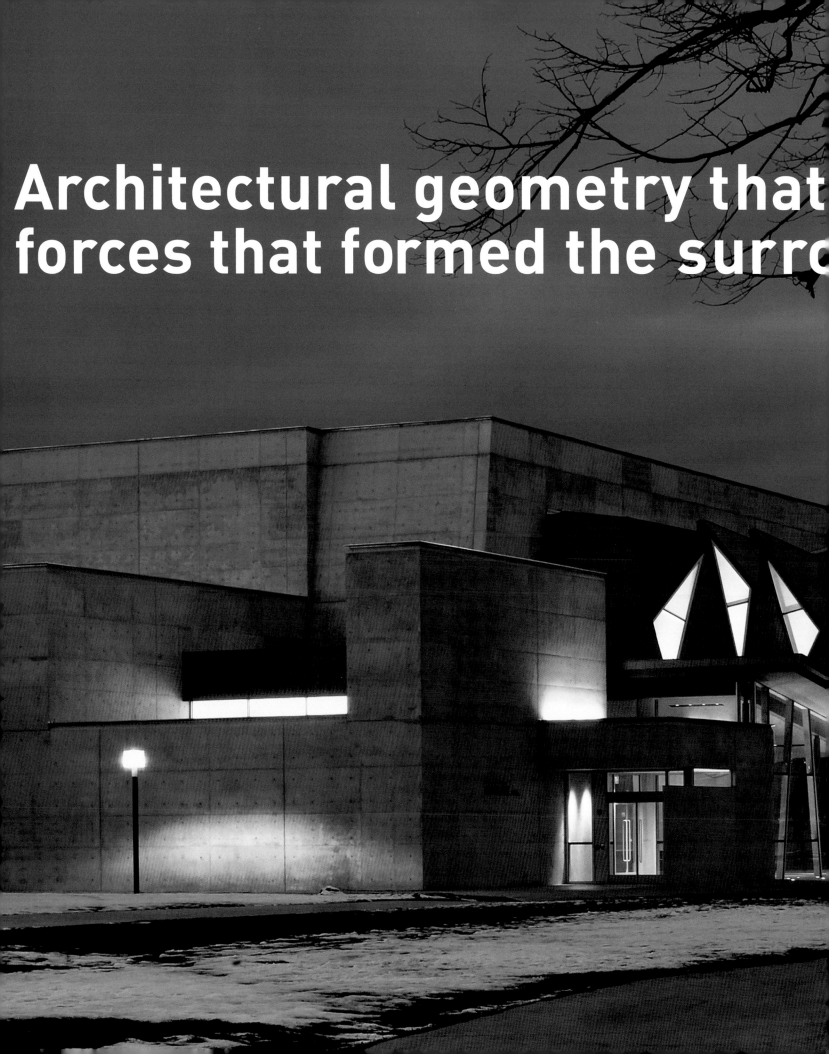

Architectural geometry that
forces that formed the surro

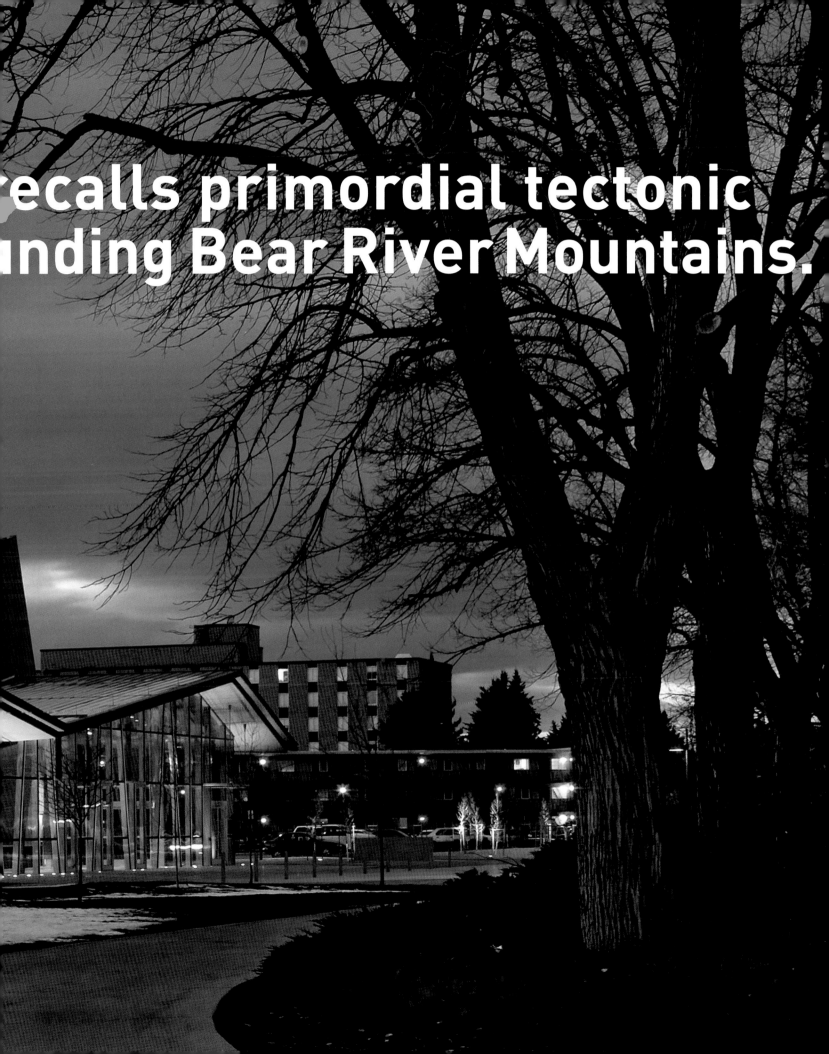
recalls primordial tectonic
...nding Bear River Mountains.

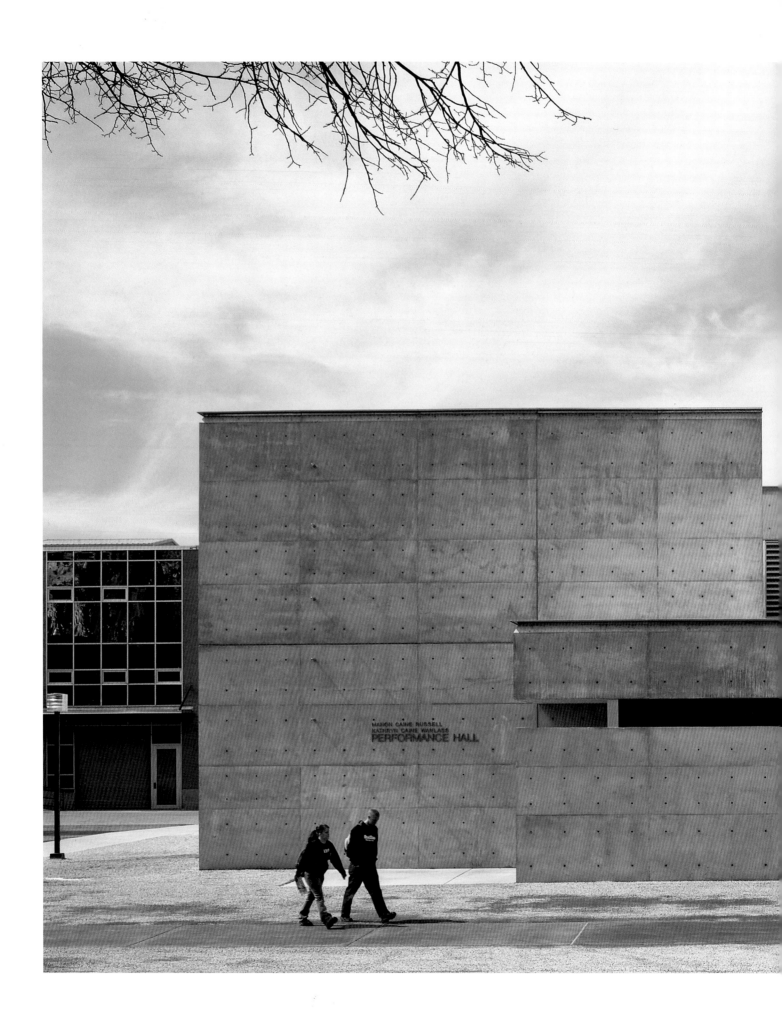

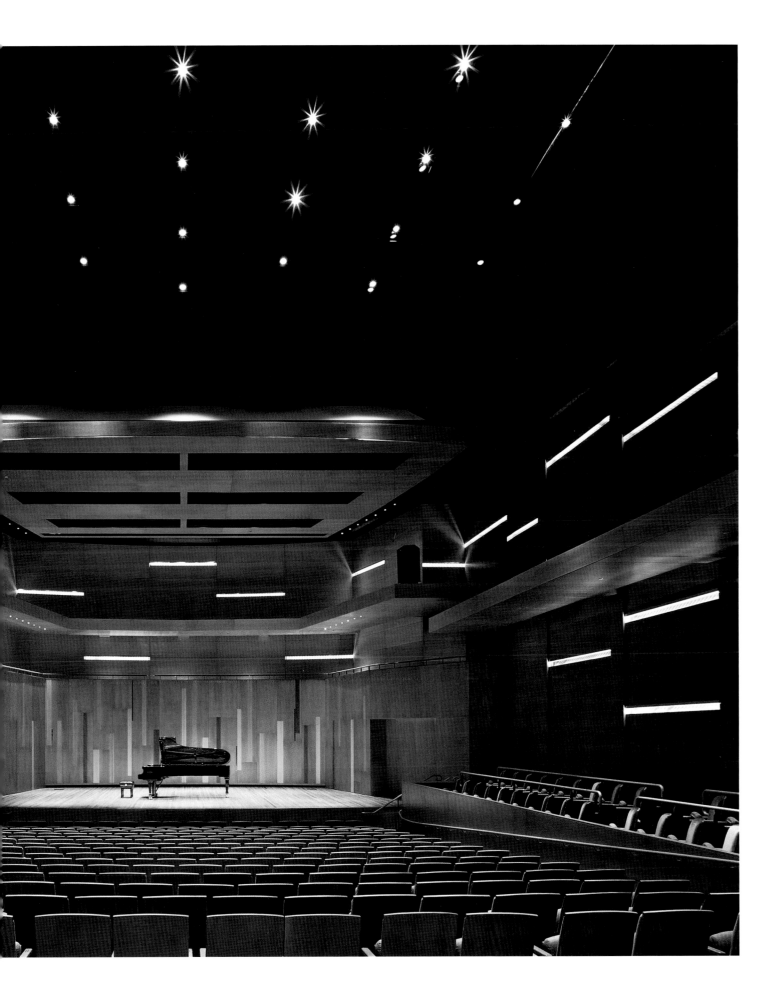

Norwegian Institute of Science and Technology, Trondheim, Norway

Trondheim, Norway is home of the Norwegian Institute of Science and Technology, (NTNU), the nation's preeminent science and technology university. Sasaki is consulting with the university in partnership with the city to bolster Trondheim's reputation as a "knowledge city," which is seen as vital to attract the kind of students, faculty, and private research necessary to compete in the realigned global economy shaped by the European Union.

But NTNU's present configuration is problematic and not conducive to the heightened competition for the best and brightest, especially as China and India emerge as intellectual strongholds and the U.S. offers a distinct higher-education experience. NTNU's science and technology programs are on an urban campus near the city center, while its arts and humanities are in a rural outpost, with associated community colleges scattered throughout the city. Sasaki's ongoing investigation seeks to integrate the university's science and technology schools with its arts and humanities, and the overall institution with its host city, while also offering a convincing alternative to the American collegiate model. One proposal brings the arts and humanities into a "collocated" campus that forms a strong axial relationship to the center of Trondheim, closely engaging the adjacent science and technology campus and bringing the dispersed community colleges into the mix. Sasaki also examined a reverse hypothesis: if it was not possible to bring the university to the city, was it possible to create a new and vibrant urban environment around the existing, somewhat suburban Dragvoll campus? An approach that created a relatively densely developed community with a rich mix of uses, with the university and related open spaces as its cultural heart, was developed.

Working with Sasaki, both university and city officials are committed to building efficient and cohesive facilities that provide good solar access and protection from winter winds, while cultivating the cosmopolitan flair that will attract the best students, faculty and researchers.

top left aerial view of existing campus

above project development

top right master plan

right seasonal heating and cooling concepts

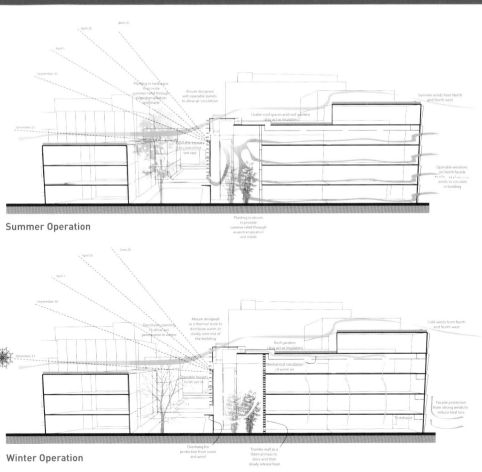

Summer Operation

Winter Operation

The old-world paradigm — a
an insular aristocracy — no

gated university educating
onger works.

Monitor

New York, New York

Sasaki Associates designed the Cambridge, Massachusetts headquarters and San Francisco office of Monitor, a leading management consulting firm. When Monitor wanted to relocate its Manhattan office, Sasaki was brought in early to help choose a site. The post-9/11 Manhattan real-estate market meant that space with stunning views could be had in the downtown Financial District at a better price than a mediocre Midtown space. The firm signed a long-term lease for two top floors at 140 Broadway, a classic SOM-designed tower known for its iconic Isamu Noguchi sculpture—titled "Red Cube"— a Financial District Landmark for 40 years.

As a primary point of departure, the views are celebrated, maximized and un-obscured, and shared by all. As in other Monitor spaces, the designers were challenged to design the space in a manner that minimizes corporate hierarchy and "corner offices," enabling encounters and collaboration among the roughly 100-person staff. Furthermore, the offices had to comfortably accommodate both clients and frequent visits by Monitor staff from other cities.

Space along the north perimeter was carved out for a double-height stairwell. This became the office's first impression, and most celebrated space. The views to the north of the iconic Woolworth Building and Empire State Building make for a memorable, even breathtaking welcome to Monitor. Existing structural beams were wrapped in drywall, becoming imposing and impressive architectural elements, and the stairway itself appears to float within the void. A sheer curtain adds a subtle sculptural quality. In contrast to the neutral, white palette, chosen as a quiet backdrop to the colorful Manhattan vistas, the reception area is defined by a "wrap"—a volume of wood paneling on the floors, ceiling, and walls. This subtly identifies it as the client space. Due to client confidentiality issues, visitors are generally not free to roam the space unaccompanied by Monitor staff.

top left, above, and right views of lobby.

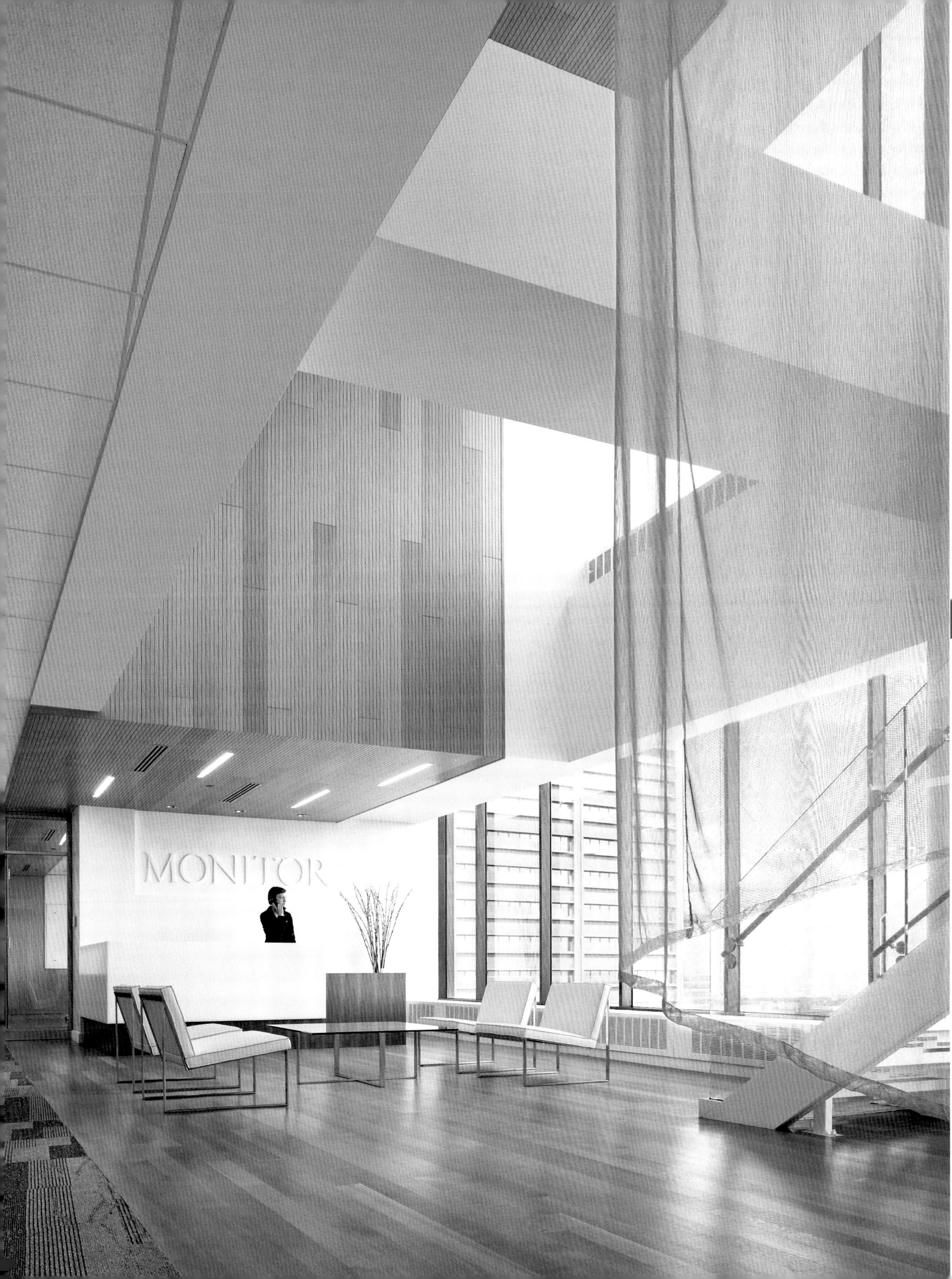
MONITOR

While there are private offices along the outer perimeter, the prime spaces at the corners are reserved for conference rooms and other common areas. View corridors and glass partitions ensure that the views are shared by all staff and visitors, and not reserved for the few upper executives. On the fiftieth floor, a café operates throughout the day and is conceived as the more "private" side of the space. It overlooks New York Harbor and the Statue of Liberty in the distance.

The extensive use of white, the dramatic double-height stairwell, and the expressed structural elements all lend a sense that the space is a void carved out of a solid. Like a loft in nearby TriBeCa or SoHo, the Monitor space has a very sophisticated, unquestionably New York feel, with all of New York on display through its windows.

above and left dramatic Manhattan views

San Francisco, California

Monitor, headquartered in Cambridge, Massachusetts, consults with clients worldwide. This 28,000-square-foot office, located at 101 Market Street in downtown San Francisco, consolidated two Northern California locations and was designed and built in seven months.

The design provides a quality, healthy office environment in keeping with the client's desire that each Monitor have its own identity. It allows the San Francisco office to maintain its own Northern California aesthetic, nurtures Monitor's appreciation of a workplace in which learning is important and social in nature, and enables insight to emerge from opportunistic and spontaneous interactions.

The focus of the design was not just on offices, but also on having a number of spaces that create areas of gathering, crossing, and social interaction. The plan is a grid of "cross streets" intersected by a diagonal "Main Street" terminating at two elliptical community spaces. The elliptical community spaces create these areas of gathering, crossing, and social learning.

The design has the quality of the Cambridge Global Headquarters but expresses its unique Northern California location. Brightly accented paint colors mimic the regional landscape: Golden Gate red, artichoke green, garlic white, poppy orange, grassy-hills gold, bay-water blue, mustard yellow, and fog gray. Local products, recyclable materials, non-toxic products, and an extensive use of glass allowing daylight to filter into all areas of the deep floor plate were employed in order to create a healthy, sustainable environment.

The resulting design has a rich texture of materials and colors, and provides an exciting visual layering of spaces and transparencies, reflecting the different personalities of the many Monitor locations coming together to collaborate and learn.

top left and top right main reception area, "client sandbox"

above and far right library and coffee bay

office plan map

- offices
- conference/teaming
- cockpits
- community space
- circulation
- support
- building care

housing

academic core

monastery

goat house

administration

student center

business and hotel
school

parking garage

elementary school

School of Theology

1–10% slope
10–20% slope
20–30% slope
>30% slope
major campus axis
minor campus axis
main landscape features
main outdoor pedestrian spaces
atrium gathering spaces
campus gateways
campus gathering points
olive groves

University of Balamand

Tripoli, Lebanon

The University of Balamand was established next to an 800-year-old Orthodox Monastery in 1988—toward the end of the civil war in Lebanon. Critical to its mission is the commitment, born out of bitter experience, to foster dialogue between Christians and Muslims in the Middle East. New faculties were created in somewhat improvised fashion to meet specific needs, but without an overall vision.

The Sasaki master plan has broad reach and is a fully integrated plan, including, in addition to the physical master plan, a comprehensive space-use analysis, a strategic academic plan, landscape plan, architectural design guidelines, and fund-raising strategies. Early architectural and landscape projects recommended by the plan, including a new dormitory, have already been undertaken, with the landscape plan for the core area of the campus and a new entry playing a central role.

The intention of the planning and design process was to create an environment that would foster dialogue and transparency, encourage interdisciplinary collaboration, and promote active and engaged learning. Outdoor spaces had to be as significant as indoor spaces and had to embody a full range of interactions, from the contemplative walk to the ceremonial gathering, from the small group to the university-wide assembly.

The concept of a "village on a hill" allows sufficient new space on the lower half of the campus to accommodate the great majority of projected academic growth for the next twenty years. Density is critical for two reasons. It encourages cross-fertilization of ideas and discourages the building of balkanized academic empires, while allowing for efficient sharing of common facilities. It creates a true learning community, with a new Library/Learning Center and outdoor academic commons at its core, directly adjacent to the new Student Center.

top left topographic and analysis plan
above existing site and view of the monastery
right master plan

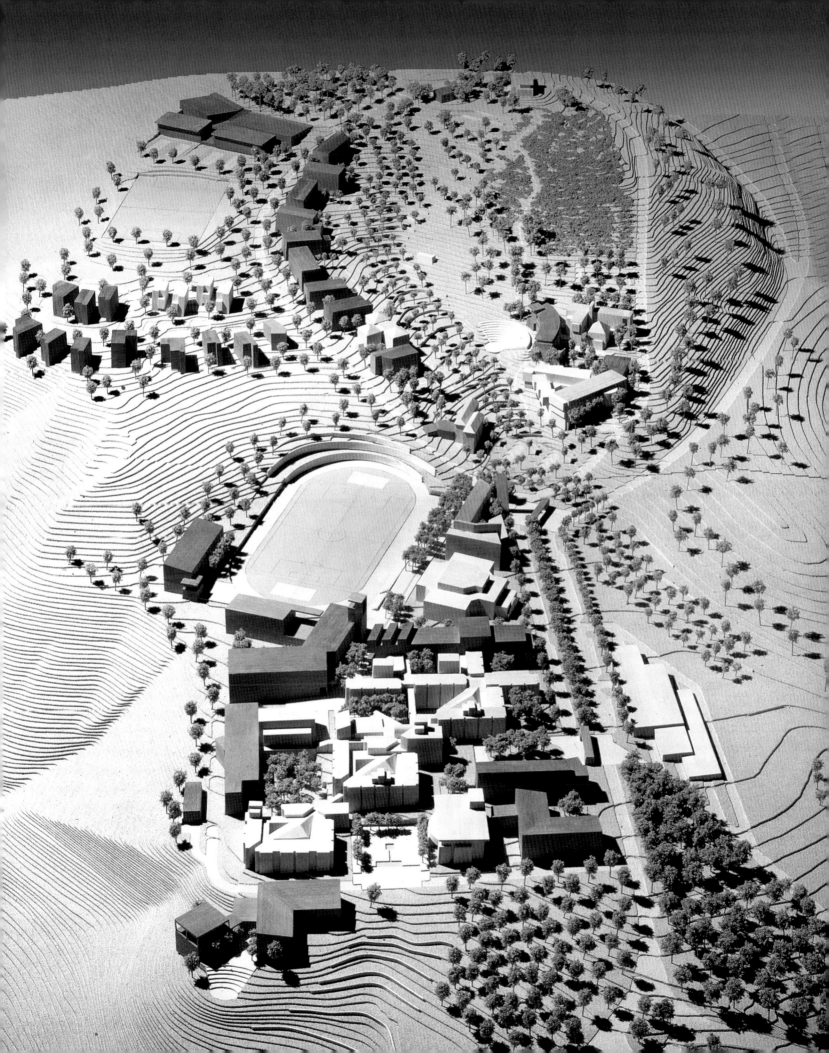

The Path of Learning is both link, seeking to bridge the sa

It also makes possible the creation of well-defined outdoor gathering spaces, at a variety of scales, which would be naturally enlivened by frequency of pedestrian traffic. Varied landscape treatments and careful choice of plant materials make these spaces more congenial for informal gathering. The landscape is an essential and integral part of the educational experience. Full advantage is taken of the topography to provide distant views to the hills and the Mediterranean Sea from the majority of gathering spaces and buildings, so that the campus celebrates and is inspired by the physical environment.

The campus was shaped around the concept of the Path of Learning, a route that extends from the hilltop Goat House (community center) through the olive groves and the campus to the Monastery. Along this path are places for contemplation, places for gathering, places for performance, places for rest and conversation, and still and moving water. Part of the path is almost urban in its concentration of academic activity; much of the path is rural, leaving room for new academic possibilities. The Path of Learning weaves together several key objectives of the master-plan process: dialogue and transparency, environmental sensitivity and sustainability, and a sense of place.

an actual and metaphorical
cred and the secular.

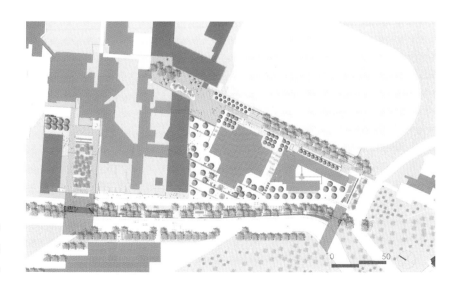

top left master plan

above path of learning

right core campus landscape plan

The landscape design seeks to establish a sense of grandeur. Key to this idea is a new entrance to enhance the sense that the university is a cultural destination. In addition, an array of public spaces are designed to repair edges, link critical new building groupings, and establish a powerful new public realm for the university. The design strategy also capitalizes on the high level of locally available craftsmanship and materials, and promotes traditional Mediterranean practices while establishing a native plant vocabulary for campus.

The new Female Residence Hall is the first building to be implemented as part of the master plan. Located along a steep rock plateau surrounded by a young oak grove, the building is conceived as a series of forms terraced along the site slope and linked by a building bar defining a ridge through the terrain. The Library/Learning Center, at the heart of the academic core, is now beginning design.

opposite entry gateway

top entry fountain at olive grove

left and above bus stop near campus entry

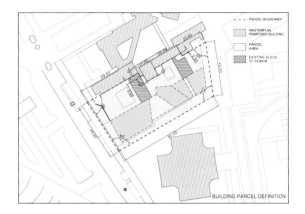

BUILDING PARCEL DEFINITION

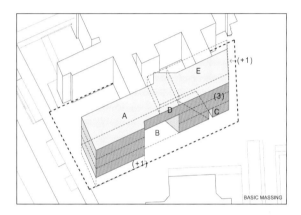

BASIC MASSING

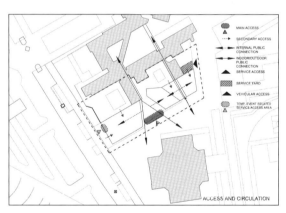

ACCESS AND CIRCULATION

above library parcel, massing and circulation guidelines

right perspective, elevation, and interior sketch of library

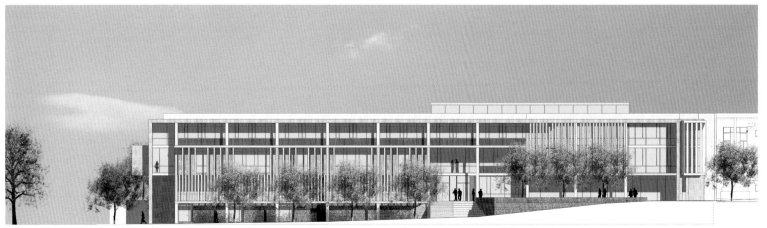

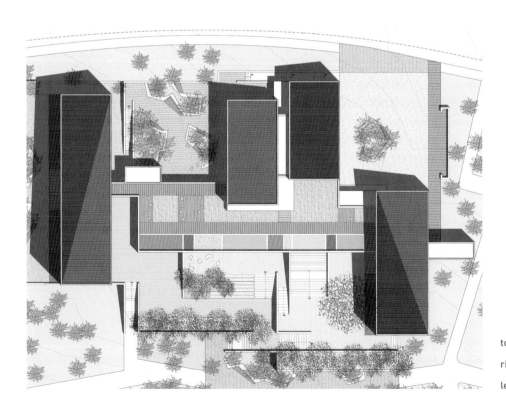

top residence hall elevation

right residence hall views

left female residence hall site plan

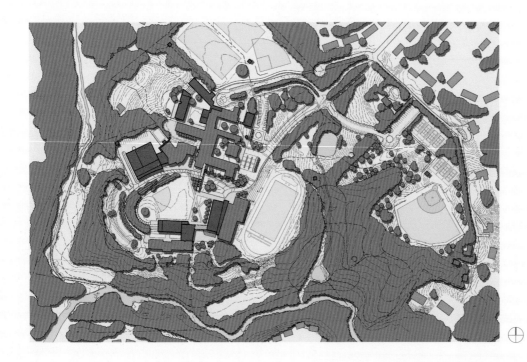

McLean, Virginia

Potomac School, founded in 1904 in downtown Washington, DC, moved its campus in the early 1950s to McLean, Virginia, then largely a rural enclave. The Country Day School Movement earlier in the century promoted the idea that exposure to nature was a critical part of educating young people. Potomac's original 1950s campus with its simple buildings, was, to quote school administrators of the day, "open to the outdoors and shared with a farmer and his cows."

Today McLean is a bustling, upscale suburb that defiantly retains as much of its rural ambience as possible. Even though suburbanization has slowly encroached on the perimeters around Potomac School, by purchasing additional land over the years, a substantial "buffer" of woodlands surrounds the campus.

Sasaki's new master plan and landscape architecture envision a village-like atmosphere that arrays the Lower, Middle and Upper Schools along an axis, culminating in a large curvilinear green—named "the Tundra," by the students because it contains only one tree—a large, old, and shading Live Oak. Sasaki's plan sited new buildings, designed by the Washington, DC firm of Cox, Graee + Spack, in the Upper School to reinforce this critical open space, while forming a new gateway to campus.

The landscaping within the heart of the campus includes stepped terraces and is purposefully angular and rational to serve as a contrast to the surrounding wooded areas. Multiple opportunities were seized to make the campus itself a living laboratory for natural systems—drainage, natural filtration and the efficacy of a green roof, which covers one of the new buildings in the Upper School. Thus, the school engages, both literally and metaphorically, its founders' desire to commune with nature while fostering in students a sense of civic collaboration and stewardship of the earth's resources.

top left site plan

above previous condition

right campus views and green roof

Wildcat Activity Center

California State University, Chico, Chico, California

At California State University, Chico, both the campus administration and student body wanted a new social venue to complement academic life. This facility would take advantage of its Northern California climate and students' increasingly active lifestyles. The new Wildcat Activity Center (WAC) is a powerful example of architecture informing, and being informed by, such institutional goals.

As the expansive name suggests, this is more than a recreation center. It is conceived as the "family room" of the campus. A broad entrance plaza is defined by the eastern façade with large glazed spaces and playful steel roof forms—the entire face of the building seems to say, "Come in and enjoy." The plaza is designed to accommodate a variety of outdoor events, from celebrations to student-government rallies. With the glazed fitness room directly fronting this broad exterior expanse, those exercising within lend color and animation to the façade.

The WAC is funded by self-assessed student fees, and student stakeholder groups were deeply involved in its programming and design. One prominent demand was for easy orientation. Immediately upon entering, a central gallery makes the entire complex readable and welcoming. Activities unfold to the left and right—a gymnasium for basketball, volleyball, and badminton; a Multi-Activity Court (MAC) for in-line skating and indoor soccer; a climbing wall; an outdoor swimming pool and spa; and a lounge featuring the desk of Outdoor Adventures, a launching point for student-led outdoor activities, including rock climbing, white-water rafting, kayaking, backpacking, hiking, surfing, biking, and skiing. The gallery is animated by a second floor incorporating a variety of balconies that overlook a running track, fitness equipment, stretching/warm-up area, and four exercise rooms.

above entrance plaza

right first floor and site plan

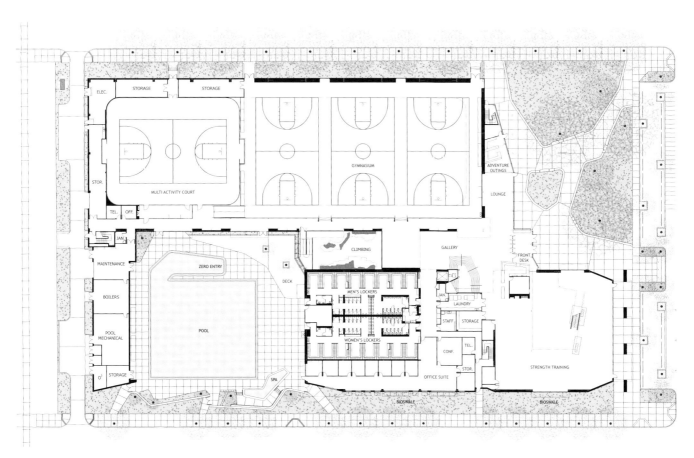

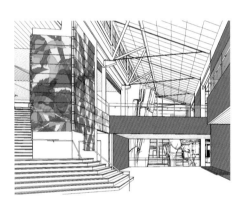 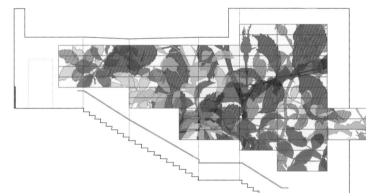

The 110,000-square-foot building is targeted to be, at minimum, LEED® Silver. Innovative, high-strength steel, long-span, "bow string" trusses reduce the amount of steel and the visual weight in the gymnasium. Reclaimed wood, from the roofs of warehouses demolished in clearing the site, is repurposed for custom casework. Bioswales around the perimeter filter stormwater to improve quality and reduce flow into the creek. Wherever possible, materials are sourced locally, as in the local clay for the brick.

Building Information Modeling (BIM) effectively brings the client closer to the design process, thus accelerating and enhancing understanding. With BIM, critical decisions can be made earlier, deliver more impact, and ultimately provide better value. Real-time 3-D representation eliminates separate multiple presentation efforts and provides a clear common understanding. The medium is instinctive and intuitive to clients, many of whom grew up immersed in virtual video-game worlds.

Throughout design and documentation, models were exchanged every three to four days, and as frequently as every three to four hours prior to deadlines. The resulting models have also been utilized by the steel subcontractor as a basis for the creation of shop drawings, and have also been reviewed by students in the Cal State Chico Construction Management Program.

left lounge and gallery stairs LED graphics

below gymnasium isometric, building program arranged around open space, and perspectives of entrance lobby

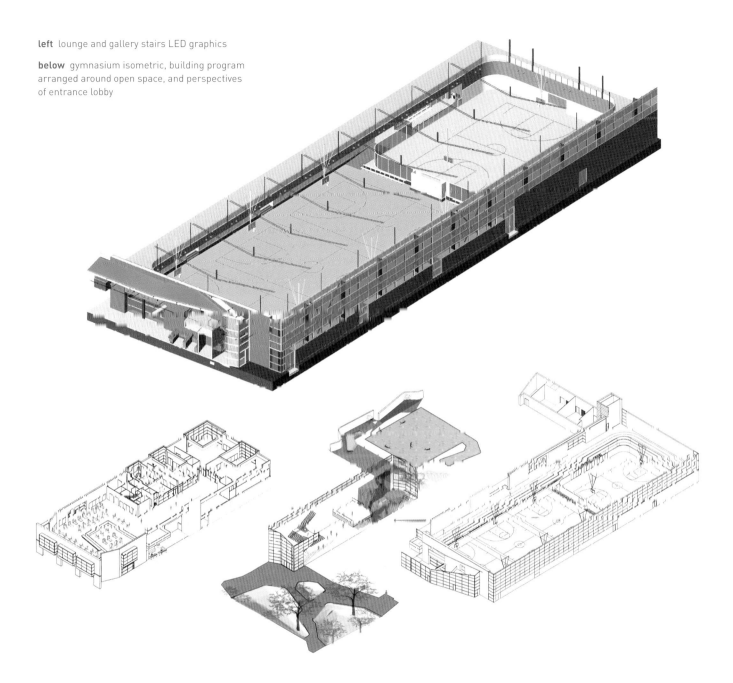

Cal Poly Residential Suites

California State Polytechnic University, Pomona, Pomona, California

Based on a precinct plan developed by Sasaki for the South Campus, the Cal Poly Pomona Residential Suites project is the first phase of a multi-phase residential community that will ultimately result in 1,400 beds of undergraduate housing and a commons building offering food service, resident parking, and various recreational amenities.

The Phase 1 design creates a cohesive neighborhood by routing primary pedestrian paths for non-residents around the project's perimeter. These project edges are defined by the buildings, which vary from three to four stories in height. Internal community spaces shaped by the buildings take the form of a series of linked courtyards and open spaces. An existing, mature sycamore grove was incorporated into the project's site design. Complemented by a newly landscaped open space, it serves as the community's front door for residents and their guests.

A mix of unit types includes four-bedroom/four-occupant units, three-bedroom/four-occupant units, and two-bedroom/two-occupant units. While student privacy is typically achieved through individual bedrooms, the rent structure afforded by the occasional double occupancy bedroom of the three-bedroom/four-occupant unit broadens the community's market capture. Each suite has shared interior spaces composed of a living area, kitchen center, storage closet, and two compartmentalized bathroom facilities. All units are equipped with data, telephone, and cable TV in each bedroom; shared living and kitchen spaces are also equipped with data and cable TV connections. Common study spaces available for group, individual study, and seminar use are clustered at prominent building corners. Aligned with vertical circulation, these stacked commons spaces act as glowing beacons at night, providing residents with a sense of identity and orientation.

top left and right courtyard views

above campus context

**The Residential Suites foster
community identity, create a
residents, and merge indoor**

a sense of community and safe environment for all and outdoor spaces.

An integrated approach to sustainability is reflected in the sensitive siting and orientation of the buildings, the shading of south- and west-facing glazing, an energy-efficient central plant, and careful selection of interior materials and finishes. The Residential Suites have fully achieved key project goals, including fostering a sense of community and community identity, creating a safe environment for all residents, merging indoor and outdoor space, integrating living and learning opportunities, and providing residents with technology unavailable off-campus. The continuing benefit to Cal Poly Pomona's student recruitment and retention is the clearest indicator of the suites' success.

above, left, and right suite and courtyard views

University of New Haven, West Haven, Connecticut

The University of New Haven's new Henry C. Lee Institute represents an important moment in the school's history. Its namesake, Henry C. Lee, is a faculty member and key figure in the development of modern forensic science as a criminal investigation tool. He has figured prominently in such pivotal cases as the O.J. Simpson trial and various war-crimes investigations. This new facility will contain three primary program components: teaching labs and faculty offices for the Forensic Science Department, research labs and offices for the Henry C. Lee Institute of Forensic Science, and a visitor's interpretive center displaying the history and development of the field of forensic science.

A main glazed space overlooking the city is defined by a dramatic C-shaped concrete surround. An interior stair leads to the lower level and the forensic-science interpretive center that will chronicle the developments of forensic science from its roots in Victorian England to the field's current high-profile, high-technology status. The building's Crime Scene Rooms, where students comb through evidence in recreated scenes, are designed to be used not just in the academic program but by local law enforcement as well.

Taking advantage of the opportunities the site affords, the building will contain a dramatic promenade and terrace on the top floor overlooking the city of New Haven. A large interactive graphic display will stretch the length of the building, establishing the building as a visual anchor and landmark. The building's north elevation, facing the rest of the campus, is sheathed in contextual red brick, but also repeats the main façade's geometric themes on a smaller scale.

From a distance, the building will have a dynamic presence—designers are investigating several high-technology digital mural systems for the main space. The building is anticipated to receive a LEED® Silver rating when it opens in 2010.

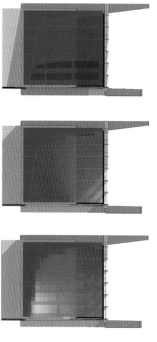

top left and right main façade

above solar heat study

right section, first floor, and site plan

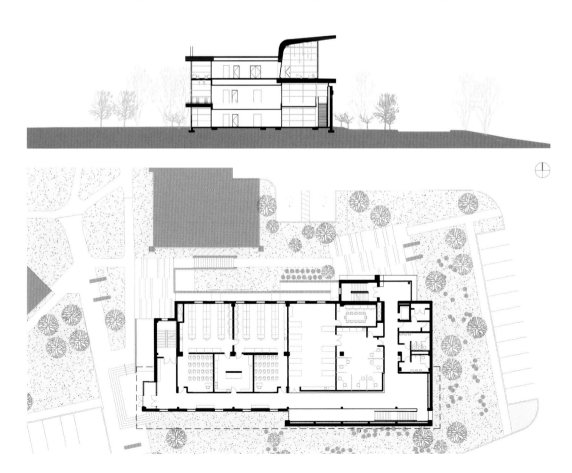

Sacred Heart University

Fairfield, Connecticut

A major building project at a Catholic university offers profound opportunities for expression of ideals that underpin the institution, as evidenced by Sasaki's transformative work at Sacred Heart University in Fairfield, Connecticut. In the many meetings Sasaki planners, architects, and landscape architects had with school officials, church leaders, students, and faculty, the richness of the Catholic tradition suffused the discussion—ideas about pilgrimages, beacons, bridges, and agoras.

Just as Catholicism offers a universal view of life, Sasaki's multiple disciplines joined to form a universal concept for a building program that will change Sacred Heart and allow its facilities to match its twenty-first-century aspirations. The building program is ambitious—an expanded library, a new humanities center, and a new chapel. The expanded library and humanities center form the main edge of a new Great Quadrangle. The lawn is banked with steep inward slopes to create sightlines and seating for spectators and to give visual strength to the Platform, an exterior gathering spot.

While two separate buildings, the library and humanities center are joined by a bridge. The gently inflected "V" shape of the humanities center seems to surround and embrace a space called the Forum, which is akin to a great plaza or meeting place. The library façade is a wall of glass that will be animated day and night with students, staff, and faculty moving about within. Along this wall, the main reading areas seem to rise slowly—the building has an outward expression of the idea of moving, rising, and reaching a destination. The campus's major pedestrian street will penetrate the library/humanities complex, passing under the bridge. This will be a modern iteration of the classic campus sequence of passing under an arch or gateway and arriving at the institution's Great Quadrangle.

top left daily chapel

left Stations of the Cross, and interior perspective

above exterior perspective

below chapel façade elevation and sections

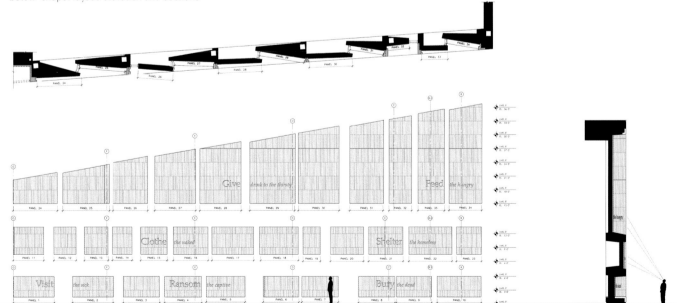

The new chapel is set at the opposite side of the new Grand Quadrangle. Its gently angled roof suggests a tent—a metaphor for the long history of pilgrimage within the Jewish and Christian traditions. The stone floor of the Platform projects out onto the lawn, creating a "welcome carpet" for the community and a seamless transition between inside and out. The Grove, a secluded chapel garden, provides a quiet, elegant, contemplative outdoor space.

It is a building that is both inward-looking and hospitable. The narthex, the traditional entrance space of a church, is roomy and conducive to casual fellowship before and after services. However, its ceiling is relatively low, making the sacristy and the ceiling's apex just above the altar all the more dramatic. The pews are arrayed around the altar so that the occupants have a sense of gathering as a community. A campanile bell tower becomes the iconic structure visible both within and from outside of the campus.

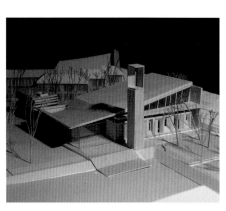

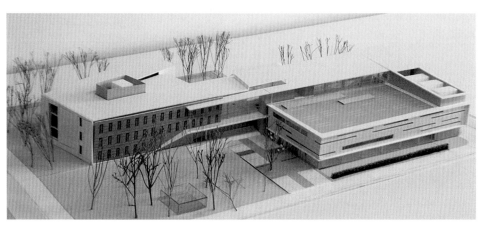

top left chapel interior model

above chapel models

left humanities and library models

right first floors and site plan of the Great Quadrangle

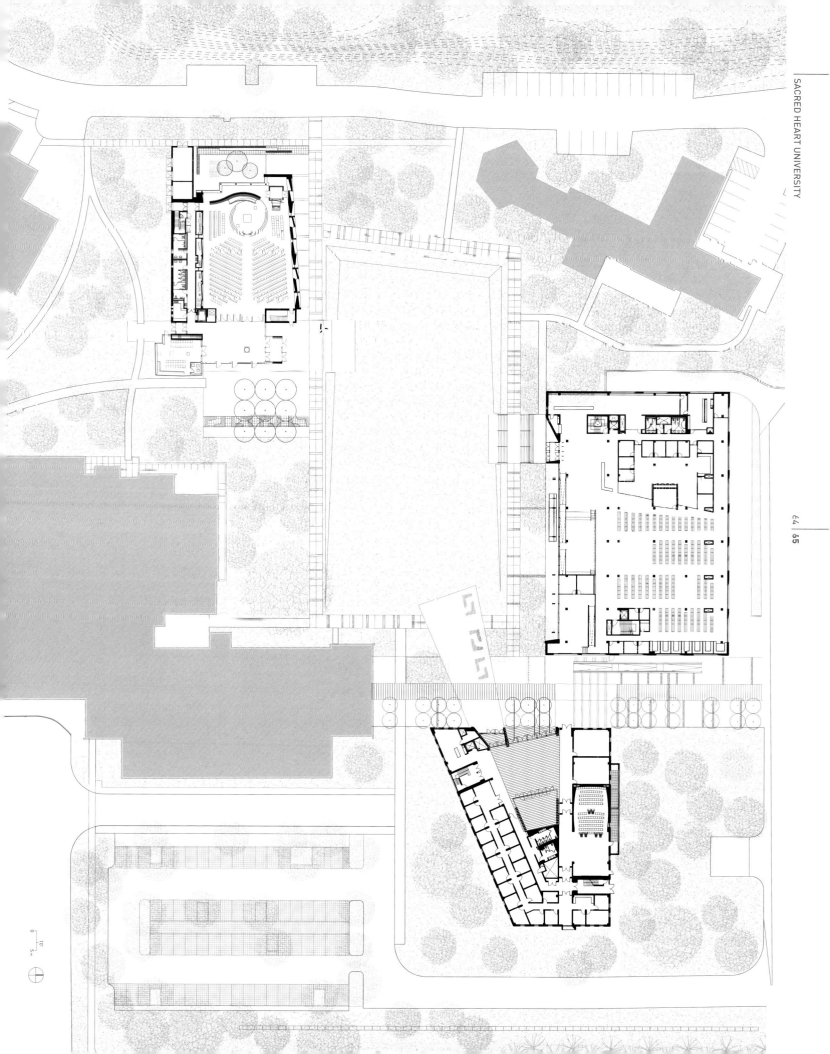

The design includes a bridge
the classic campus sequence
gateway and arriving at the i

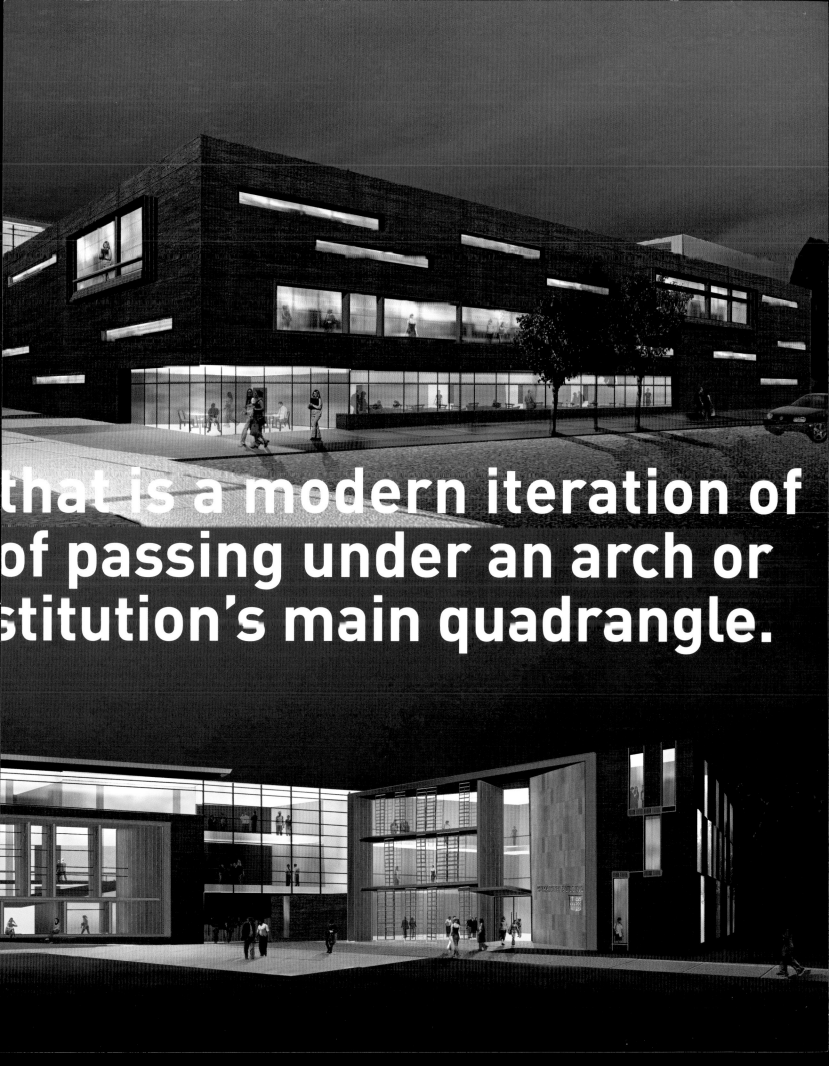

that is a modern iteration of of passing under an arch or stitution's main quadrangle.

Morgan State University, Baltimore, Maryland

Morgan State is one of several historically African-American institutions in Maryland that has worked hard to achieve financial parity with other campuses in the state with assistance from the U.S. Department of Education. Morgan Commons is a tangible example of this increased investment. This formerly underused parcel of land between the university's academic core and its residential precinct to the south now comprises two new buildings—the Student Center, and the new Soper Library.

The new Student Center's most distinctive architectural feature is "the Amble," a curvilinear central path through the building. An open, airy organizing space that orients users within the building, the Amble helps direct campus foot traffic along the important north-south path connecting the traditional North Campus to the newer Central Campus. The Amble redirects student movement through the Center, creating a feeling of energy and liveliness, and functions as a "crossroads" for everyday interaction.

The interior of the three-story Amble is flooded with natural light, open to surrounding public space with outdoor views. Glass walls facing west have shading devices to limit the sun's heat, which otherwise tax the central air-conditioning system. All the public areas of the Center are arrayed directly off the Amble, allowing physical and visual connection of all users to all aspects of the building's program.

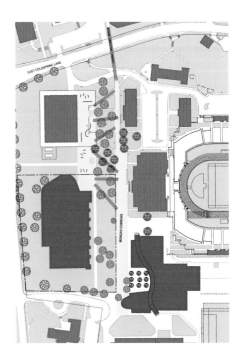

top left Student Center Auditorium

above campus plan with the new Soper Library and Student Center

right Student Center entry

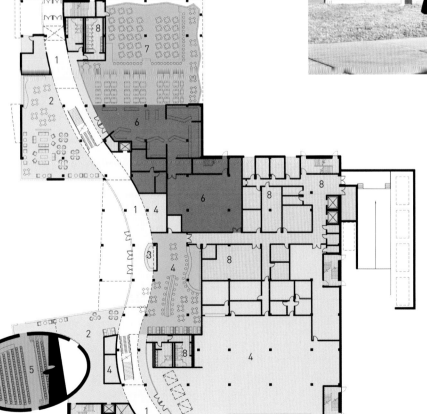

legend

1 lobby/circulation
2 lounge
3 office
4 retail
5 meetings
6 food service
7 dining
8 support

top and above Student Center exterior

left Student Center plan

opposite Student Center interior view

The library is multidirectional, with no wall serving as the back of the building. To the north, it visually connects to the academic campus, specifically to Holmes Hall—Morgan's most iconic building. To the east, the building serves to strengthen and animate the pedestrian mall with a broad glass curtain wall that gives a sense of openness and animation—a real feeling that this is the new epicenter of campus. Along the south, the building establishes an edge to a lawn that visually links Morgan Commons to Hillen Road. The west elevation of the library creates an edge between the campus and the adjacent residential community. There are different areas of the library designed specifically for the way Morgan students tend to study—some open public areas permitting talking and group study, other areas designated for quiet "honors" study.

above, left, and right the new Soper Library interiors

top right library exterior

following spread library interior

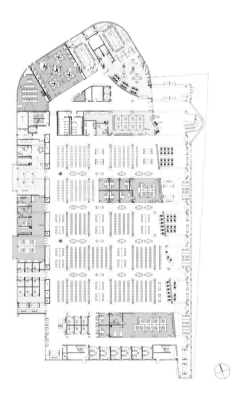

left, top, and right library exteriors

above library plan

University of Missouri, Kansas City, Missouri

Kansas City, Missouri has a tradition of philanthropy and civic pride matched by few U.S. cities, and nowhere is this spirit more in evidence than along the Brush Creek Cultural Corridor, which contains institutions like the Nelson-Atkins Museum, the Kauffman Foundation, and the Kemper Museum of Contemporary Art. The University of Missouri, Kansas City is located within this vibrant district, and the administration decided to leverage the redesign and expansion of its library with a larger institutional initiative to increase its local profile and provide a fitting presence for the university on the corridor.

The original Miller Nichols Library was a closed, fortress-like structure typical of the Brutalist architectural style of the 1960s. Sasaki's addition to and redesign of the building inverts this image—solids become voids, and voids become solids. A dense central core of book stacks is transferred to a new wing holding an advanced Automatic Storage and Retrieval System (ASRS). The former stack space is thus freed up to become hundreds of study seats in a wide variety of configurations—private, group study, and impromptu student/teacher collaborations. To the west, the new, contiguous academic building has carefully modulated large and small classroom areas, multiple light-filled atria and other spaces to make it the new social center of campus.

top left narrative screen inspired by ASRS and local culture

left interactive classroom addition

right massing concept of library addition

ASRS will make Miller Nichols a truly modern library that takes advantage of cutting-edge systems and technology. In keeping with the Cultural Corridor theme of enrichment in the humanities, the library will contain within it some important regional programs such as the Western Missouri Historical Manuscript Collection and the Marr Sound Archives, which detail the city's rich jazz history and include material about "Kaycee's" famous son, saxophonist Charlie Parker.

The orthogonal and cube-like massing of the original library is retained, although the dense and severe limestone panels are replaced with large expanses of glass set back at various lengths from the concrete bays to form lively and syncopated façades. The new classroom wing also takes its massing cue from the original, while expressing on its exterior the different classroom configurations within. Instead of reading as "old" and "new" wings, the completed complex will be visually seamless and establish a strong signature presence for UMKC along Rockhill Road.

Sasaki also designed the landscape that steps down toward Rockhill Road, retaining surface parking but minimizing its visual impact in favor of a dramatic green mantle fronting the refurbished building. Glass, wood, limestone, and fieldstone mix along the façades as gestures both to the natural setting and the predominant architectural materials of nearby museums and other institutions.

top and left regeneration of existing library

right floor plans

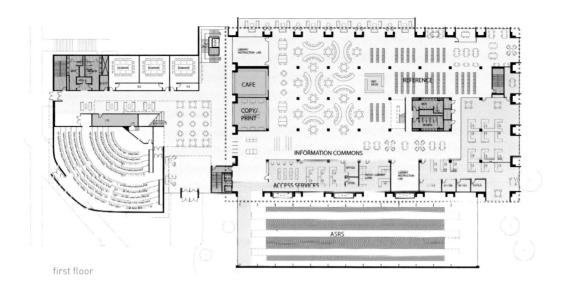

first floor

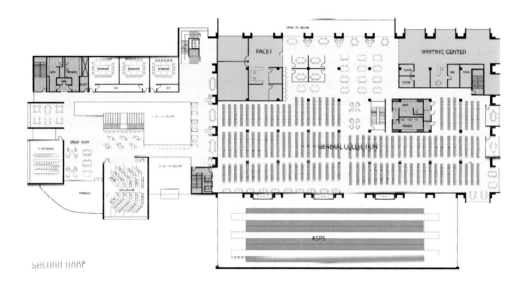

second floor

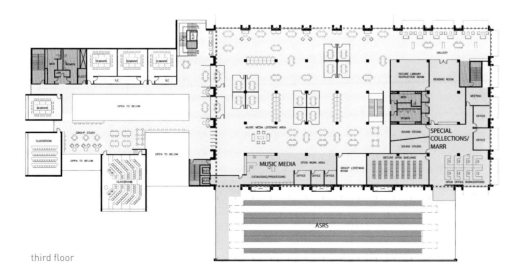

third floor

collection	classrooms	building support
patron resources	perimeter of existing MNL	circulation
interactive learning space	library staff space	Western Historical Manuscript Collection

Segundo Commons

University of California, Davis, Davis, California

With its flat Central Valley topography and temperate climate, the city of Davis, California, is one of the most bicycle-friendly college towns in the United States. The Davis campus is organized by a series of "bike highways," which are two-way, medium-speed, bike paths that effectively delineate campus precincts.

For the Segundo Commons dining hall, the social center of a residential neighborhood reserved for freshmen, Sasaki chose to incorporate one of these bike paths into the design, literally stretching it across the southern perimeter of the building. The resulting symbiosis between stationary architecture and the kinetic bicycle is evident in a sweeping curved façade, animated by hundreds of bicycles whizzing by—visible both outside and from within. Continuing this circular theme, the entry courtyard is also round, and the resulting open space becomes the epicenter of the community. Although programmatic concerns dictated a single story building, the massing around the court describes a two-story volume—befitting its civic presence. Taking advantage of a northern exposure, a sheer wall of glass presents the bustling scene within, blurring the line between inside and out, promoting the concept of food as theatre, and beckoning students to come in and enjoy.

top left, top right, and right circular entry courtyard

far right first floor and site plan

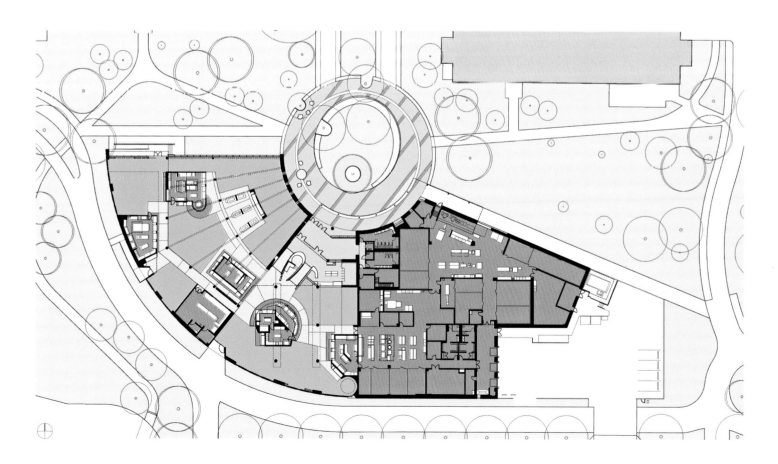

The interior is arranged as a series of streets and squares. The dining areas are activated by the various food service platforms, some of which are treated as destinations, and others that appear as storefronts around the perimeter. Interior spaces are open, with exposed beam ceilings adding a sense of drama and spaciousness. The 49,000-square-foot, one-story building provides marketplace dining for as many as 900 patrons simultaneously, as well as a full cook/chill facility supplying other dining facilities on campus. The materials palette emphasizes natural finishes; hues and values are intensified at the serving platforms, where the food is set against a backdrop of mosaic tile walls.

above and right dinning room views

University of Calgary, Calgary, Canada

The West Campus at the University of Calgary is a tract of land approximately a third of the size of downtown Calgary. The eighty-acre parcel was given to the university by the Province of Alberta in 1995 with the understanding that it would be developed with academic, research, and related uses. The West Campus Master Plan proposes a new mixed-use urban district adjacent to the main campus that reflects the university's academic mission and its commitment to building a better, more sustainable urban environment.

The urban design for the West Campus Lands responds to topography, natural conditions, and adjacent developments. The northern part of the site, aligned with 32nd Avenue, and including the Middle Campus, is a close-knit urban grid, oriented to maximize potential for passive solar power and to shield public spaces from northerly winds, creating an intimate, compact scale. The grid responds to streets in the vicinity, encouraging a seamless transition into the new district. The community centers on a main plaza, forming an urban center, with shops and cultural activity, as well as outdoor amenities for summer and winter. The plaza is connected back to the main campus of the university via a wide boulevard. Public transportation along this spine will provide easy access to existing light-rail stations and other public transportation. Buildings along the boulevard will be higher density, with structured parking concealed on the interior of each block, and will support a mix of uses, sometimes with retail at street level. Between the boulevard and 32nd Avenue, buildings will be on more modest scale. At the campus end of the boulevard, on the Middle Campus, student housing and university-related activity will be concentrated. Non-student housing will explore innovative approaches such as live/work space, as well as attached rental units that might serve a child-care provider, graduate student, or aging relative while potentially relieving the owner of some part of the cost. The community will aim to be multi-generational, and will comprise a blend of university-related inhabitants and the general public.

top left 32nd Avenue

above existing conditions

top right eco hotel

right master plan

South of the boulevard, the higher density housing will give way to R&D space, adjacent to the Children's Hospital. Significant park-like, open space will be maintained adjacent to the university's existing playing fields. South of the Children's Hospital, beyond a buffer of medical-related R&D and office space, a more natural environment dominates, taking advantage of the rolling topography and existing water. This area, with its walks and vistas, will be an attractive outdoor resource not only for the new area to the north, but also for surrounding neighborhoods. The dominant built feature will be an Eco-Conference Center and Hotel. The tower of the hotel takes advantage of the escarpment and will be a visible

landmark for the university. As a green high-rise, exploiting exciting new technologies in the construction of sustainable towers, it will become something of a focal point for the neighborhood and will provide important amenities for the university and city, and beyond, as they work together to develop sustainable approaches to urban development. This area will also include some residential and business development, exemplifying innovative or "model" approaches to living space and working space, and may also be something of a laboratory for new approaches to living and working.

above civic plaza

left central park

St. Edward's Landscape

St. Edward's University, Austin, Texas

St. Edward's is a private Catholic institution whose main campus is on a hilltop overlooking Austin, Texas. In keeping with institutional goals set by the client, Sasaki's landscape master plan seeks to guide the campus landscaping over the next two decades while instituting conservation measures that respond to the unique climate and conditions of the Texas Hill Country.

The plan develops a regionally appropriate landscape based on water conservation and microclimate enhancement. Over 60% of the campus will be maintained as a non-irrigated dry-climate landscape. At the same time, the scheme creates inviting, shaded outdoor spaces that respond to solar and wind orientation as well as to the year-round outdoor living style of Austin. To this end, among the elements proposed are new courtyards, gateways, and informal, tree-shaded gathering spots located throughout the campus.

At the perimeter of the university's property, where town meets gown, the plan strengthens the campus's edges along Woodward Street and Congress Avenue with perimeter trees and street tree plantings that help mitigate urban heat island effect.

top left, above, and right campus walkways, residence hall courtyard, and vine-shaded trellis

The scheme creates inviting
to solar and wind orientatior
outdoor living style of Austin

shaded spaces that respond
as well as to the year-round

Glen Mor Student Apartments

University of California, Riverside, Riverside, California

The new Glen Mor Student Apartments at UC Riverside provide apartments for 505 students, as well as a variety of community amenities, including a computer lab, study lounges, laundry facilities, a convenience store/grille, and three high-performance play-fields. Located at the far northeast corner of the Riverside campus, the project was carefully sited to complement an existing student-housing community to the west, capturing the natural beauty of an environmentally sensitive arroyo to the south. It now sets the stage for future phases of development, as the residential needs of the campus continue to grow. Given the project's campus-edge location, the siting of the buildings favors close pedestrian connections to the academic core, while its playfields offer off-campus neighbors a visually attractive, green transition from Glen Mor's student residences.

Within the project itself, commons facilities and building entries are oriented toward outdoor plazas and courtyards, fostering social interaction and taking full advantage of the Southern California climate. For the sake of construction economy, the four residential wings composed of four stories of four-bedroom apartment units, were designed as two proto-typical buildings. However, each façade exhibits carefully modulated fenestration, which responds to solar orientation while avoiding the monotony often seen in low-cost housing.

Glen Mor Housing represents a notable example of integrated project design and delivery. Sasaki's interdisciplinary architectural, landscape, and interior design capabilities were complemented from the beginning of schematic design by the participation of an exceptionally capable construction manager. This early teaming permitted a fast-tracked, phased delivery of the project by multiple prime contractors, ensuring on-time completion and minimized costs during a period of unbridled construction cost escalation. The team's successful, under-budget performance allowed UC Riverside to exercise a number of project enhancements.

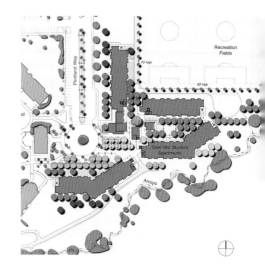

top elevation

above site plan

right exterior view

top left and right courtyards

above view from arroyo

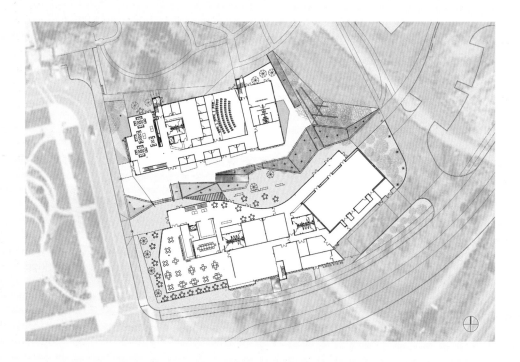

University of California, Davis, Davis, California

The new Graduate School of Management (GSM) complex represents intersection on a number of levels—locational, economic, and pedagogical. It is the new home for a top-ranked business school that actively cultivates alliances with Northern California's globally influential business sector. The two-building complex forms an important new gateway to the campus as it mediates between a rather formal south-entry quadrangle and the UC Davis Arboretum, which is envisioned as a linear park that will weave its way along the campus's southern edge. The GSM complex simultaneously relates to its important setting while forming within itself a place of interaction between the academic and "real" business worlds.

A four-story GSM classroom and administrative building anchors the northern edge of the site. A glass bridge connects to the conference center/restaurant building, which will host multiple lectures and programs and serve as a place of inter-action between students, as well as regional and global business executives. Beacon-like glass volumes, with horizontal fin louvers, flank the bridge and form the GSM's new iconic image. Far more than "leftover space," the courtyard between the buildings has along one edge a sinuous shape driven by the morphology of the site. As the conference center building inflects gently, it forms an outdoor space that also mediates the grade change across the site; this grade change optimizes outdoor functionality, providing both separa-tion through planning and connectivity through steps and ramps. Angular landscaping forms also take their cue from the shape of the site and the desire to make the courtyard space a dynamic and interesting space for gatherings and special events.

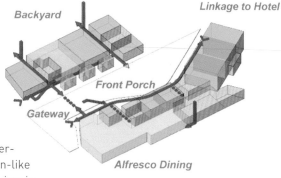

top left first floor and site

above building massing and circulation

right courtyard

Numerous sustainability components are integrated into the design. A ground-source heat pump utilizes an underground water loop to reject heat to, or absorb heat from, the ground, eliminating the need for traditional chillers. The radiant loop also charges the floor slabs for primary heating and cooling. Raised-access flooring acts as a plenum for low-velocity ventilation air, supplemented by operable windows. The building also has a layered façade assembly that provides a ventilated cavity behind the primary cladding. This cavity tempers the transfer of thermal bridging, virtually eliminating the potential for condensation, which can lead to the formulation of molds. It also allows a variation in the "depth" of the façade based upon solar orientation—for example, windows on the south and west are set deeper in the wall than on the north and east, minimizing heat gain in summer.

As part of an intensely competitive, sixty-day competition, UCD awarded the project to the Design-Build Team of Sasaki Associates/Sundt Construction. A key element of the team's success was utilization of Building Information Modeling and Management (BIM) technology. BIM allowed the team to have a real-time, full electronic model of the entire building and all of its components. This in turn reflects on a daily or even hourly basis, material costs and delivery strategies, allowing both client and team decisions to be made quickly and efficiently as they arise.

Natural day-lighting is passively controlled based on orientation and introduced deep into the building via clerestory windows:

- Reduces energy loads associated with artificial lighting

- Fosters views to the outside

- Is modulated based upon program demand

above façade along courtyard

top right iconic entrance

right selected sustainability components

A ground-source heat pump serves radiant floors and ceilings:

- Less energy use for cooling and heating
- Less energy use for pumping water vs. large volumes of air
- Better thermal comfort

100% outside ventilation air is delivered via under-floor diffusers and wall-mounted displacement diffusers:

- Low velocity results in low fan loads and small AHU
- Excellent air quality
- Operable windows allow for individual comfort control

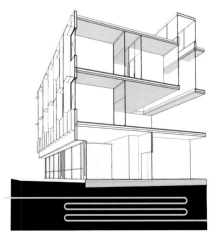

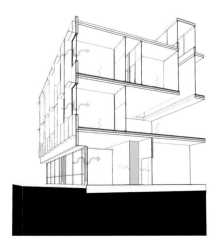

A full building information mo
and all of its components ref
delivery strategies in real tim
decisions to be made quickly

del (BIM) of the entire building

ects material costs and

e, allowing client and team

and efficiently as they arise.

Grumbacher Sports and Fitness Center

York College of Pennsylvania, York, Pennsylvania

York College of Pennsylvania is responding to its growth needs by expanding its campus into a formerly industrial zone of the city and using the parcel as a link between its main campus to the east and a growing residential campus to the west. At the heart of this new development is the recently completed Grumbacher Sports and Fitness Center.

The building accommodates both the college's general student fitness facilities and its intercollegiate athletic programs. An interior "Main Street" bisects the north and south areas of the building and provides a logical continuation of the pedestrian path that connects the two campuses. Students pass through the light-filled building and can glimpse virtually all the activity taking place within. Linking these major spaces is a naturally lit concourse that has at its focal point a dramatic, two-story climbing wall. Other features of the building include an extensive weights and fitness room with cardiovascular equipment and weight machines, a racquetball court, a wrestling room, two multi-purpose rooms with sprung wood floors, and all the facilities to run the college's ambitious athletics program—including offices for the coaches, team rooms, locker rooms, and a well-equipped training room. The outdoor facilities include a 400-meter running track, two synthetic turf fields, and a throwing area.

In plan, the building reads as an orthogonal structure to the south with a more free-form northern wing. In elevation, the flat-roofed north pavilion features a curved façade that helps maximize views out to the athletic fields, while the southern portion that houses the field house, arena, and natatorium features an arching roofline. This curved roof is spanned by custom-designed steel trusses with skylights above. The unique form of the trusses gives the space a distinct character, while the skylights flood it with natural daylight. Exterior aluminum panels lend a sense of machine-like simplicity while subtly evoking the parcel's industrial past.

above left public circulation area

above right natatorium

bottom right field house

above window detail

top soccer field

left climbing wall, café

right basketball arena

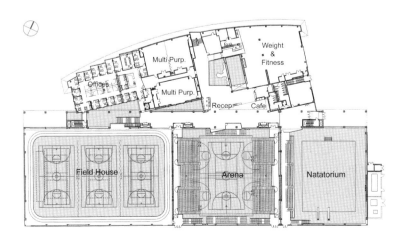

Offices
Multi Purp.
Multi Purp.
Weight & Fitness
Recep.
Cafe
Field House
Arena
Natatorium

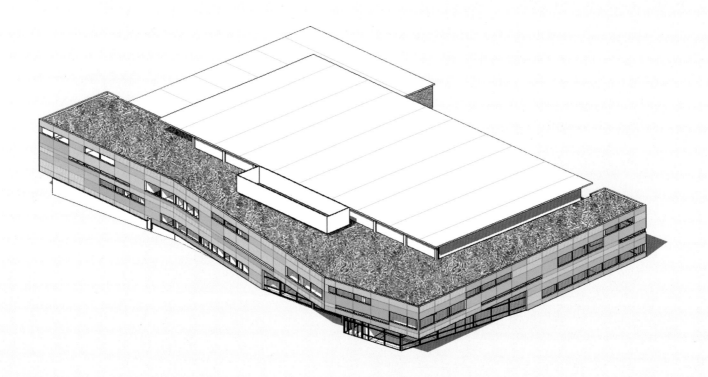

Stony Brook Recreation Center

Stony Brook University, Stony Brook, New York

The new recreation center for Stony Brook, part of the State University of New York, is on an extraordinarily tight site. Both to accommodate an aggressive program and give the building a prominent visual presence on campus, the overriding architectural idea is to set two orthogonal volumes, housing the gymnasium and Multi-Activity Courts (MAC), against a more freely shaped pavilion that houses the cardio and fitness facilities.

Each of the building's façades reacts to a different context. The "big box" elements of the three-court gymnasium and MAC are placed to the north and east of the site. These façades are clad in brick masonry, and along one edge, given a playful jagged shape that mitigates heat gain while providing natural light. The L-shaped pavilion forms a circulation pattern around the building and is clad in a multi-colored, cementitious-panel rain screen in a syncopated grid. Its colors change from predominantly blue to green as the façade wraps from Toll Road toward the university's Ken Lavalle Stadium, in a sense from "urban" to "rural." The earthy color of the gym and MAC, coupled with the blues and greens of the glass façade, recall the landscapes and seascapes of Long Island.

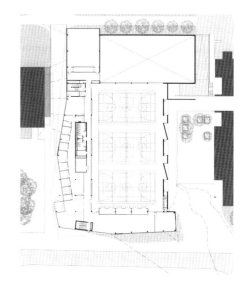

The "big box" elements appear as anchors set against the more free forms of the pavilion, whose façade is slightly canted in plan at one point so that the second floor cantilevers out to signal the main entrance to the building. The entire pavilion is covered in a green roof to mitigate the heat-island effect. The glass is carefully patterned so that movement of students within is visible from the outside. Thus, students exercising within become kinetic sculptures that animate the façades of a complex dedicated to movement and fitness.

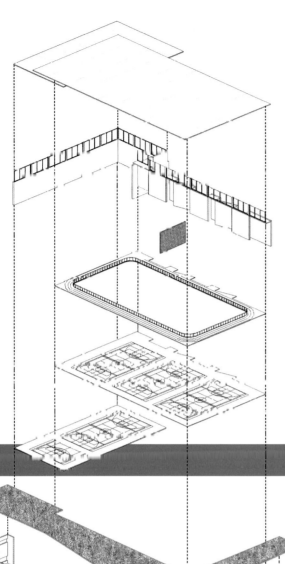

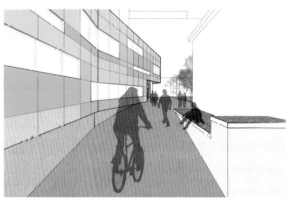

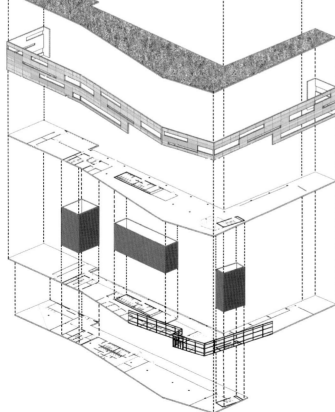

top left isometric showing the green roof

bottom left first floor and site

above and below perspectives

left exploded isometric showing relationship of major program elements

bottom rain-screen panel pattern

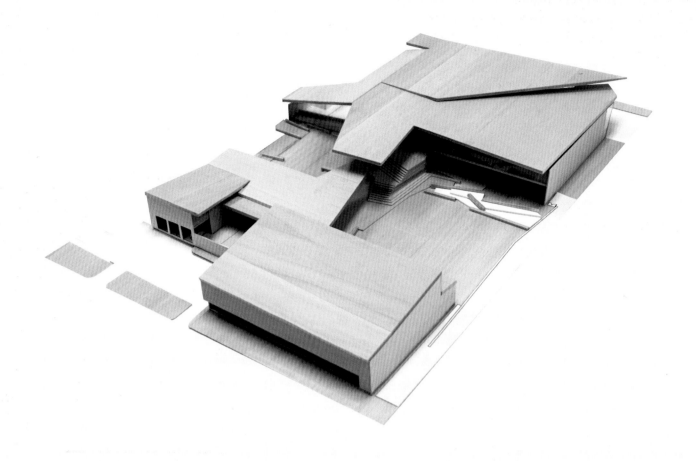

University of Arizona, Tucson, Arizona

Much of twentieth-century architecture was concerned with a vibrant relationship between indoor and outdoor spaces—transparency, visibility, permeability, light, and shade were all part of this elemental design dialectic. Nowhere is this more evident than in the desert Southwest, where the outdoors can be forbiddingly hot at one point in the day and cool and inviting at another. The intersection and convergence of indoor and outdoor spaces deeply informed the architecture of the expansion of the University of Arizona's Student Recreation Center, designed in collaboration with M3 Engineering & Technology Corporation. The addition connects directly to the existing recreational facility via an indoor street. The building wraps around and defines outdoor spaces, and the extensive use of glass allows interior occupants to view activity outdoors, and vice versa. A particular transparency is given to the fitness center, a large indoor space that looks out onto the very active Sixth Street Corridor, in effect displaying the students exercising within as a means of encouraging fitness throughout the university community.

A central courtyard is defined by two intersecting roof elements. A bathroom wing, envisioned as a sculptural element and rendered in concrete, divides the space and provides casual seating for spontaneous viewing of sand volleyball and rock climbing. Defined in large part by its outdoor spaces and rendered in planes of bold angles and juxtapositions, the Recreation Center expansion becomes a contrast and foil to the current, rather inward-looking and orthogonal Recreation Center.

The ecological imperatives of the desert location are addressed throughout the building, currently slated for LEED® Gold. Water efficiency is of particular concern in Tucson, and water harvesting and stormwater management techniques include bioswales, the use of the volleyball court as a percolation bed, and capturing HVAC condensation for irrigation.

top left and below models showing intersecting roof elements and central courtyard

top right and right perspectives

far right floor plan

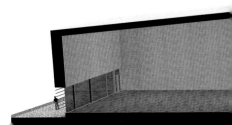

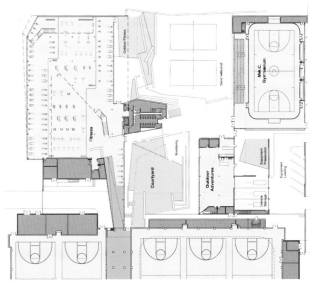

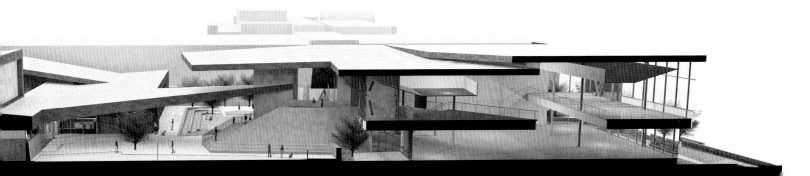

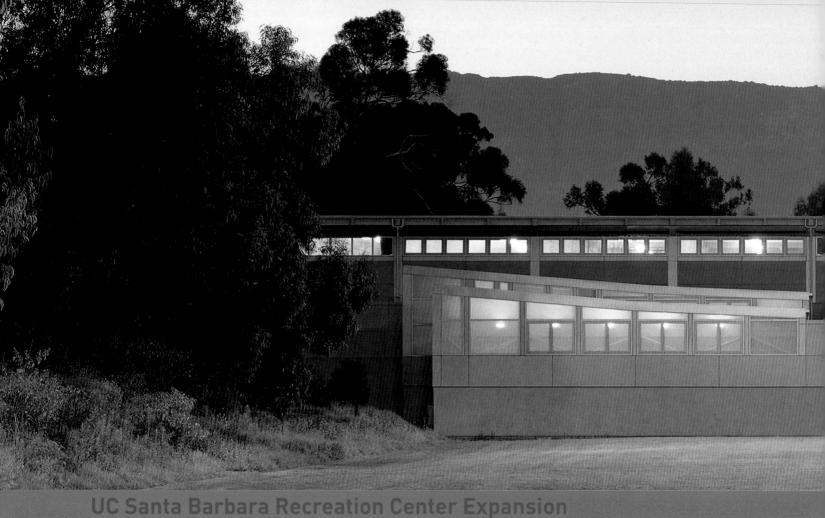

UC Santa Barbara Recreation Center Expansion

University of California, Santa Barbara, Santa Barbara, California

The 54,000-square-foot expansion of the University of Santa Barbara's Recreation Center completes a nine-acre recreation quadrangle, landscaped with historic California live oaks, walking and running paths, volleyball courts, and social areas. The expansion is the second phase of the recreation and aquatics complex designed by Sasaki.

The building is organized in two wings, academics and recreational activities. A sunny, south-facing loggia dominates the academic wing. The loggia is lined with a classroom, offices, multipurpose room, and a pottery studio, and is distinguished by a full-height wall of California ceramic tiles. The spaces along the loggia are glazed for controlled day lighting and to open the activities to view.

The activities wing terminates the loggia and contains a multipurpose activities court (MAC), lockers, and a climbing wall. The climbing wall dominates the entrance to the activities wing and overlooks the quadrangle from behind a three-story glass wall, creating an alluring landmark. The cardio/weight room is a transition between the two wings of the building. The room is expressed on the exterior as a truncated pyramid, sheathed in glass. The ceiling of the room rises toward the Santa Ynez mountains, affording dramatic views and filtered sunlight.

This building is the background to expansive grass practice fields, and the foreground to the dramatic mountain vistas. The building's cool green and lavender colors reflect this transitional place in the landscape. The clerestories are irregular, permitting a visible accent of the brilliant yellow and red walls, as well as providing natural light and ventilation to the locker rooms.

above expansion against the back-drop of Santa Ynez Mountains

left lobby/reception and aerial view

right cardio/weight room exterior

above cardio/weight room

left pottery studio, locker room, cardio weight/room
mezzanine, and multi-purpose activities court

right climbing wall

The climbing wall is given pro
exterior as it is centered on a
curtain wall overlooking the

minence on the
large glass
courtyard.

Valparaiso University, Valparaiso, Indiana

Valparaiso University's most iconic landmark is the modernist Chapel of the Resurrection, built in 1959 to celebrate the school's centennial. The chapel is located in the center of the campus. It is a well-known local landmark, visible from the highway. The new Student Union is the final addition of three new buildings that will array around the chapel and form the new core of the campus, the other two being the recently completed library and performing arts center.

The Union will provide a social and administrative hub for faculty, staff, students and visitors to the campus. The 205,000 square-foot building is organized in three levels and is home to the university's main dining room and café, bookstore, post office, ballroom, meeting rooms, career center, student organizations, multicultural and administrative suites, and a series of lounge and recreation spaces.

The University Union building is positioned directly opposite the Chapel, across the dominant open space known as the University Commons. The building looks out onto the landscape of the Commons and the surrounding buildings, relating indoor social destinations with outdoor gathering spaces. The Union plan is turned inside out, internalizing support areas and services at the building's core. By externalizing all public functions, the plan defines an active periphery for the building, where each use becomes a destination. This notion is further reinforced by the massing and envelope of the building, where the string of public destination uses is defined by an undulating organic skin clad in limestone, granite, brick, and glass.

A series of portals carved into the building mass serve as entrances to pedestrian pathways from around campus. These portals project the pathways into the building defining a major pedestrian crossroads around which most program spaces are organized.

top left exterior perspective

above model of main reading room

right first floor and site

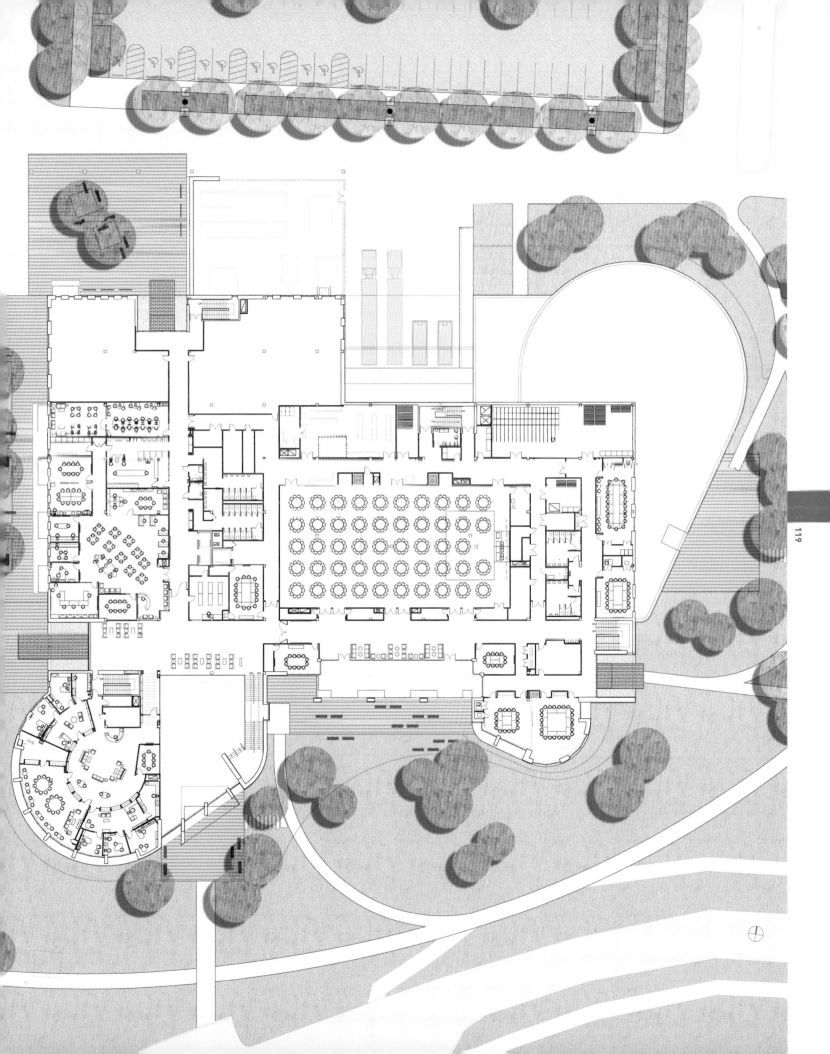

The building has multiple fr different approaches from v also to act as exterior expres place within.

top left and top right exterior perspective and early model study

left, above, and far right cafeteria, building section, and piano lounge

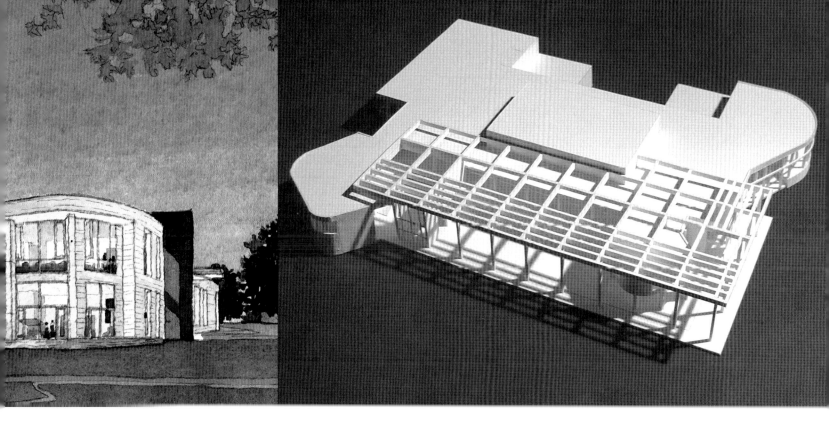

nts to address not just the
rious campus directions but
sions of the usages taking

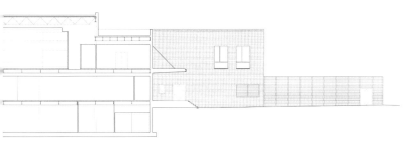

Purdue University, West Lafayette, Indiana

The master plan for the main campus of Purdue University in West Lafayette directs growth for the next twenty years and beyond. As Indiana's Land Grant University, Purdue has considerable land holdings in the areas north, south, and west of the existing campus. Viewing these lands as an irreplaceable natural resource, the master plan seeks to prevent encroachment into them—"campus sprawl"—by advocating increased density in the campus core. The plan also proposes an intermingling between formerly segregated "academic" and "research" precincts of the campus and a series of terraced open spaces that array around the center and that will serve as armatures around which future building will occur. The result will be a strong, vibrant and pedestrian-friendly center supported by a preserve of surrounding reforested lands that will offer innumerable recreational, research and environmental opportunities for the university community and surrounding city.

To mediate the campus's large scale, the master plan creates identifiable neighborhood districts that are linked to one another by a central, unifying spine: State Street. This important artery is evolving from a heavily used vehicular road into a more urban and pedestrian-friendly thoroughfare. State Street is thus reconceived as a "Collaborative Spine" along which a variety of campus uses are organized.

The master plan dissolves traditional segregated campus uses and distinctions and instead integrates academic and research uses and surrounds them with vibrant student-life amenities, such as housing, recreation, dining, and collaborative spaces. The result is a series of dynamic, mixed-use districts arranged around a series of new iconic open spaces. Early university planning established a strong Beaux Arts axis in the academic core, around which future development occurred. The planned new open spaces organize future development but also relate to the larger open-space concept through a series of diagonal stepping quads and well-designed streets that follow the Midwestern grid system.

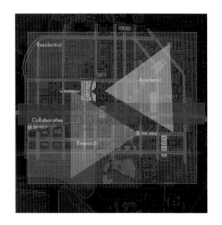

America's Land Grant universities were founded on the idea of environmental stewardship. With this master plan, Purdue moves to preserve this legacy while encouraging the development of a vibrant academic and research core and distinct university districts defined by discrete green open spaces.

top left topographical model

top right master plan in context

right master plan aerial view

left proposed district interaction

 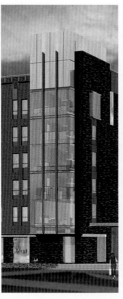    

Tower

Bay/Vertical

Crenellation

Fordham University, The Bronx, New York

Fordham University, the Jesuit university of New York City, has its main campus in the Rose Hill section of The Bronx. Sasaki undertook a master plan for the university with a special focus on residential and student life. These investigations yielded a vision for an upper-classmen residential complex and a student life precinct that will combine a new campus center with all of the university's recreational and athletic facilities. Sasaki is providing the full range of services to Fordham including planning, architecture and landscape architecture.

The campus's main entry point is formed by the intersection of East Fordham Road and the Metro-North commuter rail line. While anchored on one side by the William D. Walsh Family Library, this entrance at present lacks another building that could make it a true celebratory gateway to the eighty-five-acre Fordham campus. Two new upper-classmen residential halls designed by Sasaki will provide this missing link. They will also complete the university's main quadrangle, at present open on one side.

A historic pedestrian path along the gateway is articulated with a new allée of oak trees, which also links to a curvilinear strand of oaks in the main quadrangle. The buildings themselves are set on "terraces." Closest to the gateway, the terraces are a hardscape with a sidewalk café overlooking the quad; gradually, this "public" zone gives way to varied paving patterns, more trees and a greener and more intimate zone that includes a quiet courtyard formed between the new buildings and an older residential building immediately adjacent.

The buildings will be coed by floors. At the heart of each building are double-height lounges that offer opportunities for socialization between students of two consecutive floors. The southern building, to be named Campbell Hall, expresses these social spaces on the exterior by a fully glazed tower structure that will be a new beacon on campus.

top left neo-gothic context and proposed residence hall façades

above master plan

top right exterior perspective

right residential life first floor and site

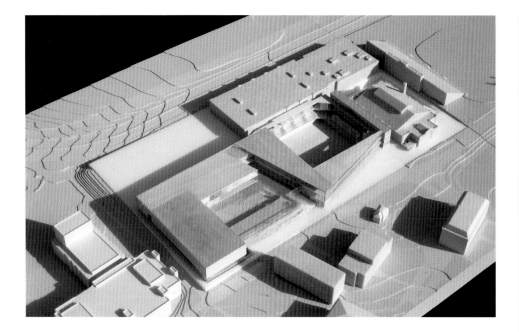

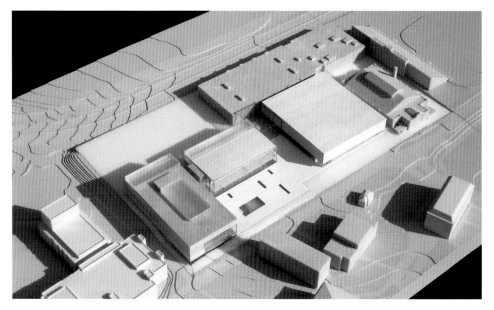

The new student life precinct lies to the north and east of these new residential buildings, forming another perimeter of the campus. At present the three buildings include an outmoded 1960s-era student center, a field house and a historic gymnasium.

The strategy was to create a cohesive new student life complex arrayed around a lively outdoor piazza. To accomplish this, a completely new campus center will be built on the site of a relocated tennis court and soccer field. After this is done, the outmoded McGinley campus center will be torn down, freeing up space for the piazza, which will then be surrounded on three sides by the new campus center, the new recreation center and a 6,500 seat basketball arena.

Like the new residential buildings, the new campus center will pick up both materials and subtle Gothic architectural patterns from existing buildings on campus while forming a modern and forward-looking profile; the most active programs—such as meeting rooms and lounge areas—will be clustered along the building perimeter so as to lend animation to the façades overlooking the piazza. A lit tower element will identify this new student life complex as the social crossroads of the Fordham campus.

top left schematic student life study models

above perspective of student life piazza

right interior perspectives of atrium, sports arena, and natatorium

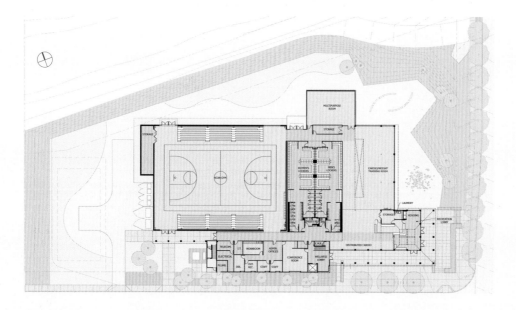

University of California, Merced, Merced, California

The Joseph Edward Gallo Recreation and Wellness Center occupies a key transitional site on the new UC Merced campus, situated between the academic core and the residential precinct. In response, the building is set back from the street, creating an arrival plaza and preserving views. Significantly, the plaza also serves as a bus stop for the parking-lot shuttle, providing a gateway presence to the pedestrian nature of Main Street along the academic core.

Engaging the arrival plaza is a covered walkway/colonnade, which, while integral to the building's design, also serves as a protective transition between inside and out. The colonnade is punctuated by the building's entries—the Recreation Center entry, which serves as the focal element of the plaza, and the Wellness Center entry, a more visually subdued but equally accessible destination off the public space.

The center's highly active programmatic elements (cardio/weight training/multipurpose room/gymnasium) are organized around a central core of support spaces (locker rooms/ rest rooms). Rather than being a discrete series of individual rooms, spaces flow together, presenting an engaging, participatory user experience while providing flexibility for future use. The most active spaces (such as cardio and weight training) are located in highly visible areas of the building, enhanced by liberal use of glass. The resulting transparency contributes to a more meaningful connection to the exterior landscape gardens outside, as well as to the campus as a whole.

top left first floor and site
top right arrival plaza
right multi-purpose room

The most active spaces are l[ocated]
of the building, resulting in a
exterior landscape and the ca[mpus]

The history of California's Central Valley is evident in its agricultural structures, which remain comfortably rooted to the surrounding landscape. The elegantly spare forms, simple construction, and lack of pretense that characterize these structures served as fertile inspiration for the character of the Recreation and Wellness Center. A series of simple shed, gable, and hip roofs were utilized to create an informal composition, each shape a reflection of its internal function. Light monitors crown the hip roofs, presenting a diffuse glow of daylight to the deepest part of the rooms below, while acting as lanterns at night. The roofs are clad in zinc-colored metal, a nod to their agricultural roots. The goal was to create a composition that evoked the inherent qualities of these functionally driven forms in a visually provocative manner, while engaging a dialogue with both the residential and academic campus districts.

cated in highly visible areas
meaningful connection to the
mpus as a whole

The American University in Cairo
Cairo, Egypt

Auburn University Master Plan
Auburn, Alabama

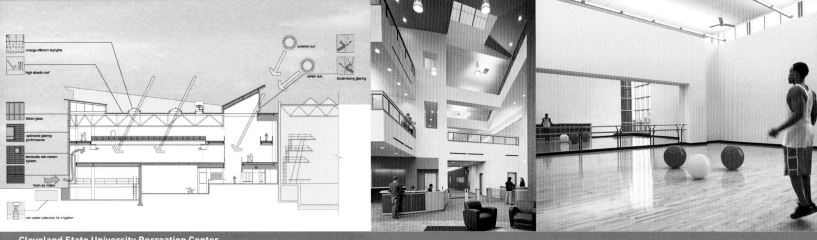

Cleveland State University Recreation Center
Cleveland, Ohio

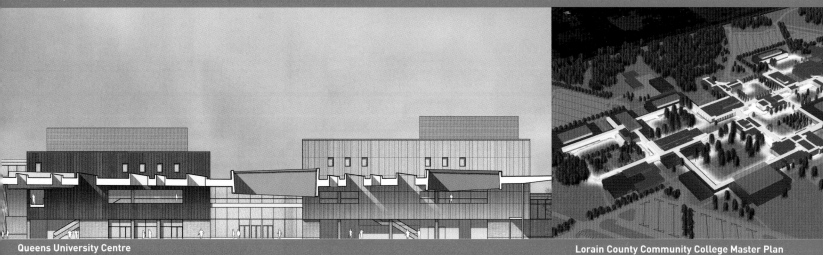

Queens University Centre
Kingston, Canada

Lorain County Community College Master Plan
Elyria, Ohio

University of Maine Master Plan
Orono, Maine

University of Massachusetts Recreation Center
Amherst, Massachusetts

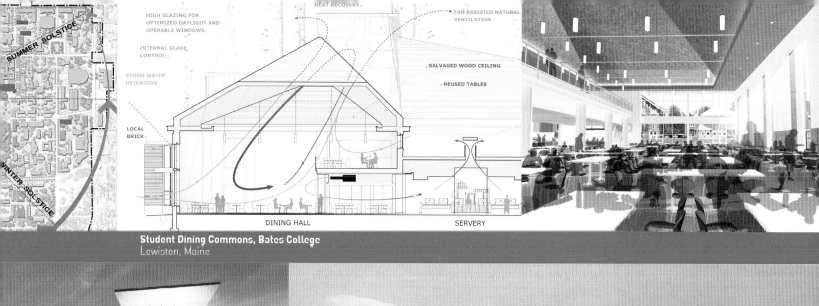

Student Dining Commons, Bates College
Lewiston, Maine

Sacred Heart University Gallery Building
Fairfield, Connecticut

Bryn Athyn College Residences
Bryn Athyn, Pennsylvania

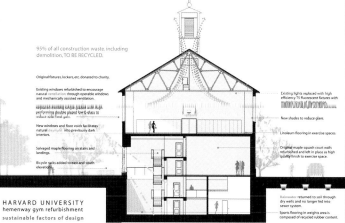

Hemenway Gymnasium, Harvard University
Cambridge, Massachusetts

University of Balamand Engineering
Tripoli, Lebanon

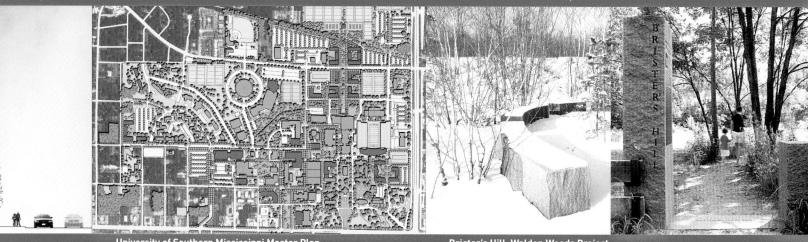

University of Southern Mississippi Master Plan
Hattiesburg, Mississippi

Brister's Hill, Walden Woods Project
Concord, Massachusetts

regenerative
cities

The human-centered design of Sasaki aims to benefit the public realm and foster regenerative cities that are conducive to human growth and potential. Indianapolis's virtually forgotten industrial past is resurrected with a revitalized canal, once abandoned but now lined with cultural institutions, hotels, and housing. In Philadelphia, the University of Pennsylvania is reconnecting both to the riverfront as well as to the city's central business district by a series of real and conceptual "bridges." The site of a great Chicago lakefront steel mill, idle since the 1980s, offers the opportunity to design a vibrant new mixed-use community that ensures lakefront access to the adjacent neighborhood, nurtured for more than a century by the mill during its heyday. In Dallas, the most automobile-centric of cities, a Transitway designed by Sasaki in the mid-1990s has convinced a highly skeptical city of the value of light rail. At the Port of Los Angeles, the Sasaki plan shows that the presence of an economically vibrant international seaport—the nation's largest—can coexist with an abutting residential neighborhood—and make both thrive, especially when the plan calls for generous green and waterfront space for the local community and waterside linkages to adjacent coastal neighborhoods.

Charleston, South Carolina

The east side of the Charleston peninsula borders the Cooper River. By the latter part of the twentieth century, this shoreline had declined into a stretch of rotten, and largely abandoned piers. Sasaki was hired to transform this waterfront into a park worthy of the city's great tradition of elegant urbanism.

Reconnecting the city and its people to the waterfront required connecting the city's human systems back to the natural systems of the river. The city grid extends into the park, making physical and visual connections to the Cooper River. This framework creates site lines for landmarks and active areas at the terminus of primary streets. Shaded by a tree canopy, quiet garden rooms of varied design connect to the city's edge to create extensions of the urban form. The large public lawn frames the central fountain, bringing water into the park and thereby strengthening the visual land/water connection. The 1,200-foot, palmetto-lined esplanade follows the natural water line, ensuring public access to the water's edge. Restored salt marshes sweep out into the river from the esplanade edge, creating valuable habitat and a rich visual experience, while retaining the memory of the port with the pattern of pilings and inevitable deposition at the mouth of the river.

The completion of the park spurred both public and private investment, proving once more that a truly great public park yields benefits across a wide economic spectrum.

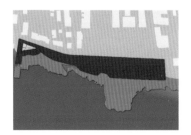

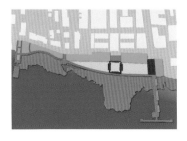

Ashley River

Cooper River

Charleston Harbor

top left restored salt marsh

left middle previous conditions

left bottom pervious surface
analysis before and after

top right aerial view

above location map

right integration of city grid into park

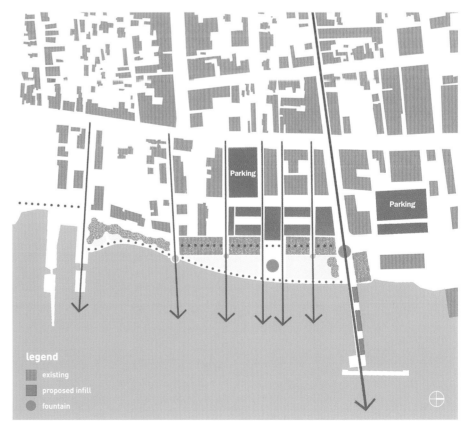

Parking

Parking

legend

existing

proposed infill

fountain

Adgers Wharf

Crushed stonedust

Recycled granite to line park edge

Handmade local brick

Restored Salt Marsh

Restored salt marsh

Old pier piles, preserved for bird habitat and aquatic life

The River

Marine wood (Ipe), with natural resins that obviate use of toxic maintenance products

Urban infill
and regeneration

Shaded Walk

Connecting the city to the waterfront

Walk/Bike path

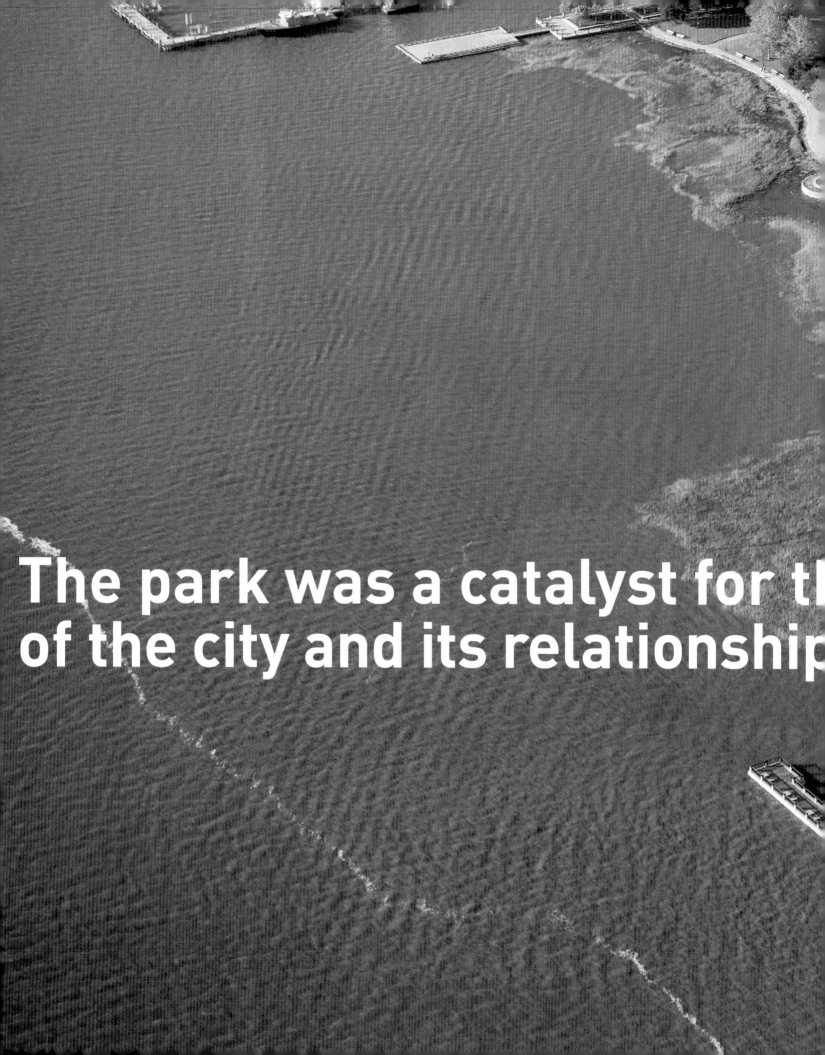

The park was a catalyst for t[...]
of the city and its relationship[...]

e regeneration
to the waterfront.

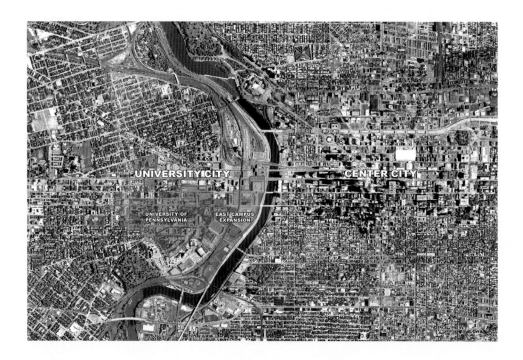

Penn Connects: A Vision for the Future

University of Pennsylvania, Philadelphia, Pennsylvania

University of Pennsylvania President Amy Gutmann's inaugural goal was to "engage locally and globally." Penn's 269-acre West Philadelphia campus has always been isolated from the downtown business district and residential neighborhoods across the Schuylkill River. With the university's acquisition of 24 acres of former Post Office facilities and under-utilized surface parking, a new opportunity emerged to connect these two communities. But there were daunting obstacles: irregular and triangular land configurations, multiple levels of adjacent streets and blocks, lack of direct roadway access, and numerous working rail lines. By identifying a series of virtual "bridges of connectivity", a strategy was conceived for the growth of the academic and research campus while seamlessly integrating urbane mixed-use development along key city streets.

The "Bridges of Connectivity" serve as the conceptual armature for organizing the major land uses and development zones proposed for the East Campus area: A "Living/Learning Bridge" re-establishes an active Walnut Street and connects to Rittenhouse Square and Center City; A "Sports/Recreation Bridge" proposes a dramatic new pedestrian-only cable-stay span and incorporates student-life programs like a series of sports and recreation areas along the river adjacent to the historic Franklin Field stadium; A "Health Sciences/Cultural Bridge" at South Street and future "Research Bridge" accommodate health-care and research endeavors that are critical for both the university's and city's growth. The plan celebrates East Campus's industrial history while establishing a real physical presence for Penn along the banks of the Schuylkill.

top left city context

above existing conditions

top right vision for East Campus area

near right existing condition and campus armature

far right Walnut Street corridor

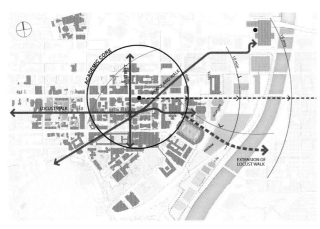

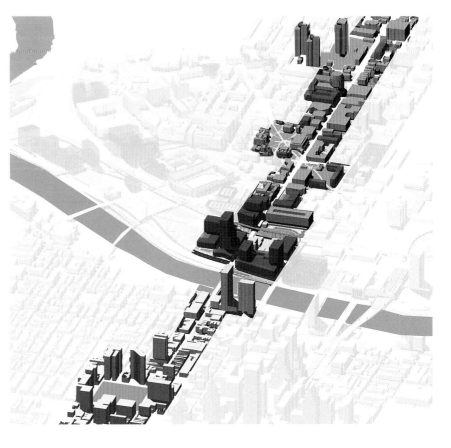

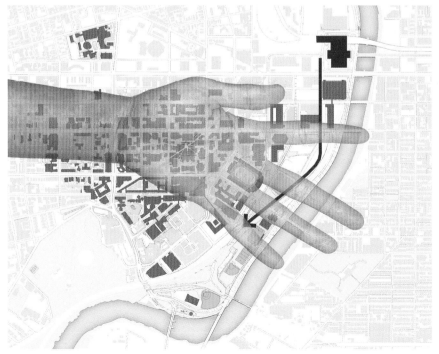

above Penn Park and Fields

right connections concept

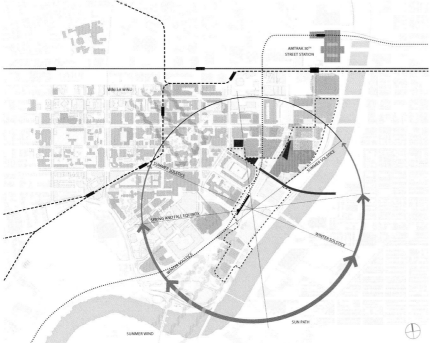

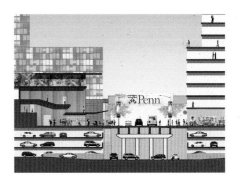

above Walnut Street gateway

left environmental analysis

C College House Hill Square

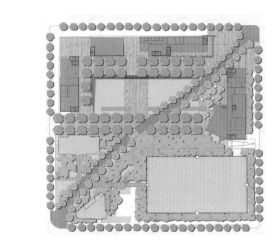

C College House Hill Square

above and below Walnut Street

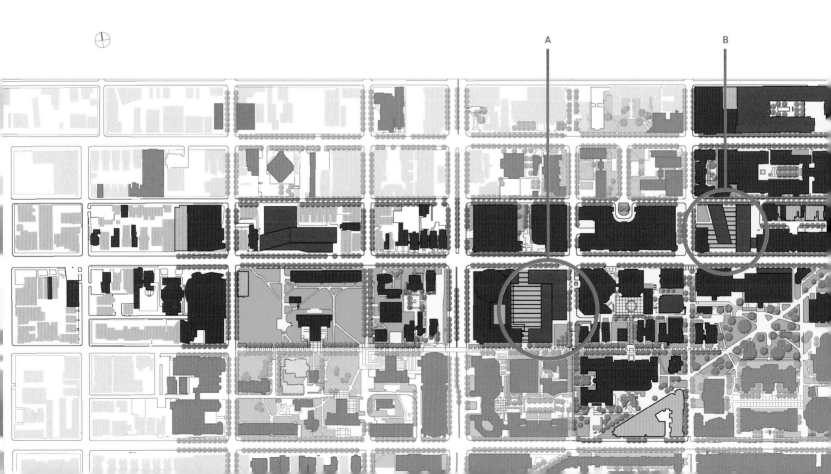

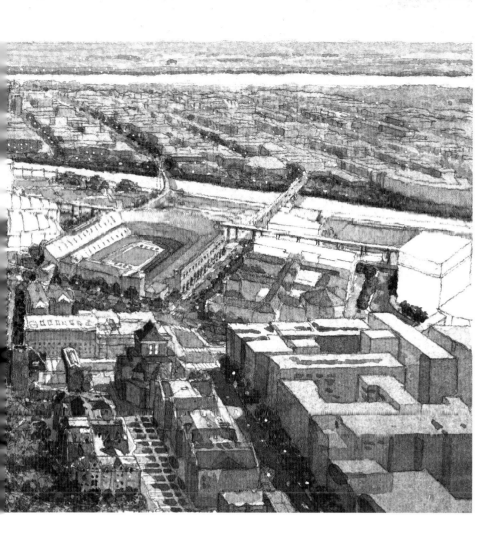

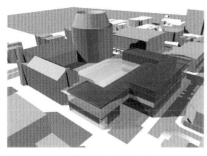

A academic: 3700 Walnut Street

B academic: 3400 Walnut Street

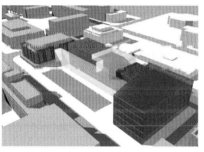

D research/nanotechnology: 3200 Walnut Street

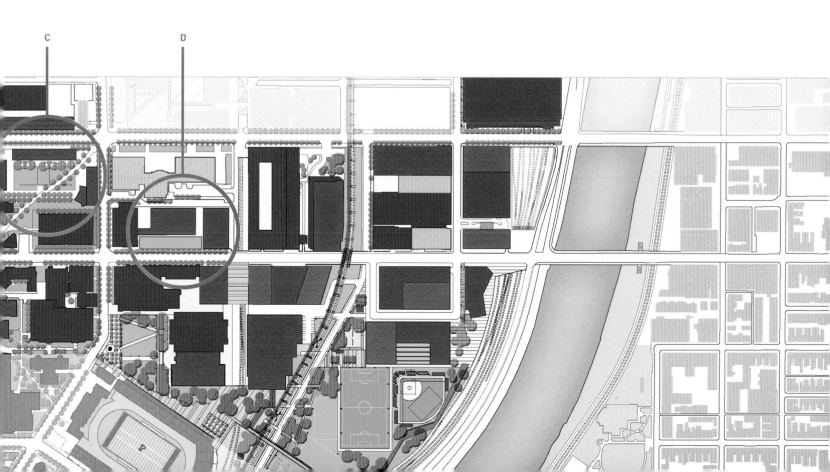

New recreational opportunities were identified to permit a contiguous expansion of the athletic precinct. A new urban park, defined as a public realm for community and campus interaction, will accommodate a series of carefully planned venues for intercollegiate and intramural sporting events. The design vocabulary and framework of the new open space are based on an extension of the existing image-defining public spaces, Locust Walk and College Green. Direct access to transit and improved pedestrian and bicycle routes will reduce the need for vehicular movement in the campus environment.

Critical to the idea of a sustainable campus, strategic sites throughout the university were investigated for regeneration and densification by academic programs, housing, research and sports. A phased plan is proposed as a natural growth of the campus in planned steps of realizable development, thoughtfully staged in coordination with the university's capital planning, real-estate and development goals. It addresses the immediate facility needs as well as strategic priorities that may arise over the next thirty years.

above and far right Penn Park and Fields

right stormwater vegetation trench

additional flood area for larger storm events

storm water infiltration tanks under athletic field | sidewalk | vegetated swale | grove of riparian trees | sidewalk | roadway

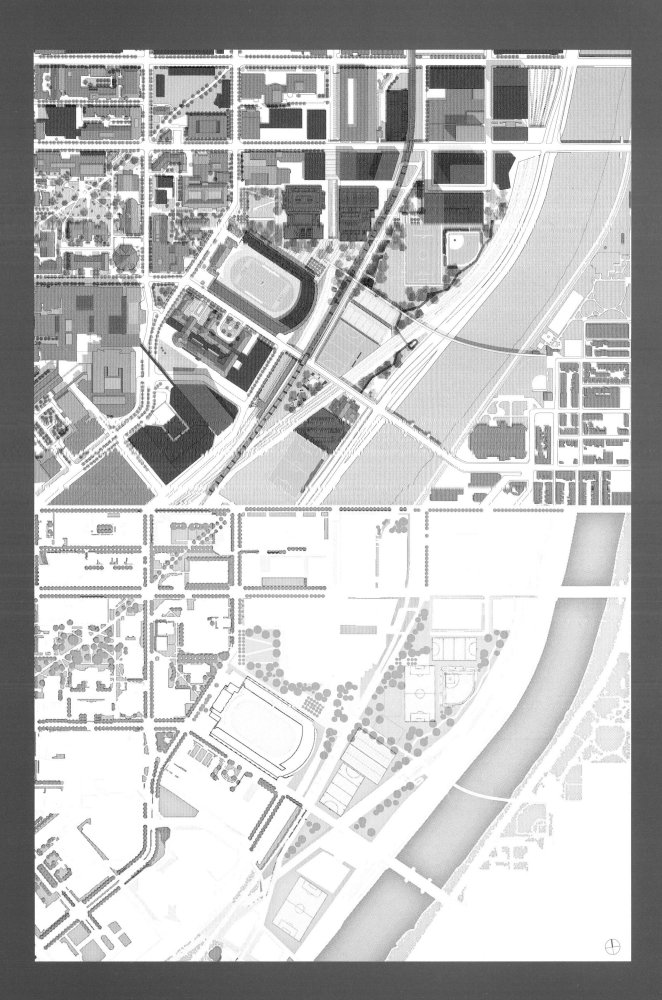

Dallas Area Rapid Transitway

Dallas, Texas

When the first phase of the Dallas Area Rapid Transit (DART) system opened in the summer of 1996, it was largely considered by this automobile-centered city an admirable undertaking with limited appeal to tourists and conventioneers, but not a system that could offer a sizable impact on the vast, booming metropolitan area. Defying naysayers, DART and the City of Dallas proceeded with their forward-thinking plan.

Working with the client groups, including abutting property owners and community organizations, Sasaki conceived the Transitway as a "Ramblas of the Southwest," the famous linear park in Barcelona. The entire length of the Transitway is unified with street trees, streetscape features unique to it, and a dynamic public-arts program. Public squares embrace distinct locations of each transit station, while the blocks between stations are designed to clearly define the Transitway, local access, and pedestrian zones. The design employs a unique paving design, lighting and vibrant public art, such as clock towers and 3-D area maps to support the development of ground-level retail, animate the street, and provide a safe environment during off-peak use.

Dallas, a city that always thinks big, is now reaping a big payoff from its investment. DART has gone from carrying 1.4 million passengers in 1996 to 17.5 million passengers in 2005. The vibrant urban and landscape accoutrements lining the core 1.2-mile downtown path of DART Rail, known as the DART CBD Transitway, are now firmly part of Dallas's urban character. DART is moving forward with a $2.4 billion expansion plan that is expected to more than double the size of the system, at present forty-five miles total. System-wide, more than $3 billion in private development along DART lines is taking place or being announced. According to the *Dallas Morning News*, DART can boast that it is not only the first light rail system ever in the Southwest, but now the fifth largest in the United States, behind Los Angeles, Newark, New Jersey, San Diego and Portland, Oregon.

top left and right station views

above transit system from above

The elements that line the d
are now firmly part of Dallas

wntown path of DART
urban character.

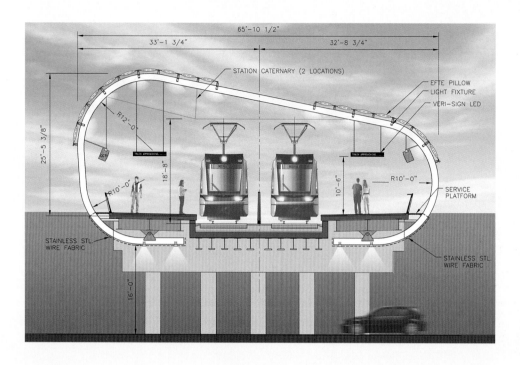

Diagram labels:
65'-10 1/2"
33'-1 3/4"
32'-8 3/4"
STATION CATENARY (2 LOCATIONS)
EFTE PILLOW
LIGHT FIXTURE
VERI-SIGN LED
R12'-0"
25'-5 3/8"
18'-8"
TRAIN APPROACHING
TRAIN APPROACHING
R10'-0"
10'-6"
R10'-0"
SERVICE PLATFORM
STAINLESS STL. WIRE FABRIC
STAINLESS STL. WIRE FABRIC
16'-0"

Charlotte Light Rail Transit

Charlotte, North Carolina

The South Corridor project for the Charlotte Area Transit System (CATS) is an eleven-mile-long traffic infrastructure, landscape, and architecture undertaking aimed at providing an alternative transit and urban solution to a significant fraction of Charlotte's metropolitan area. Sasaki Eco-Technologies—working in concert with the firm's Architecture, Planning, and Landscape Architecture practices—has been charged with designing stations and streetscapes for the fifteen stations along the corridor.

The most significant station along the corridor is the Charlotte Transit Center (CTC) Arena Transit Station in downtown Charlotte. The station is conceived as a "light beam" bridging Trade Street and wrapped around a former trolley-system street bridge. The elegant and simple asymmetrical shape of the station echoes the asymmetrical section of downtown Charlotte's development while providing a transparent canopy over the station's public platform space. Instead of glass, the station is glazed with a system of ETFE panels, providing transparency, daylighting, and shading as part of a unified cladding system. Versatile lighting systems will allow the station to change color keyed to major civic, business, and sports events—this is especially important given the station's location directly adjacent to a major sports arena. The color display in conjunction with the movement of people, cars, and trains provides an urban spectacle for a vibrant section of Charlotte's downtown area.

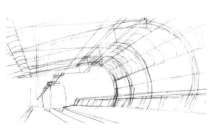

top left station section
left station sketch
right station night views
top right station day view
far right station site

Beijing, China

As contemporary China emerges on the world stage, Beijing's 798 Arts District is poised to become a center of the country's creative culture. The district's modern bohemian style, combined with its historic industrial architecture, makes it one of Beijing's most distinctive neighborhoods—a kind of SoHo with an Asian spirit. The challenge presented is to preserve the character and spirit of the district while infusing additional revenue-generating programs, in an effort to ensure that it remains a vibrant and innovative destination.

The 798 Vision Plan seeks to regenerate the area as a high-quality, mixed-use district with a distinct focus on the arts. Planning and design principles include emphasizing the arts as a central theme, retaining the qualities of the historic industrial aesthetic and developing strategies that increase visibility and encourage a wide variety of creative industries and complementary uses. The framework plan for the district seeks to incorporate modern facilities such a new school for the arts, theaters and performance spaces, hotels and conference centers, parks and outdoor space for gatherings, and live/work housing for local artists. Emphasizing the pedestrian character of the district, including its distinctive courtyards, corridors and passageways is another critical component of the plan. Increased connections to adjacent neighborhoods and better integration with the city are key aspects of the strategy. The positioning of new civic plazas and other open spaces adjacent to the proposed cultural institutions adds opportunities for indoor and outdoor events, and art installations.

A Bauhaus-style factory building from the 1950's was recently transformed by French architect Jean-Michel Wilmotte and the Chinese firm MADA, into The Ullens Centre for the Arts. This stunning space is one of the first privately supported arts institutes in China. With this addition, as well as the infusion of arts-related uses, clearer access and exposure, additional affordable studios for local artists, and new parks and plazas, the district will continue to sustainably regenerate itself as a dynamic center of culture in Beijing.

top left Railyard Park

above top Ullens Centre for the Arts

above bottom existing structures

top right theater

right proposed program

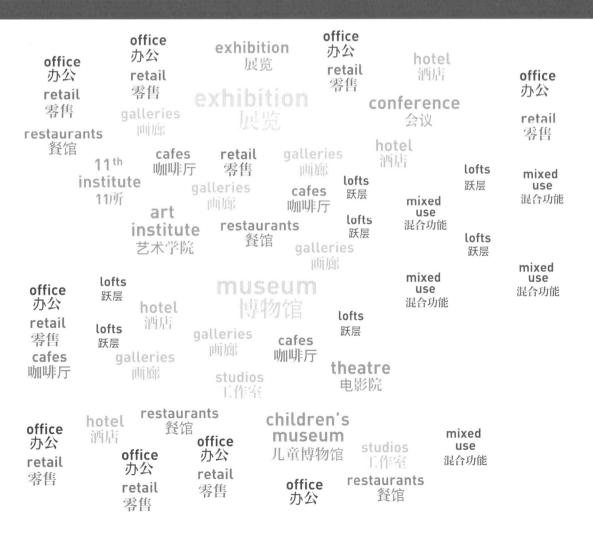

office
办公

office
办公

exhibition
展览

office
办公

hotel
酒店

office
办公

retail
零售

retail
零售

retail
零售

office
办公

exhibition
展览

conference
会议

restaurants
餐馆

galleries
画廊

hotel
酒店

retail
零售

11th
institute
11所

cafes
咖啡厅

retail
零售

galleries
画廊

hotel
酒店

lofts
跃层

mixed
use
混合功能

galleries
画廊

cafes
咖啡厅

lofts
跃层

mixed
use
混合功能

lofts
跃层

art
institute
艺术学院

restaurants
餐馆

lofts
跃层

mixed
use
混合功能

galleries
画廊

lofts
跃层

office
办公

lofts
跃层

museum
博物馆

mixed
use
混合功能

mixed
use
混合功能

retail
零售

hotel
酒店

lofts
跃层

cafes
咖啡厅

lofts
跃层

galleries
画廊

cafes
咖啡厅

galleries
画廊

studios
工作室

theatre
电影院

office
办公

hotel
酒店

restaurants
餐馆

children's
museum
儿童博物馆

mixed
use
混合功能

retail
零售

office
办公

office
办公

studios
工作室

office
办公

retail
零售

restaurants
餐馆

retail
零售

The district's modern bohem
historic industrial architectu
most distinctive neighborhoo

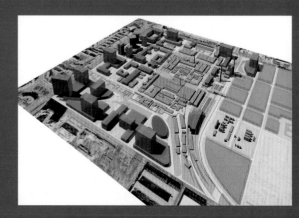

above master plan

top right northwest entry

left and right development strategy

an style, combined with its
re, makes it one of Beijing's
ds.

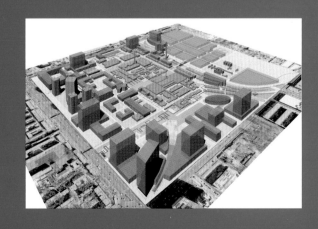
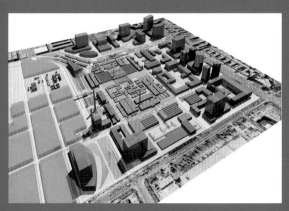

Drexel Recreation Center

Drexel University, Philadelphia, Pennsylvania

The Drexel campus straddles both sides of Market Street in Philadelphia's University City section, adjacent to the University of Pennsylvania and 30th Street Station, the city's primary train terminal. The project site houses a 1960s-era athletic complex, the Daskalasis Athletic Center (DAC), surrounded by one of Drexel's few outdoor landscape spaces.

Given the compact and dense nature of the campus, the DAC addition had to accomplish several institutional and programmatic goals: increase the university's visual presence along Market Street, integrate existing and new buildings into a unified complex, group all of the recreation facilities—as distinguished from varsity athletics—into a new building wing, and maximize the preservation of the site's open landscape areas wherever possible. The new building wraps around two sides of the DAC building, providing a new urban presence for the complex along Market Street. The new façade is treated as large glazed screen with meandering folds shaded by the extension of the building's floors. The folded enclosure provides alcoves along the exercise areas, where active users and equipment add a sense of color and movement to the building's façade. The building provides space for a Multi-Activity Court (MAC) gymnasium, fitness, weights and group exercise areas, squash courts, and locker rooms, linked by an "interior street" connecting the Market Street entrance and a new entrance at the site's north end.

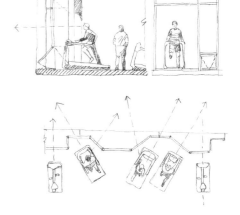

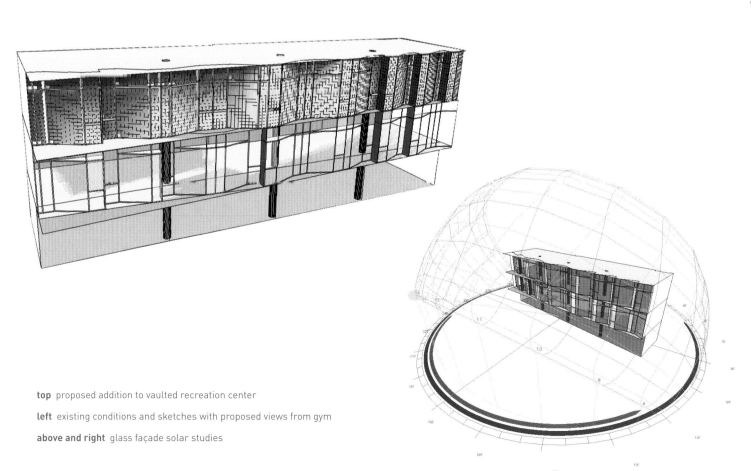

top proposed addition to vaulted recreation center

left existing conditions and sketches with proposed views from gym

above and right glass façade solar studies

Complementing the kinetic animation of the floor above, at street level the building engages the passing urban scene. At the far eastern edge, paving patterns echo the angular folds of the building, and a café is placed among trees preserved and integrated into the design. Along this edge, a restaurant will engage the larger community as well as students. At the opposite western end, a previously nondescript corner is brought to life through the combination of a landscaped plaza and the center's climbing wall framed in glass—a further outward expression of a building whose very purpose is movement, dynamism, and promotion of the academic ideal of a trained mind and a trained body.

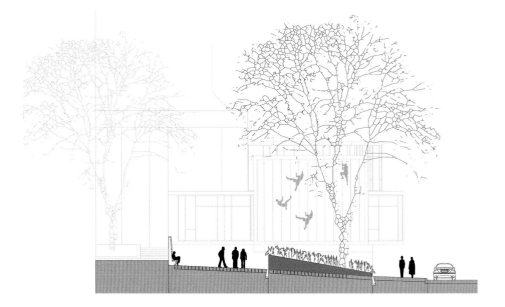

top left first floor and site

above view along Market Street

right early strategy sketch

below glass façade model studies

bottom left street section

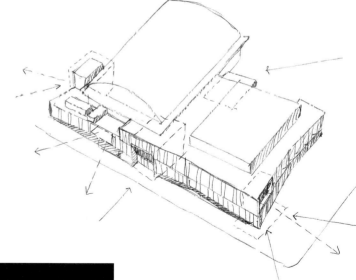

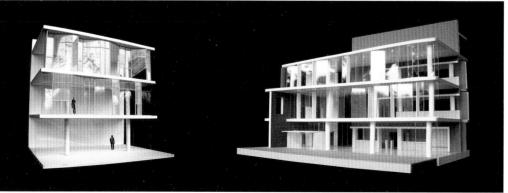

East Baltimore Neighborhood Plan

Baltimore, Maryland

With the dramatic transformations of the harbor and many inner-city neighborhoods, Baltimore has experienced an urban renaissance in recent years. Many of Baltimore's historic rowhouse neighborhoods have, however, continued to suffer from abandonment and disinvestment. In East Baltimore, despite the presence of the internationally recognized Johns Hopkins Medical Center, the adjacent neighborhoods have not benefited from the tremendous economic prosperity at their doorstep. It is hoped that plans to redevelop a new Life Sciences district next to the medical center (the Phase I area) will contribute to the neighborhood's regeneration and break down existing barriers between the medical campus and the surrounding neighborhoods.

The East Baltimore Neighborhood Plan, Phase II and III, builds on the opportunities created by the Phase I redevelopment to guide the regeneration of the surrounding neighborhoods. The plan creates a transition in scale and uses from the large institutional buildings within the medical center and Life Sciences district, to the two-, and three-story rowhouses that define the East Baltimore neighborhoods. The plan preserves viable blocks of historic rowhouses while sensitively integrating new, mixed-income housing on in-fill sites. A reinvigorated "Main Street" will serve as a mixed-use corridor linking the medical center through the Life Sciences district to a new commuter rail station on the Maryland Rail Commuter (MARC) line. Transit-oriented development is planned around the station. Workplace uses, including life sciences spin-offs, will be integrated along the Main Street corridor, and within renovated industrial buildings adjacent to the rail corridor. Tree-lined streets will restore the green canopy of the neighborhood, and many small parks will provide convenient and safe public spaces near homes. At the eastern area, a new community school campus will be a center for neighborhood activity, revolving around life-long recreation, cultural activities, and family support services. To the north, a proposed MARC station will anchor higher-density housing, retail, workplaces in renovated warehouses, and new development along the rail corridor.

top left existing row houses

above community workshop

top right major transportation corridors

right abandoned property

far right civic analysis

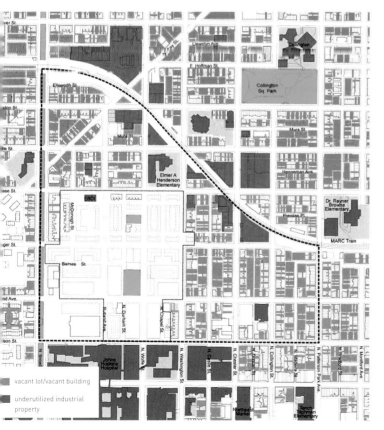

vacant lot/vacant building

underutilized industrial property

civic features

- landmark
- school
- hospital
- church
- community center
- park
- retail
- other
- train/subway

The Neighborhood Plan is fou
sustainability: social, econom

The East Baltimore Neighborhood Plan is founded on three pillars of sustainability: social, economic, and environmental. The development of a new community school provides the foundation for community development intended to bring together existing and new residents of all generations. Nearly forty percent of the area's rowhouses will be rehabilitated, allowing many residents to remain in their homes. Areas that are too far deteriorated will be redeveloped with housing for a mix of incomes, family types, and ages. The Life Sciences district will generate new economic opportunities that will be accommodated on infill sites and within renovated industrial buildings. High-density urban form and transit-oriented development will support a multi-modal transit service and walking, reducing the need for cars. A connected open space system will enhance neighborhood character. Thoughtful design of parks and the addition of a canopy of street trees will reduce storm water run off, and further mitigate the heat of summer. The design of the parks will feature special porous paving, tree species, and other vegetation, providing both ecological value and stormwater elements.

above Life Sciences district

top right sustainability plan

right master plan

Legend:
- public open space
- porous hardscape
- parking courts
- roof gardens
- bio-retention swales
- special streets
- T transit corridors
- sustainability focus area

MARC Line

5 minute walk

Wolfe Street Bus Route

Washington Street Bus Route

nded on three pillars of
c, and environmental.

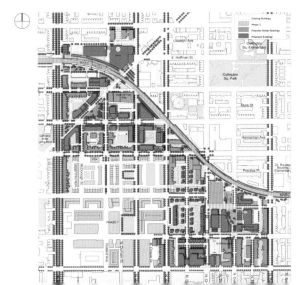

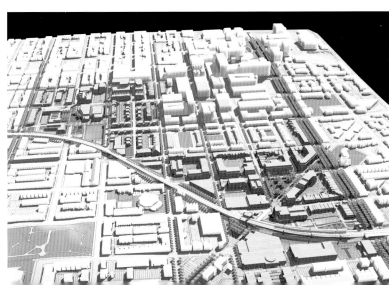

Detroit Civic Center Riverfront Promenade

Detroit, Michigan

Despite its importance and history, for many decades Detroit's waterfront was a neglected remnant of the city's industrial past. Sasaki was brought in to collaborate with Albert Kahn Associates, based in Detroit, to reimagine a thin strip—3,000 feet long but less than 100 feet wide—along the Detroit River adjacent to the Detroit Civic Center. It was here that the French explorer Cadillac first landed and established a fort in 1701, naming it "Detroit" from the French word for "strait," referring to this stretch of water joining Lake St. Clair with Lake Erie.

In addition to the site's compact size, there were challenges presented by the presence of the overhead "people mover" light-rail system that bisects the site as it snakes through downtown Detroit. The design strategy yielded an elegant solution that playfully engages with this massive piece of infrastructure while referencing the site's maritime history. A stepped concrete helix resembles a coil of rope unwinding and morphing into a gently undulating serpentine seat wall. Despite its jaunty presence, this nautical allusion has a practical side—as the seat wall meanders down the site, it weaves among the twenty-five-foot columns supporting the people mover above, creating a usable civic environment out of what would otherwise be dark and forbidding leftover space. As an iconic image for the site, the helix is envisioned as a pedestal for future major sculptural installation. Light- and dark-grey striped paving forms a dramatic backdrop.

Completing the scene, landscaped berms and groves of river-birch trees recall the sylvan riverfront first encountered by the French explorers more than three centuries ago. All up and down the site, a variety of commuter, tourist, and personal watercraft dock along the waterfront as visitors and locals enjoy a reclaimed part of Detroit's natural and historic legacy.

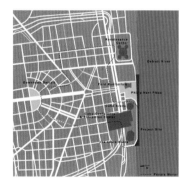

top left riverfront promenade

above context plan

right promenade park

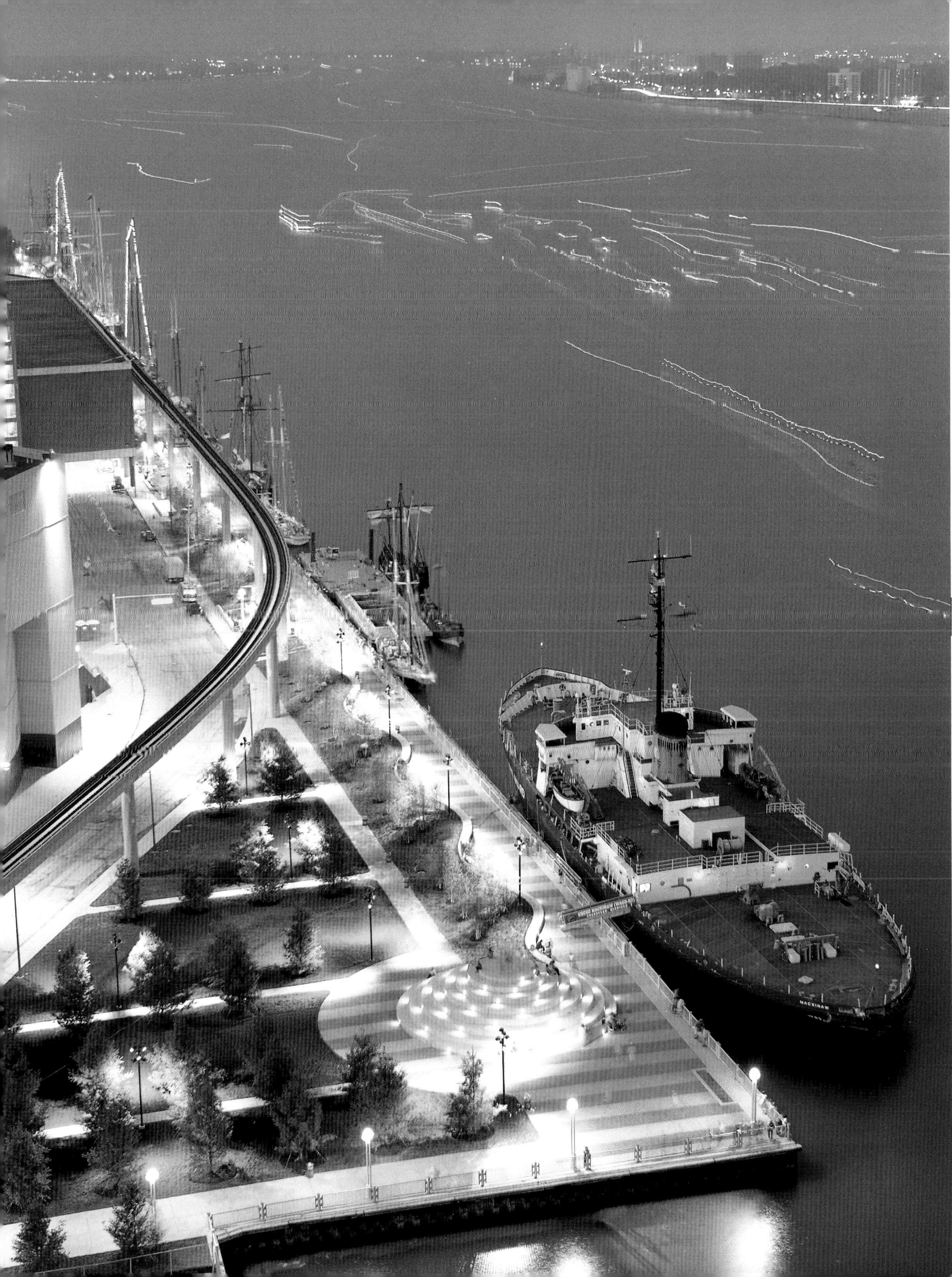

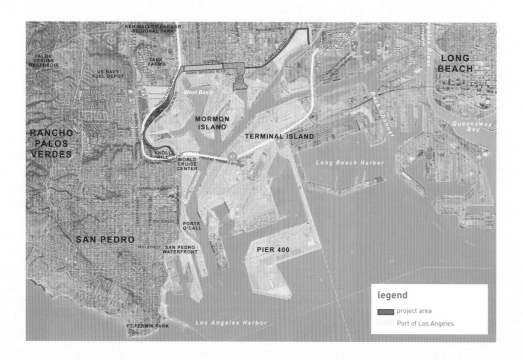

Port of Los Angeles, San Pedro and Wilmington, California

Wilmington is a working-class neighborhood adjacent to the Port of Los Angeles (POLA), the nation's largest seaport. In another era, just this combination alone would be a recipe for enmity between a huge industrial operation and its economically and politically powerless next-door neighbors. But POLA, deeply aware of its civic and environmental responsibility, hired Sasaki to master plan ninety-six acres that would separate Wilmington from the noise and emissions of port operations, create a community amenity that provides regional linkages, connect Wilmington with its waterfront, incorporate sustainable design strategies, and increase economic opportunities. POLA remains a viable contributor to the local economy, directly or indirectly responsible for more than 2,600 jobs.

The first step in the analysis set aside two overlapping zones: one zone is parallel (east/west) with the waterfront, and one is perpendicular to it (north/south). Wilmington's immediate southern neighbor is a terminal dedicated to container traffic, one of the port's twenty-seven terminals. The terminal operates on a 24/7 schedule, with diesel truck traffic coursing principally along its boundary with Wilmington. In response to this, the program establishes a thirty-acre parcel, "the Buffer" as a physical separation from the terminal. The parcel will consist of a set of raised landforms—offering elevated views over the container terminal and to the waters of the extensive coastline beyond—that will act as a scenic backdrop for a large, public, green open space oriented east/west. The design vocabulary is at once contemporary yet also referential to the cultural ties of the community— for example, a plaza for large gatherings is culturally compatible with Wilmington's Latino population. The sculptural, faceted quality of the landforms in the Buffer is repeated at the finer grain, evident in the architecture of the pavilions, the selection of the site lighting and furnishings, and in the design of the joint patterns on the ground plane. Integral to the visual expression of the design is a complement of sustainable landscape strategies.

top left and above site context

top right master plan

right section at waterfront tower and tower night view

These strategies include reduction of greenhouse gas and heat-island effect via establishment of a generous tree canopy, water conservation and biodiversity through the use of native and ecologically appropriate plant materials sustained by reclaimed water, reduction of air pollution with titanium-oxide coatings, and green energy production via solar canopies.

The north/south linkage to the water's edge will take place through the zone perpendicular to the waterfront. It begins at the crossroads of the Industrial District and the historic commercial corridor along the east/west zone. The urban design framework of the program promotes commercial and industrial development that builds on the existing marine-related businesses, as well as those that provide public-serving amenities. From there, one will move into the Waterfront District along a processional series of green parks, plazas, terraces, water features, and promenades that provide a landscape narrative featuring the natural history of the shoreline, the rich maritime industrial heritage, and the essential reconnection of the community to its waterfront.

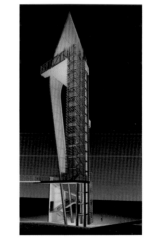

above and below waterfront tower

near right phase 1

far right phase 2

**The design vocabulary is cont
a plaza, for example, for larg
compatible with Wilmington'**

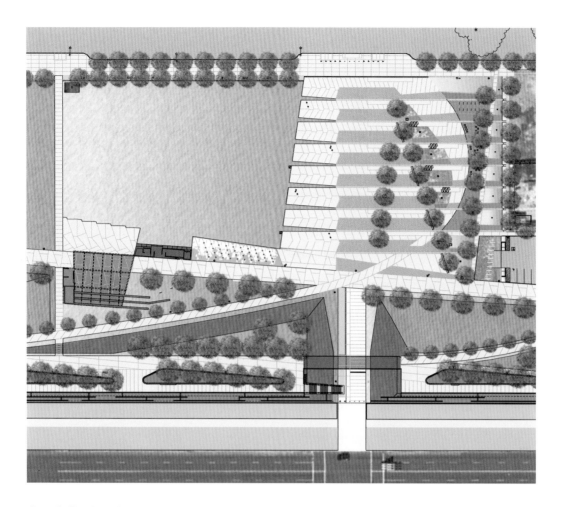

above buffer plaza plan

top right buffer plaza

below buffer grading

15'–20'

2'–25'

26'–30'

above 30'

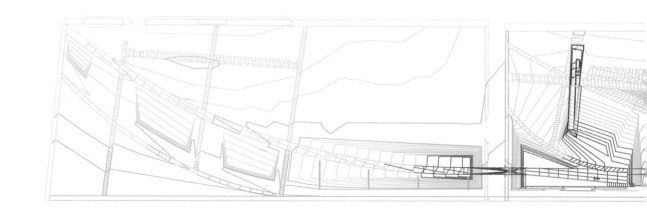

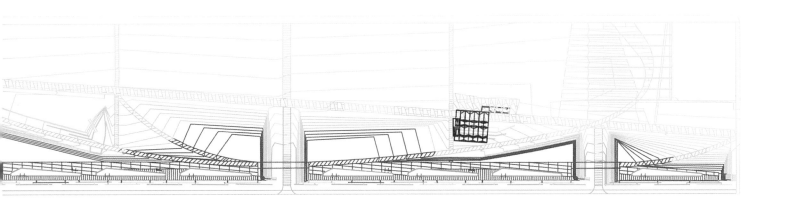

top left and above east pavilion

right C Street promenade

left west buffer pavilion

opposite middle left C Street great lawn

opposite middle right main plaza great lawn

Auraria Higher Education Center Campus Plan

Denver, Colorado

The Auraria Higher Education Center (AHEC) campus in downtown Denver began in 1970 as a then-untested idea—why not serve the needs of three institutions of higher learning by grouping them together, and then blurring the boundaries among them? The idea was to promote social and academic synergy among the schools, save money with shared facilities, and capitalize on the adjacency of downtown Denver to generate jobs, research, and mutually beneficial intellectual capital.

It is an urban success story—AHEC is now a community of more than 37,000 students, faculty, and staff—that's about three times the original size projections that were made when it was formed almost four decades ago. Located in a triangular-shaped district that used to be the separate town of Auraria, Colorado, AHEC accommodates the University of Colorado at Denver Health Sciences Center (UCDHSC), Metropolitan State College of Denver (MSCD), and the Community College of Denver (CCD). Each school has its own distinct identity but shares resources like the library, student center, and recreation facilities. Numerous historic buildings have been preserved, including churches, townhouses, and a landmark brewery.

Sasaki's role was to revisit a master plan done several years ago and establish a pattern for growth to accommodate AHEC's success. The master-plan update builds on the idea of giving each of the institutions its own distinct quarter within AHEC. UCDHSC, MSCD, and CCD will now have an identifiable home within the campus, where each can direct visitors and attract donors to build specialized space. Furthermore, the plan establishes a Campus Crossroads that strengthens the idea of a common mission and shared territory. This district is the site of the library, student center, recreation facilities, and other common services—in other words, it is the heart of AHEC.

top left proposed urban district

above site context

top right view from downtown Denver

near right framework

far right context plan

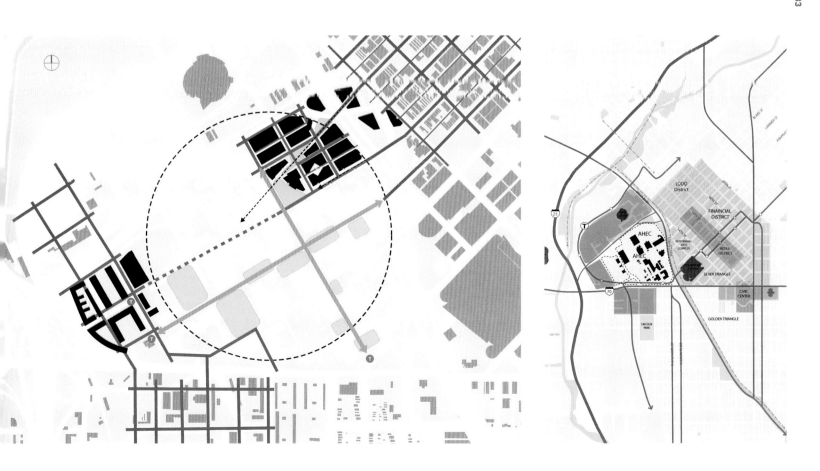

In order to offer more students the option of housing, the plan establishes a Campus Village at the far western end adjacent to a new light-rail station. At the opposite end, a new Urban District—comprising a mix of student and market-rate housing, offices, research space, hotel rooms, cafés, and shops—is placed closest to the city's central business district. This strengthens the connection to downtown and offers the potential for AHEC to partner with private developers, maintaining control of the content of the development while potentially creating new sources of revenue for the institutions and the public entities that support them. To this end, the plan also lays out different economic scenarios to create an administrative structure to fuel the level of capital investment needed to make this urban district a reality.

top left campus-city connection

bottom left master plan

above core campus

Indianapolis, Indiana

The Indianapolis waterfront is an epic story of urban regeneration. A short four decades ago, it was a decrepit riverfront and an abandoned industrial canal—residents of Indiana's capital scarcely thought of themselves as living in a riverfront city. Today it is a vibrant mix of commercial, cultural, and institutional destinations.

The Capital City Landing is the principal park link between the downtown civic/commercial core and the river. The principal organizing element of the landing is the extension of the historic Central Canal. The extension flows into a terminal basin that narrows into a mill flume, recalling the original flume that was on the site, then discharges over a fountain weir into the river. An abandoned sluice was incorporated into the waterfall feature, whose walls are made of Indiana limestone. The landing site, as found, was layered with other remnants of roads, bridges, industrial and commercial buildings, utility corridors, and canals, evidence of 175 years of growth and change within the city. The park design radically rethinks the topography of the site and reinterprets the found-site conditions using contemporary design forms. The planning strategy was analogous to the practice of navigation. Historic routes—waterways, roads, and river bridging points were plotted on the site. These navigation lines became the organizing structure of the new park. The park was made using the operations of cutting and layering—a principal goal was the preservation of river views from as many points in the city as possible. The land was cut into a series of terraces of varied widths that step down to the river from the city, revealing the riparian landscape from the moment one enters the park. The urban walls that were created as part of this cutting and stepping process were arranged in several layers. Limestone cladding, metal trelliswork and pergolas, and vine plantings create a textured, living edge to the spaces of the park.

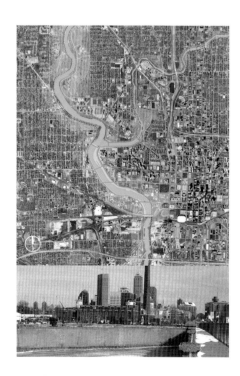

top left Capital City Landing

above waterway and open space context, and existing water wall

top right and right canal promenades

The park design radically reth
site and reinterprets the found
contemporary design forms.

nks the topography of the
site conditions by utilizing

The planning, design, and construction of new public space in Indianapolis exemplify how urban open space can be a key factor in civic regeneration and social sustainability. The site has attracted both the public and private sectors to invest in, or on the edges of, the park. It has instilled a sense of pride in Indianapolis residents, creating a more stable and sustainable population, one that reinvests in its own city, ensuring a high quality of life for future residents. The current buildings around the site include the NCAA Hall of Champions, the Indiana State Museum, the Indiana Historical Society, the Indiana State Library, the Indiana Government Center, Historic Landmarks Foundation of Indiana, new medical research facilities, new housing for the private sector and local academic institutions, a minor-league baseball park, and additions to the Indianapolis Zoo.

top left Capital City Landing

right canal promenade on the 4th of July

Loyola College in Maryland, Baltimore, Maryland

Webster's Dictionary defines palimpsest as "a tablet used after earlier writing has been erased", and "something having diverse layers apparent beneath the surface." Both definitions could apply to the Woodberry section of Baltimore, a rich and multi-layered neighborhood whose striations read like a manuscript of urban history. Along the site of textile mills and quarries, the area is physically isolated due to surrounding parks and expressways. After the mills and other industry moved elsewhere, parts of Woodberry became a much-loved urban forest; the Jones Falls River that once nourished industry now meanders through woods and hiking paths. And yet, even with this reforestation, one corner of Woodberry became a landfill. Loyola College, located a few miles to the east, asked Sasaki to conduct a feasibility study of this seventy-one-acre landfill as a possible site for a sports complex to accommodate the college's soccer, lacrosse, and other programs. This "Field of Dreams" is now moving toward realization though a concerted and committed vision shared by the client and Sasaki for innovative use of infill sites—urban regeneration that uses existing land without further encroaching into greenfield sites.

Among the site's program elements are a 6,000-seat complex with athletic support spaces and a special-events area; a competition lacrosse/soccer field with natural turf; a practice lacrosse/soccer/rugby field with synthetic turf; and a multi-purpose field with natural turf and a 400-meter track. The hilly, irregular site posed a somewhat contradictory challenge: much of the area over the old landfill had to be "packed down" to further isolate buried waste and meet local and national environmental standards. But to flatten the site to accommodate athletic fields, earthen infill had to be brought in. Sasaki collaborated with Haley & Aldrich on this project, and the team designed a complex subsurface system that controls and isolates any gases and other matter from the previous landfill use while allowing the complex infrastructure required for the new multi-athletic use.

top left site slope section

above site slope construction

top right site and plaza plans

right site systems

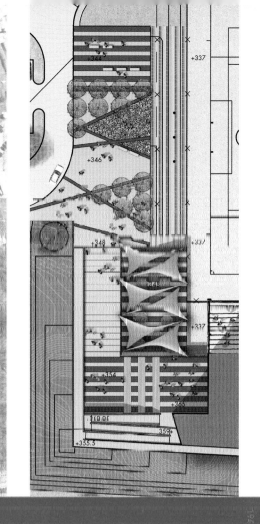

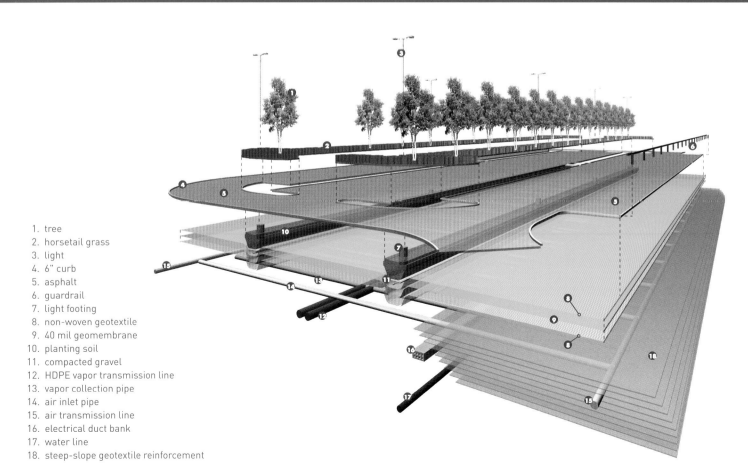

1. tree
2. horsetail grass
3. light
4. 6" curb
5. asphalt
6. guardrail
7. light footing
8. non-woven geotextile
9. 40 mil geomembrane
10. planting soil
11. compacted gravel
12. HDPE vapor transmission line
13. vapor collection pipe
14. air inlet pipe
15. air transmission line
16. electrical duct bank
17. water line
18. steep-slope geotextile reinforcement

A complex subsurface system
previous landfill while allowin
required for the new multi-a

controls and isolates the
g the complex infrastructure
hletic use.

Providence, Rhode Island

Providence, the capital and largest city of Rhode Island, is blessed with a dramatic setting—residential neighborhoods on surrounding hills overlooking a dramatic waterfront on Narragansett Bay. As railways and highways began to pierce the city in its heyday, each district developed its own personality, with each complementing all of the others.

As a means of reinvigorating this post-industrial New England city, Providence 2020 brings all of these districts together while retaining their individuality and character, and relating them to a greater whole: downtown Providence. A continuous waterfront greenway will weave through the different neighborhoods that make up downtown: Promenade, Capital Center/Downcity, Jewelry District, and Narragansett Bay. A strong linear connection will be established through a series of parks that reinforce the city's identity, link districts, and are integral to the surrounding development. Furthermore, a continuous transit spine will link all of the districts together and to downtown and the waterfront.

Each district's historical and architectural attributes are celebrated. Promenade, a former industrial district with a wealth of loft-style buildings, will become a center for innovation and research. Downcity/Capital Center will build on its strengths as the city's traditional financial and political hub. Jewelry District, another former industrial zone, will take advantage of its proximity to universities and hospitals to generate jobs in biomedical research. And the Narragansett Bayfront, a working waterfront, will offer the potential of becoming a dynamic waterfront district ripe for residential conversions and new building development.

As Providence 2020 begins to be implemented, Providence is already showing signs of reinventing itself as a thriving post-industrial city, maximizing its attributes as a university center and nexus of creativity and human innovation.

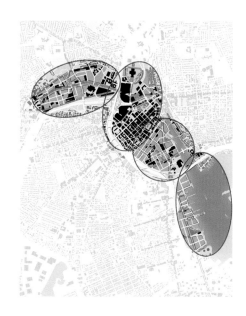

top left site context

above districts

right master plan

existing buildings

proposed buildings

development blocks

top and middle existing highway

bottom proposed highway relocation

right new waterfront district

A series of parks reinforce the
and are integral to the surrou

legend
- proposed buildings
- development blocks

above waterfront park

top right mixed use research district

left park system

right zoning

far right transit

city's identity, link districts, nding development.

legend

▬ proposed transit spine

▬ gold line trolley

▬ green line trolley

▪▪▪▪ proposed trolley

⭕ 5 minute walk radius

Savannah East Riverfront Public Spaces

Savannah, Georgia

Savannah is defined by its beautiful urban squares. In 1733, Georgia's colonial governor, James Oglethorpe, laid out four squares and an urban grid to create the nation's first planned city. Eventually, these four grew to twenty-four squares, each shaded by the city's signature oak trees. There have been no new squares since the 1850s.

For undeveloped land east of the city's main historic district, as part of a 2007 invited competition, Sasaki prepared designs for three new squares. The East Riverfront Neighborhood is more low-lying than the city's historic district, which is somewhat isolated from the riverfront due to the high bluff on which the city is built. This natural condition led to a key design decision by Sasaki to orient these new squares to the river.

While Savannah's historic squares are linked like a series of inward-looking individual green jewels, the new squares and public spaces of the East Riverfront will acknowledge and express their connection to a greater open-space network—both the river to the north and the wetlands to the south. So as the visitor to old Savannah is drawn from one square to the next by glimpses of a dense mass of green, the visitor to the East Riverfront will instead be drawn through the squares' open centers by the prospect of greater views beyond. In a sense, the relatively small spaces will leverage the wider landscape around them, giving them an identity and impact on a scale comparable to the architecture that will surround them.

above Preston Square street elevation and plan

opposite site in relation to historic Savannah, and Preston Square plan

near right environmental graphics and Preston Square perspectives

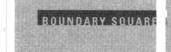

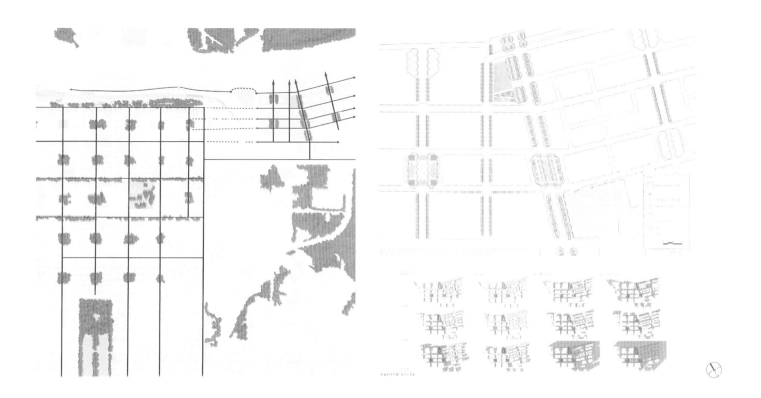

SHADOW STUDY

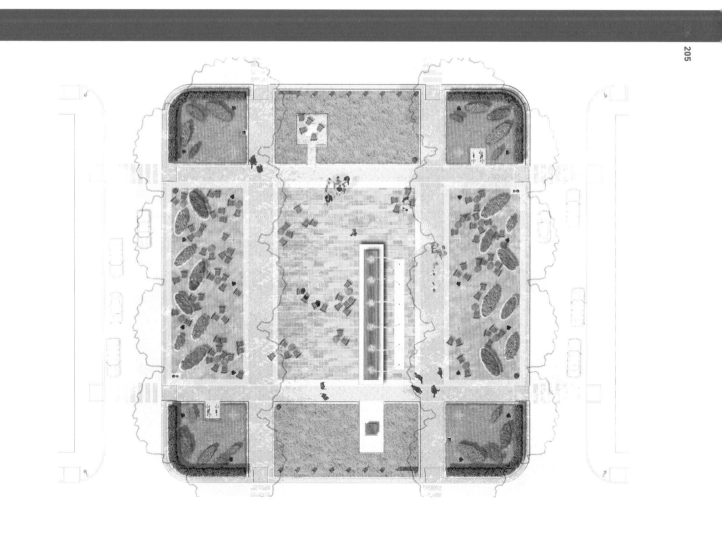

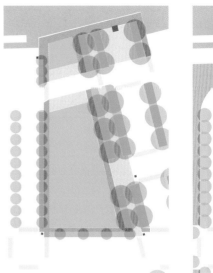
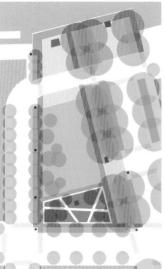

Preston Square will be the district's true urban plaza. In the center of the square is a richly paved blue stone plaza. To the south is a vertical granite pier spilling water over its four faces. Boundary Square sits east of Preston, at a point of transition between the busy commercial center of the new neighborhood to the west and the primarily residential areas to the east. Also designed to have a view toward the river, this square serves as a small neighborhood park with a central lawn flanked by shading oak trees.

Riverfront Park will be the primary gathering space for the East Riverfront neighborhood and a waterside destination for residents throughout Savannah. A sweeping double row of oaks will run the full length of Boundary Street. A third row at the park makes the last piece of the journey to the river not merely a place of passage, but a destination in and of itself. The park provides a place for casual recreation and can accommodate events ranging from private tented events for 250 to small concerts for 350. The park physically engages the river by cantilevering over a portion of the riverfront and offering dramatic views across the river and back toward the city. Like the two smaller squares, it is designed so that future monuments, sculptural installations, and historic markers can be integrated into these vibrant democratic spaces in future decades and centuries.

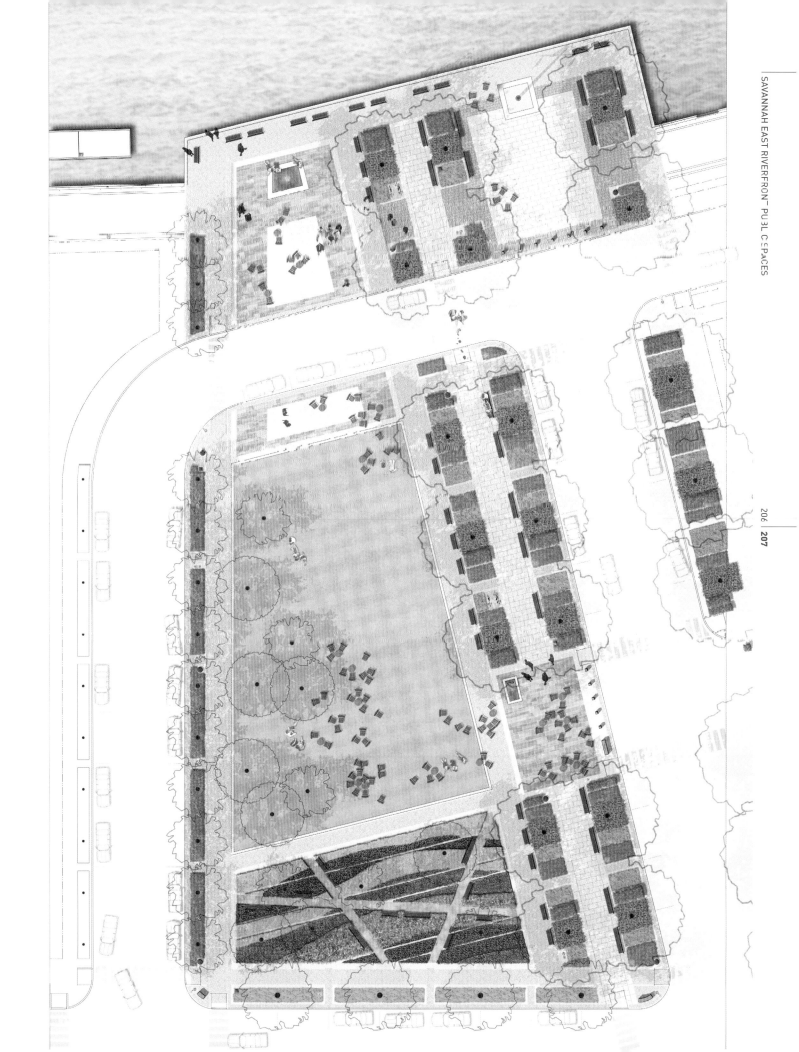

601 Congress Street Roof Garden

Boston, Massachusetts

Sasaki designed the roof garden, atrium planting, and streetscape of the new headquarters building of a major financial services company located in the Seaport district of Boston, collaborating with architects Skidmore, Owings & Merrill (SOM). The building has a double-glazed curtain wall and numerous other sustainability components, making it one of the most advanced green office buildings in Boston.

The fourteen-story building is stepped at the twelfth floor, leaving an open roof area with direct access from adjacent offices, visible from the floors above. The pursuit of LEED® certification was identified as an objective by the owner and SOM. The design team saw this space as an opportunity to create both a terrace and green roof garden capable of serving as an amenity for company employees, as well as a sustainable design component of the building.

The plants used on the terrace and green roof are mostly drought-tolerant, ornamental grasses and sedums. A drainage/water, storage/aeration system was installed over a layer of closed-cell extruded polystyrene insulation. The drainage system consists of lightweight panels of 100% recycled polyethylene, molded to form water retention cups and drainage channels, and engineered to promote irrigation through capillary action and evaporation into the soil/vegetation layer. A layer of filter fabric separates the drainage system from the planting soil. The structural concrete roof slab was waterproofed with a hot, rubberized asphalt monolithic membrane, produced with a minimum twenty-five percent recycled content.

The green roof area provides additional insulation, minimizes stormwater runoff, and reduces the heat-island effect of the building. The green roof's carefully designed coastal flora sightline gives occupants of the terrace a welcome respite from the urban location, and the juxtaposition of the garden against the harbor views lends the impression of being at a seaside location.

top left roof garden view with building behind

above roof garden detail

top right roof garden plan

opposite middle left installation

far middle right view to harbor

right materials detail

CONGRESS STREET

D STREET

CONNECTOR ROAD

INTERSTATE ROUTE I-90

N

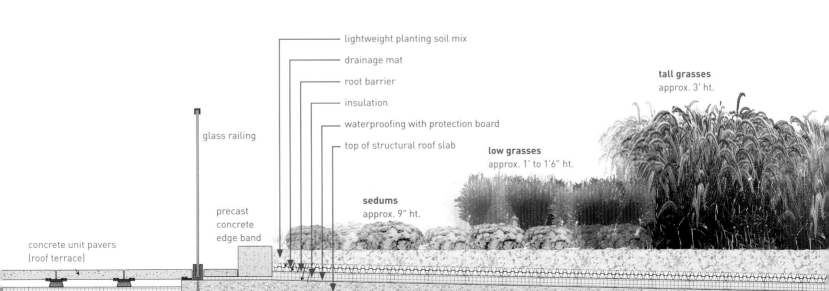

lightweight planting soil mix

drainage mat

root barrier

insulation

waterproofing with protection board

top of structural roof slab

glass railing

precast
concrete
edge band

concrete unit pavers
(roof terrace)

tall grasses
approx. 3' ht.

low grasses
approx. 1' to 1'6" ht.

sedums
approx. 9" ht.

Harbor Point

Stamford, Connecticut

Harbor Point will transform eighty-two acres of former industrial brownfields in Stamford's South End into a dynamic new mixed-use waterfront district. The master plan envisions a new framework of public realm—parks, plazas, and streetscape improvements—to overcome the flood-control walls and levees that have proven historic barriers to the waterfront. In reconnecting the city to the water, the project celebrates the historic and essential relationship between Stamford and Long Island Sound.

By establishing an armature of streets, blocks, and public spaces, a phased strategy for development is proposed for this critical site just a short walk from the major transit station serving Stamford and the metropolitan region. A series of new public parks provide much-needed open space to the South End, make connections to the larger park systems of Stamford, and help to integrate and define unique neighborhoods within the new district. A waterfront square and plaza, lined with retail, hotel, restaurant and office uses, provides a local and regional destination from both land and water. The Commons, an actively programmed urban park, and the Coastal Gardens, a strolling garden of seasonal plantings, provide distinct foregrounds to over 4,000 new units of housing. A public promenade along the water's edge provides continuous access to the water.

Realignment and streetscape improvements to key roadways such as Washington Boulevard link the district to the surrounding neighborhood and establish a network of pedestrian-friendly streets leading from the new community to the nearby transit center and downtown.

With full build-out expected over the next decade, Harbor Point will transform the image of Stamford and reinforce its identity as one of the most desirable destinations for living and working on the Connecticut coast.

top left context

above master plan in context and existing site

right landscape plan

STAMFORD HARBOR

FEDERAL CHANNEL
DREDGED BY ARMY CORPS OF ENGINEERS

WEST BRANCH STAMFORD HARBOR

left public realm activities

right Triangle Park perspective

below Triangle Park in summer, fall,
winter, and spring

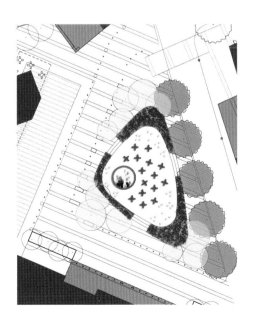

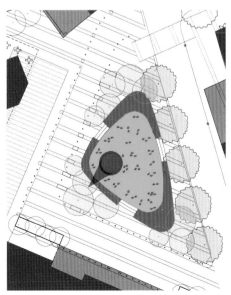

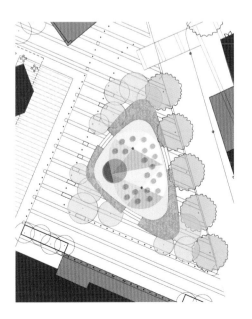

Cincinnati Riverfront Park

Cincinnati, Ohio

Cincinnati River Park aims to create a world-class contemporary setting by reconnecting the heart of the Cincinnati, Fountain Square, to the Ohio River. The thirty-two-acre park is envisioned as the remaining and largest jewel in a series of smaller public parks on the high banks of the downtown portion of the Ohio River. The Riverfront Park will complete the necklace on the Cincinnati riverfront and tie to a much larger statewide recreation trail and bike system that concludes in Columbus, approximately seventy-five miles to the northeast. The John A. Roebling Suspension Bridge, designed by the same engineer as the Brooklyn Bridge and predating the Brooklyn span by more than twenty years, is a major American architectural landmark that, before it traverses the river, neatly bisects the park.

Symbolically, the park's trees and land forms celebrate the presence of the bridge and its historic role as the gateway to the city. A series of terraces slope down to the riverfront, according different perspectives of the span; at the point where bridge meets land, the trees and land forms seem to part, as if a curtain visually unfolding the dramatic urban scene.

The park acts as a setting and catalyst for civic activities and entertainment venues such as the new National Underground Freedom Center, Paul Brown Stadium (home of the Cincinnati Bengals), and the Great American Ballpark (home of the Cincinnati Reds), supported in partnerships with private and public funds. Planned within the waterfront park district is a six-block mixed-use development that will bring roughly 400 residential units, as well as office and commercial activities. The park program includes the creation of an appropriate setting for the bridge, along with areas for large gatherings, passive recreation, and programmed events.

top café plaza

above master plan context

right master plan

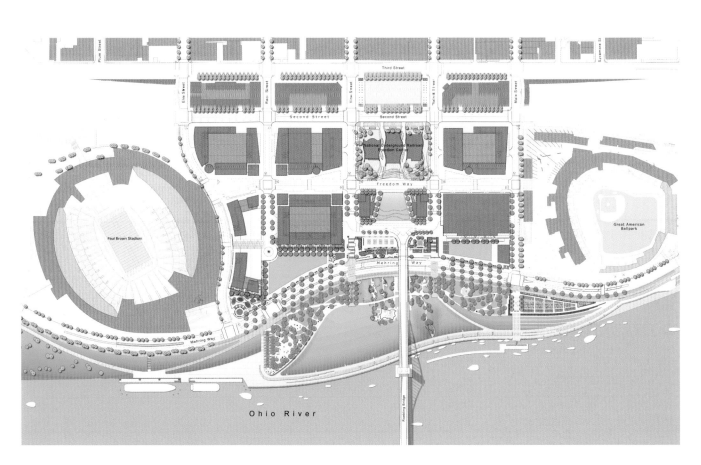

Ohio River

Where bridge meets land, the
to part, as if a curtain unfoldir

Events range from small, picnic-like activities to large national events such as Tall Stakes, which brings 350,000 visitors to the downtown area. Activities in the park include several interactive water features, a 300-foot pier overlooking the river, a sculpture play area, pavilion, bench swings, water gardens, a 100-foot-long riverfront promenade, as well as public land-ings and seasonal docking and wharves that service the commercial cruise boat traffic.

trees and land forms seem
g the dramatic urban scene.

top left aerial view

above bike path

below Race Street Esplanade,
Roebling Green

Chicago, Illinois

The redevelopment of the former Southworks steel mill, located on 575 acres on the shores of Lake Michigan on Chicago's south side, emerged from a vision that began in 1998 with city leaders, planners, commercial developers, community individuals, and civic organizations. From the outset, plans were guided by a focus on transit-oriented development; community connectivity; a mix of land uses with distinct neighborhoods; and extensive parks, public spaces, and natural areas.

In late 2004, Sasaki Associates, in collaboration with Skidmore, Owings and Merrill (SOM), was hired by a private-development consortium to prepare a mixed-use master plan for the site, incorporating the initial visioning principles. The team created a plan for a vibrant new lakefront community with mixed residential and commercial uses, civic and institutional uses, a clear street network as an extension of the neighborhood grid, and over 130 acres of parks and public spaces.

The Southworks master plan centers on ideas of connectivity and weaving the development into the existing urban fabric. Residential neighborhoods to the west of Southworks, which have long been cut off from the lakefront to the east by the steel factory, are reconnected to the lake. Existing parks to the north of the site are connected to those in the south through a new 100-acre lakefront park, which once completed, will add over three miles to the thirty-two-mile-long chain of Chicago lakefront open space.

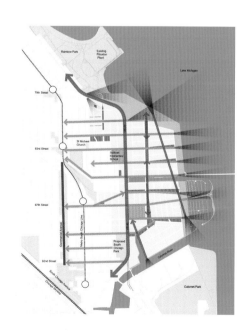

top left Southworks site in context

above view corridors and connections

right master plan

left existing conditions

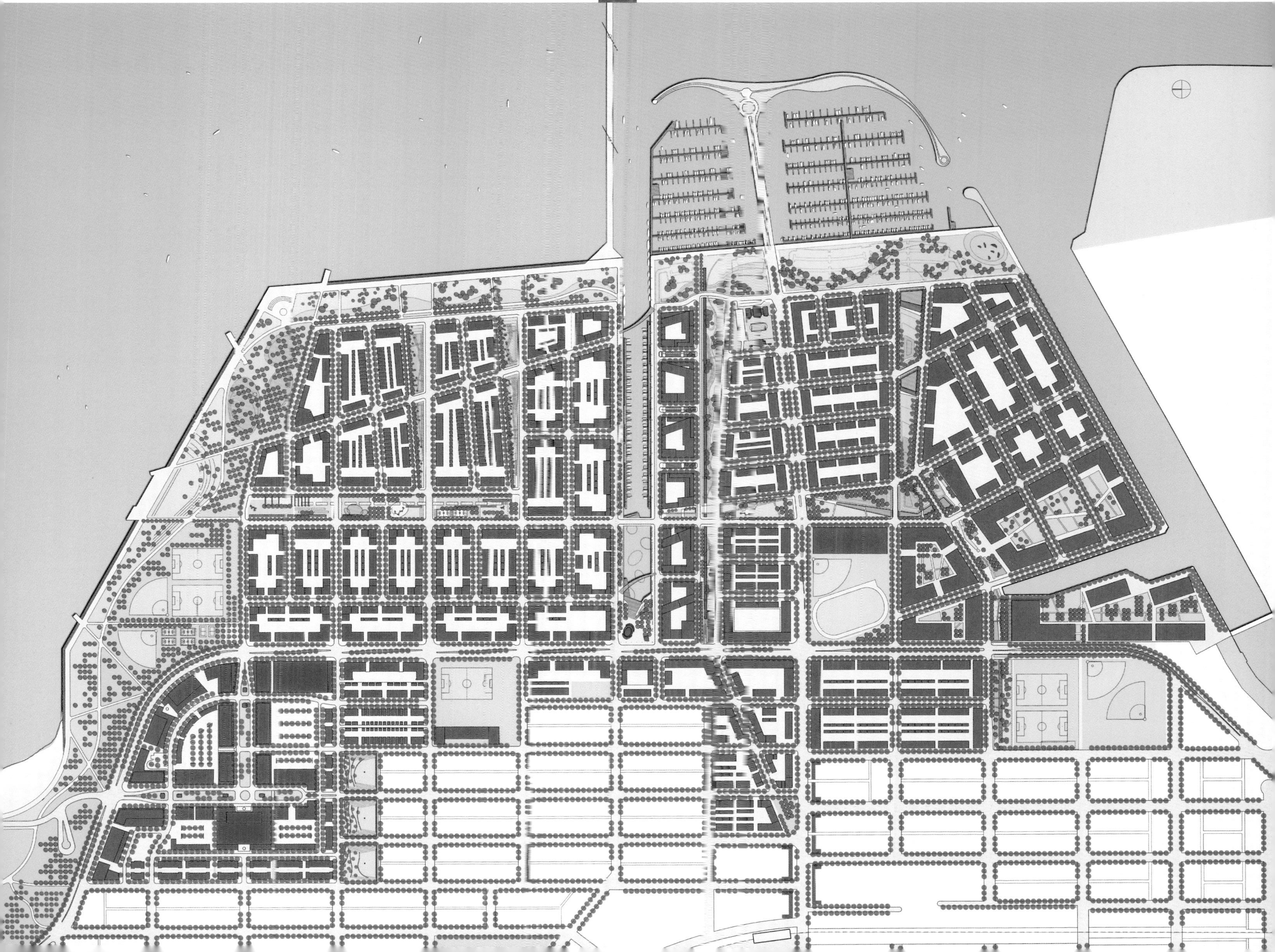

Neighborhoods that have lo[ng]
[?]mill are reconnected to the la[nd]
including the half-mile long

JUNE 21, 2007
SEPT 21, 2007
MARCH 21, 2007
DEC 21, 2007

ORE WALL PLAZA
PLANTED SWALE
100'

ORE WALL MEADOW
ORE WALL PROMENADE
100'-200' (VARIES)

ORE WALL MEADOW   WET SWALE   STREET   ORE WALL AMPHITHEATER

been cut off by the steel

kefront via a series of parks.

re Wall Park'.

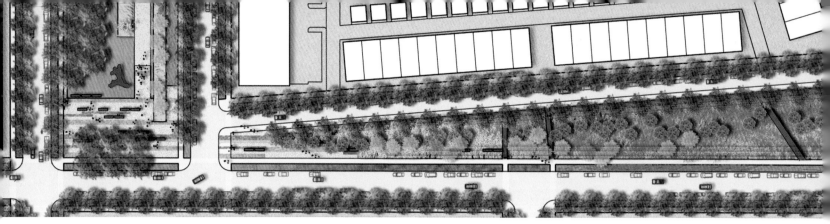

Southworks is also positioned to become a model of sustainable neighborhood development. The plan emphasizes a Low-Impact Development (LID) strategy, where creative site-planning techniques are employed to promote lake recharge. Much of the site's watershed (close to 90%) is therefore directed back into the soil or lake, bypassing Chicago's combined sewer system and lessening the burden on the existing city infrastructure. Additionally, Sasaki developed a configuration of "finger parks" that will serve as large-scale biofiltration and infiltration areas, as part of the conceptual stormwater-management plan required by the city under its newly implemented Stormwater Ordinance. Other sustainable initiatives include pervious pavements at all alleys and parking lanes (part of Chicago's new Green Alleys program), the use of rain gardens in roadway medians, and the storage and reuse of rainwater from larger roof-catchment areas.

Sasaki's recent work has focused on incorporating many of these Best Management Practices (BMPs) into the landscape network, which includes the half-mile-long Ore Wall Park, which will highlight the site's industrial past. The enormous North Slip waterway, previously used to accommodate the large barges offloading the materials in the steel-making process, is maintained and activated through commercial, residential, and water transport uses. Landscapes are planted with native vegetation, providing neighborhood-scaled spaces as well as a migratory bird habitat. Sasaki is currently investigating a strategy of early phase, predevelopment, mass tree plantings to amend the soil, to cleanse the air through carbon sequestration, and as a means for establishing tree stock on site for future use within the development.

Today, as a LEED®-ND (Neighborhood Development) pilot project pursuing Platinum certification, the plan for Southworks has become a model of collaborative, sustainable development between the developer and the City of Chicago, based on a master plan that signifies new and innovative approaches to urban growth on Chicago's south side.

above ecological finger park
below stormwater detail
right Southworks parks
far right stormwater strategy, transit

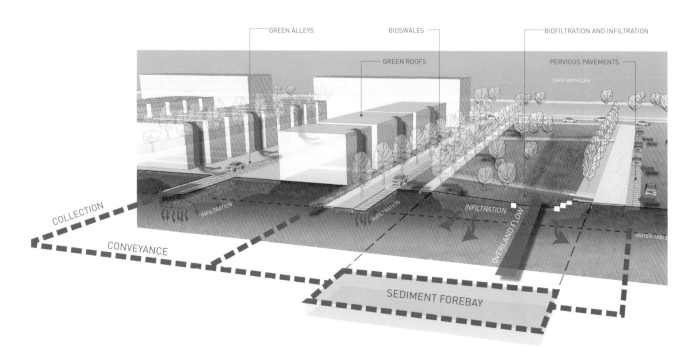

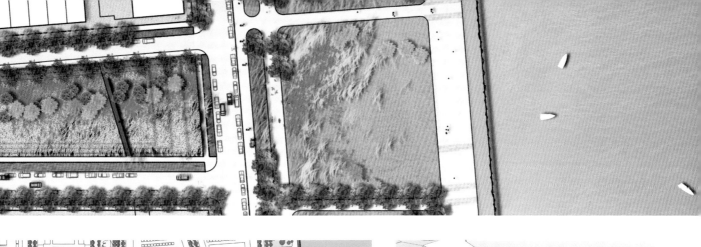

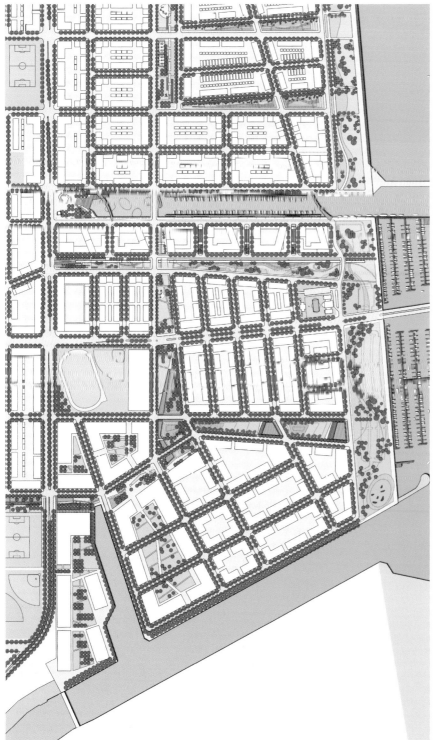

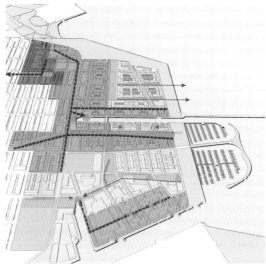

southworks stormwater management plan

9% to Chicago's combined sewer

91% filtered and returned to Lake Michigan

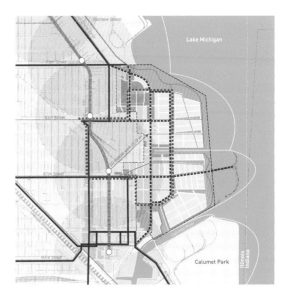

Rainbow Beach

Lake Michigan

79th Street

83rd Street

87th Street

93rd Street

Calumet Park

Illinois
Indiana

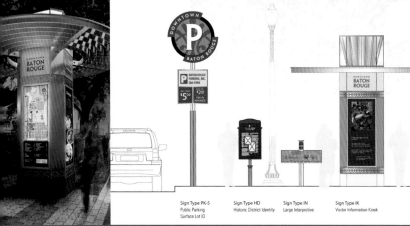

City of Baton Rouge Wayfinding
Baton Rouge, Louisiana

Channel Center
Boston, Massachusetts

Cleveland Gateway
Cleveland, Ohio

Dorchester Shores Beach Restoration
Boston, Massachusetts

North Station Train Signage
Boston, Massachusetts

Schenley Plaza
Pittsburgh, Pennsylvania

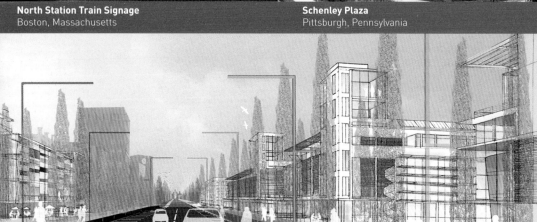

Syracuse Connective Corridor
Syracuse, New York

Charleston Maritime Center
Charleston, South Carolina

Cira Centre District
Philadelphia, Pennsylvania

Miami World Center Streetscape
Miami, Florida

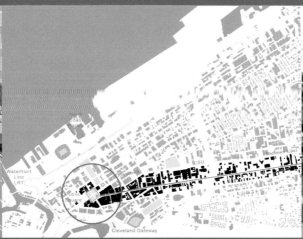

Euclid Avenue Bus Rapid Transit
Cleveland, Ohio

Cleveland RTA Waterfront Transit
Cleveland, Ohio

New Jersey Urban Parks
Trenton, New Jersey

Wheeling Heritage Port
Wheeling, West Virginia

new social
realities

Architecture and urban design are inevitably informed by new social realities. Kunming, China undertakes a massive civil engineering project that seeks to clean a polluted lake and introduce around it an array of new uses, public spaces, and parklands. A community near Houston, conceived in the 1960s as a verdant "escape" from the perceived ills of urban life, finds itself wanting a new public square that takes its cues from the excitement and interaction of big-city life. In Columbia, South Carolina, an epic collaboration between university and city envisions a live/work community to attract the best and brightest for global study and research. At UC Santa Barbara, a "new kind of student center" revolves completely around student organizations and issues important to them, from ethnic and sexual identity to sports and volunteer teams. Thus, higher education finds itself, like the rest of society, increasingly under the influence of the larger culture outside campus gates.

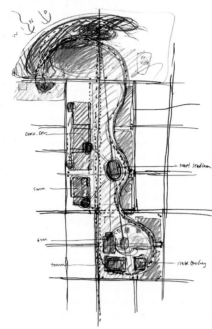

Beijing, China

In 2002, Sasaki was awarded first prize for its planning and urban design of the Olympic Green, the principal venue of the 2008 Beijing Olympics. Sasaki's proposal is deeply connected to an environmental ideal that has its beginnings in the myth and legends of ancient China. The goal was to link ancient China to the present while recognizing the contemporary imperative of sustainable development. The design is further informed by Beijing's urban history, and draws inspiration from the great urban axes of the world. It has three fundamental elements:

The Forest Park This land encompasses the area north of the central area of the Olympic Green. It is conceived as an ideal paradise from which Chinese civilization emerged millennia ago. The park is a sculpted landform of hills, forests, and meadows. Existing bodies of water are reformed into a "Dragon Lake." The pastoral nature of the Forest Park gives way to a more ordered spatial idea by using water to link the central area and the Asian Games beyond.

The Cultural Axis Beijing was founded on the basis of its north/south axis. The concept plan extends the axis some five kilometers through the Olympic Green site. The scale of the axis is monumental in order to emphasize its significance, yet it concludes with the serene simplicity of the Forest Park hills.

The Olympic Axis Set against the Cultural Axis at an acute angle, the Olympic Axis begins at the existing Asian Games stadium. It extends northwest, through the National Stadium by Herzog & de Meuron. This axis then continues to a Sports Heroes Garden, intersecting the Cultural Axis at Zhou Dynasty Plaza, which commemorates the Chinese contributions to city building. The axis terminates at the Memorial of Olympic Spirit.

top left view from Canal Park, early schematic sketch

above city context

right master plan

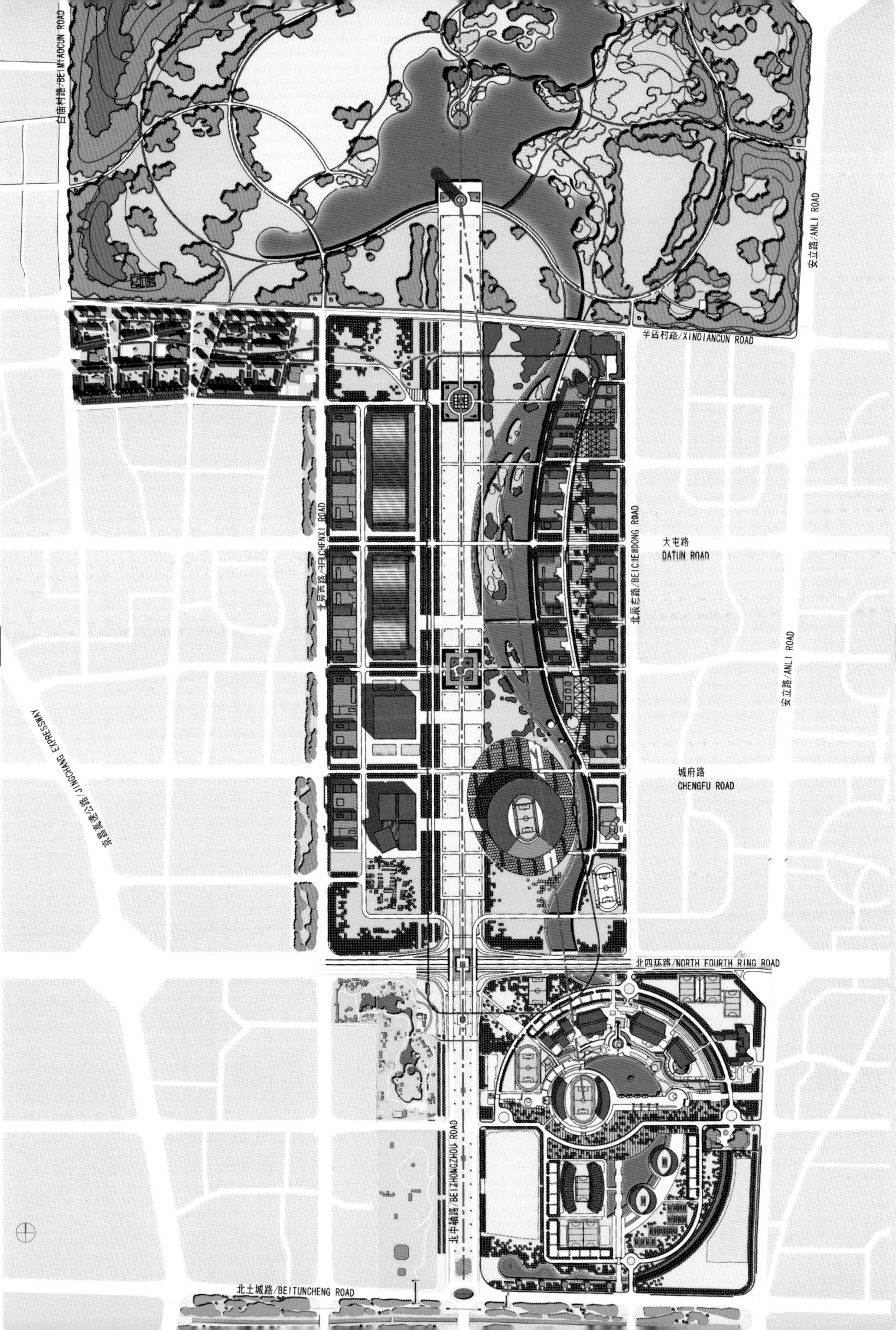

白庙村路/BEIMIAOCUN ROAD
安立路/ANLI ROAD
辛店村路/XINDIANCUN ROAD
北辰西路/BEICHENXI ROAD
北辰东路/BEICHENDONG ROAD
大屯路
DATUN ROAD
安立路/ANLI ROAD
城府路
CHENGFU ROAD
京昌高速公路/JINGCHANG EXPRESSWAY
北四环路/NORTH FOURTH RING ROAD
北中轴路/BEIZHONGZHOU ROAD
北土城路/BEITUNCHENG ROAD

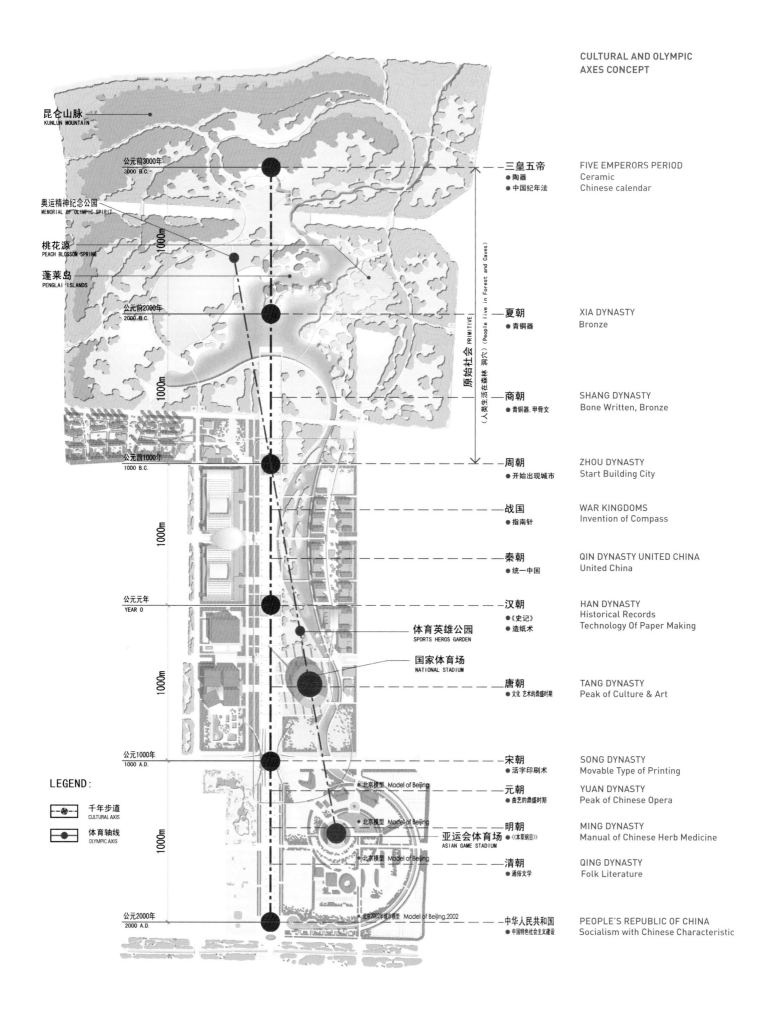

CULTURAL AND OLYMPIC
AXES CONCEPT

昆仑山脉
KUNLUN MOUNTAIN

奥运精神纪念公园
MEMORIAL OF OLYMPIC SPIRIT

桃花源
PEACH BLOSSOM SPRING

蓬莱岛
PENGLAI ISLANDS

公元前3000年
3000 B.C.

公元前2000年
2000 B.C.

1000m

1000m

公元前1000年
1000 B.C.

1000m

公元元年
YEAR 0

体育英雄公园
SPORTS HEROS GARDEN

国家体育场
NATIONAL STADIUM

1000m

公元1000年
1000 A.D.

北京模型 Model of Beijing

北京模型 Model of Beijing

北京模型 Model of Beijing

亚运会体育场
ASIAN GAME STADIUM

1000m

公元2000年
2000 A.D.

北京2002年城市模型 Model of Beijing,2002

LEGEND：

千年步道
CULTURAL AXIS

体育轴线
OLYMPIC AXIS

原始社会 PRIMITIVE (People live in Forest and Caves)
（人类生活在森林 洞穴）

三皇五帝　FIVE EMPERORS PERIOD
● 陶器　Ceramic
● 中国纪年法　Chinese calendar

夏朝　XIA DYNASTY
● 青铜器　Bronze

商朝　SHANG DYNASTY
● 青铜器,甲骨文　Bone Written, Bronze

周朝　ZHOU DYNASTY
● 开始出现城市　Start Building City

战国　WAR KINGDOMS
● 指南针　Invention of Compass

秦朝　QIN DYNASTY UNITED CHINA
● 统一中国　United China

汉朝　HAN DYNASTY
● 《史记》　Historical Records
● 造纸术　Technology Of Paper Making

唐朝　TANG DYNASTY
● 文化 艺术的鼎盛时期　Peak of Culture & Art

宋朝　SONG DYNASTY
● 活字印刷术　Movable Type of Printing

元朝　YUAN DYNASTY
● 曲艺的鼎盛时期　Peak of Chinese Opera

明朝　MING DYNASTY
● 《本草纲目》　Manual of Chinese Herb Medicine

清朝　QING DYNASTY
● 通俗文学　Folk Literature

中华人民共和国　PEOPLE'S REPUBLIC OF CHINA
● 中国特色社会主义建设　Socialism with Chinese Characteristic

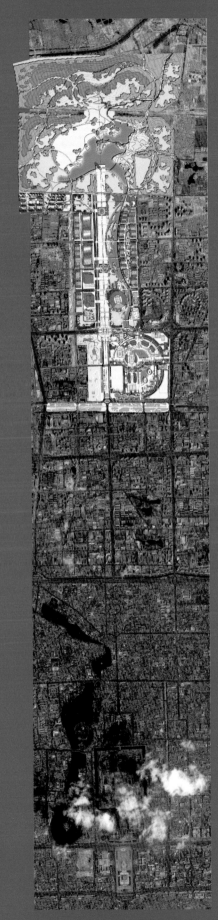

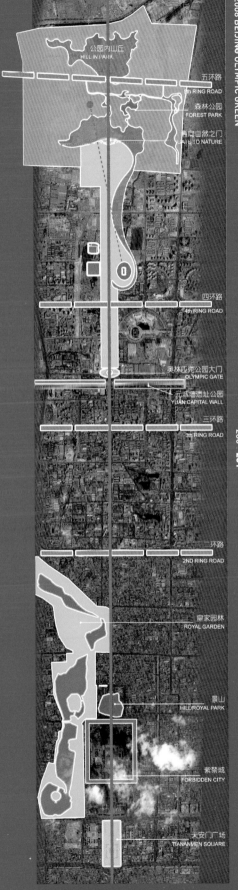

existing condition

master plan

cultural axis

五环路
5th RING ROAD

森林公园
FOREST PARK

通向自然之门
GATE TO NATURE

公园内山丘
HILL IN PARK

四环路
4th RING ROAD

奥林匹克公园大门
OLYMPIC GATE

元城墙遗址公园
YUAN CAPITAL WALL

三环路
3th RING ROAD

二环路
2ND RING ROAD

皇家园林
ROYAL GARDEN

景山
HILL/ROYAL PARK

紫禁城
FORBIDDEN CITY

天安门广场
TIANANMEN SQUARE

Olympic Green is a framework the district. Mixed-use sites wi twenty-first-century Beijing.

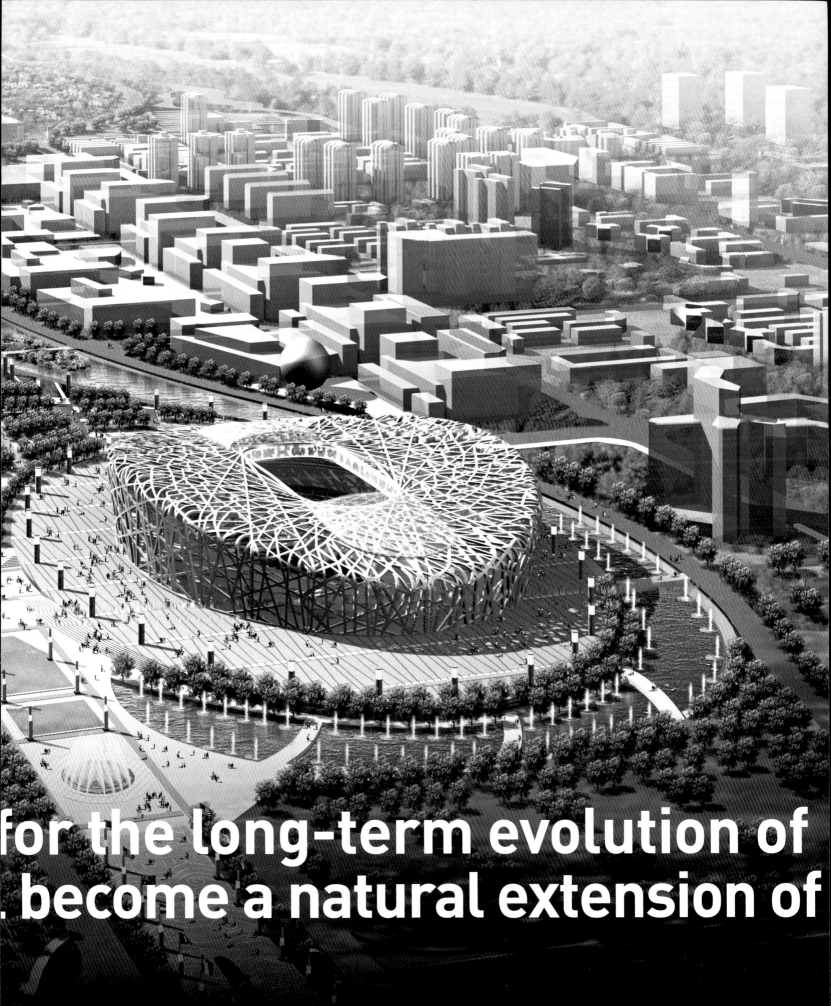

for the long-term evolution of

become a natural extension of

The urban design plan for the Olympic Green is conceived as a framework for the long-term evolution of the district. Streets and pedestrian routes extend from the adjacent districts seamlessly through the site, while public transit stations connect the area to the larger Beijing transit system. Mixed-use development sites are identified for the post-Olympic era so that the district may become a dynamic yet natural extension of twenty-first-century Beijing.

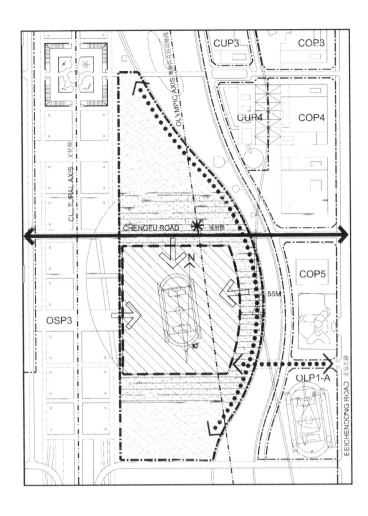

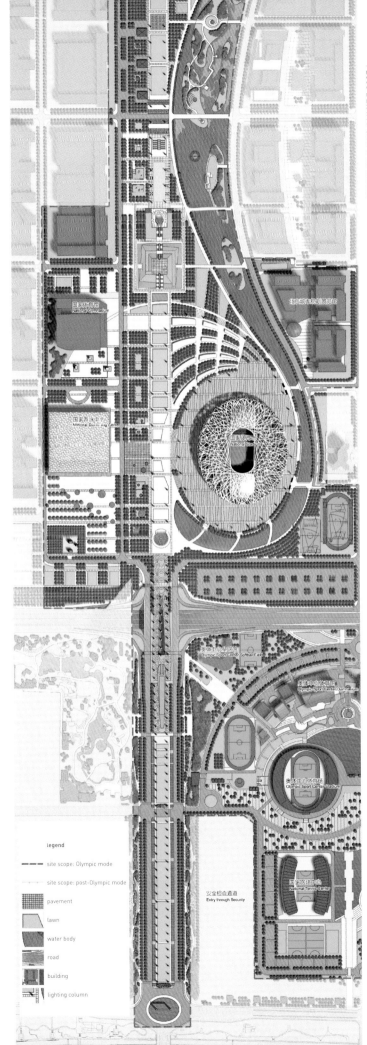

top left and left views within the Olympic Green

above guidelines for parcels and urban structure

right Olympic venue plan

below urban connections

legend

------ site scope: Olympic mode

------ site scope: post-Olympic mode

▨ pavement

▢ lawn

▨ water body

▨ road

▨ building

▨ lighting column

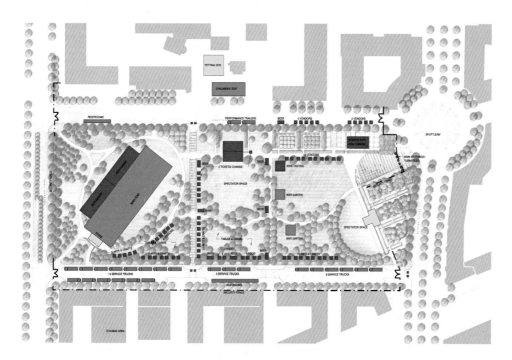

Addison Circle Park

Addison, Texas

The town of Addison, Texas is a new, high-density urban community in the northern Dallas suburbs. The town posed a challenging planning and design problem: make an inspiring and beautiful ten-acre urban park that would be ideal for everyday use but could also transform, on occasion, into a civic gathering space for festivals of over 12,000 people.

Sasaki led a detailed planning and design process with the town to make the design work both as a park and festival site. Existing trees on the site were saved, and new building sites were planned to define the edges of the park. A variety of spaces were carefully organized for maintaining good sight lines to events, queuing of ticketholders, locating tents for events, and defining spaces for food and beverage vendors. An infrastructure of electrical, water, and sewer hook-ups supports events ranging from Shakespeare in the Park to other 500- to 1,000-person events, as well as 12,000-plus person rock concerts. A contemporary pavilion designed by Cunningham Architects was integrated into the landscape composition to support the event space with a kitchen, shade structure, and restrooms.

Groves of trees and fountains make the park an oasis for the surrounding high-density residential community. An interactive fountain in the central plaza is a magnet for families and children, while a series of linear fountains between shade-offering trees create a cooler micro-climate for everyday use. A vine-covered arbor makes a shaded link to a regional transit stop, while defining distinct zones of the park during major events.

Addison Circle Park is an outdoor arts and cultural district that is a landmark in the region, helping to attract almost one million people each year to support the town's hotels and restaurants. On a daily basis, it is Addison's Central Park. At a cost of $9 million, it is a creative and cost-effective approach to establishing a civic hub that attracts people and events to the center of the community.

top left project program
top right large gathering
right and following spread park views

Agilent Technologies

Beijing, China

The purpose of the new headquarters is to consolidate the Agilent operations now housed in two locations in Beijing and to provide a more productive, environmentally sustainable, and healthful workplace for Agilent employees and customers.

The master plan for the Agilent site envisions two office buildings of five and six floors, sited around a central landscaped quadrangle. In a decidedly urban fashion, the buildings front the set-back lines to reinforce the street alignments on the south and west. Only at the entry is the street wall relaxed; the building rises from the ground to form a protected cover for the auto arrival court. The arrival court presents direct access to the lobby and to parking, and opens selective views into the quadrangle.

As the phase one headquarters building faces the streets, as well as the west and south orientations, the pierced stainless-steel façades control harsh sunlight and reduce traffic noise. The deep-set windows, two to a floor, alternately shade the interior spaces and serve as light shelves for controlled daylight. As the building faces the quadrangle, it makes a decided shift: open offices line the quadrangle within a wrapping of floor-to-ceiling glass hung from the edge of the structure. The sensation inside is one of open terraces overlooking and engaging the landscape.

The landscape design for the courtyard suggests a place of quite repose for both employees and guests. It frames the stand-alone dining pavilion, whose dramatic shape and transparency lend a sense of importance and drama to this main employee gathering space.

Low-E glass accommodates daylighting deep into the building to reduce artificial lighting. The building uses advanced, efficient mechanical systems including under-floor distribution, zoned and activity-controlled lighting, and an advanced building-monitoring system.

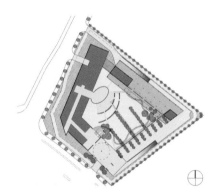

top left main stairway

above view of the quadrangle

right arrival court

next spread dining pavillion

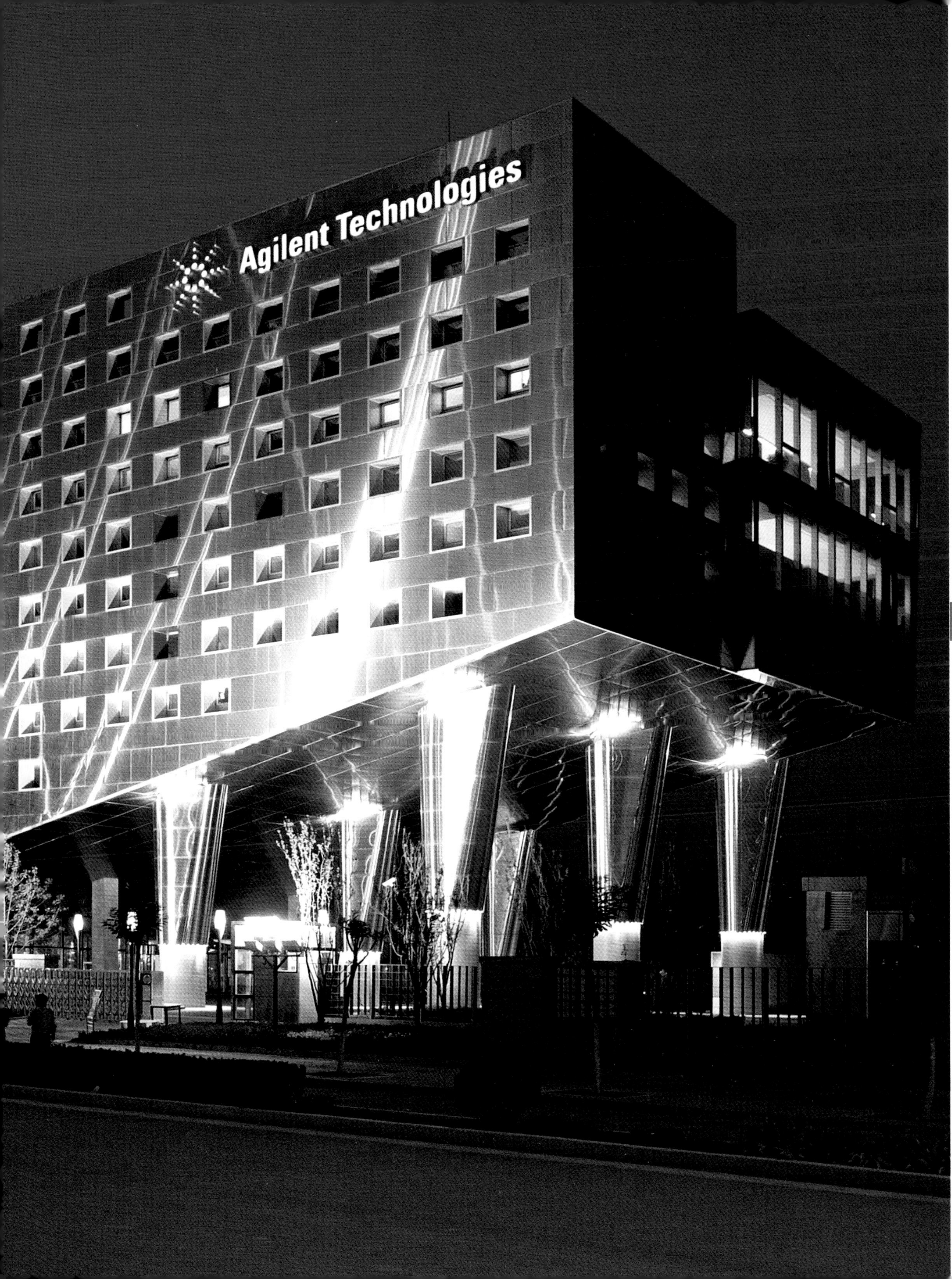
Agilent Technologies

Innovista Master Plan

University of South Carolina, Columbia, South Carolina

The University of South Carolina Innovista District in Columbia, South Carolina is one of the most ambitious town/gown initiatives currently underway in the United States. It promises to transform underused land downtown into research, residential, commercial, and entertainment districts that will reconnect both the city and the university's iconic "horseshoe" to a new park along the Congaree River.

This master plan has a rich history. A substantial portion of Innovista's land is owned by the Guignard family of Columbia, and the plan is actually a modern-day realization of an urban plan drawn up more than 200 years ago by J.G. Guignard, founder of the family in Columbia and Surveyor General for the state of South Carolina between 1795 and 1802. There is little if any precedence anywhere in the U.S. for such a venerable plan actually being executed and transformed in collaboration with the descendents of the original planner more than two centuries after it was originally conceived.

Historically known as "the Vista," the riverfront area is about 500 acres large and, once built out, will be developed at urban densities with over 3,000 new residential units and eleven million square feet of new facilities for biotech and other academic research endeavors, as well as for private partners' offices and research buildings. While the site is conceived as a mixed-use area, the focus will primarily be on research as it gets closer to the existing campus, and a wide mix of residential and retail will cluster closer to the river. A detailed, form-based code, currently being integrated in the city zoning ordinance, will guide the implementation of the plan over time.

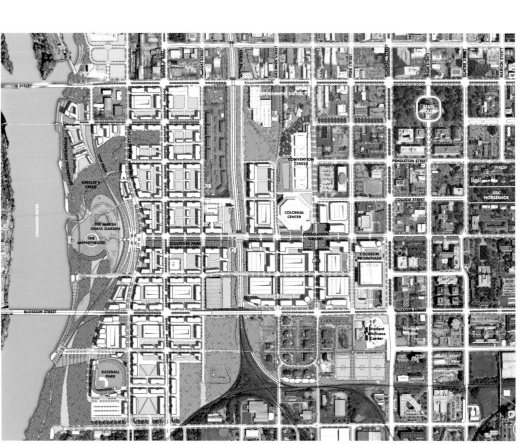

above Foundation Square

top far left historic context

bottom far left recreation network

left master plan

Currently cut off from the river by railroad tracks, a re-landscaped Greene Street will
be extended via a bridge to link the core campus and the State Capitol complex with the
waterfront. That street, as well as a couple of key north/south streets, while accessible
to cars, has been designed as a pedestrian and bike priority zone encouraging the use of
alternative transportation modes within the mixed-use district and beyond its boundaries.
Greene Street will also serve as a major public display for innovative rainwater-manage-
ment techniques, where the water will be collected and cleansed in planted bioswales
and urban water canals carrying it all the way to the waterfront park.

A new eighty-acre park will receive the city grid and provide access to and along the river
for residents and visitors alike. The entire park is located within the 100-year flood plain,
and its design and road alignment are derived from the natural topography to minimize any
river-flow disturbance. Its design features a large amphitheatre for public theater and cel-
ebration, as well as one urban edge for future hotels and restaurants. It also contemplates
the restoration of a large freshwater marsh, erosion control measures, and a massive
reforestation of the river's edge, where a power line corridor was cutting the site. A network
of trails and paths connects the park to an existing regional outdoor recreation network.

The plan has been characterized as "transformative" by *The State*, Columbia's daily news-
paper, and was unanimously approved by the city council in the fall of 2007.

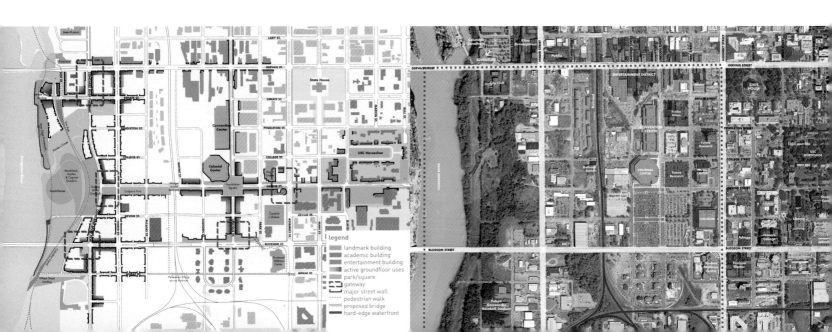

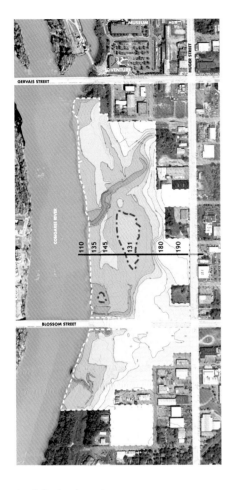
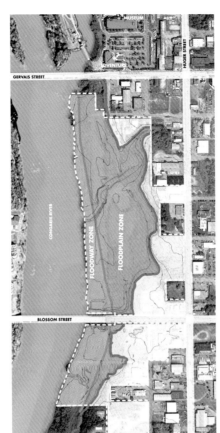
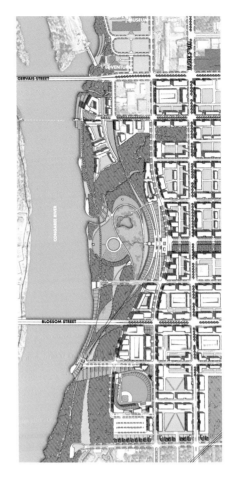

top left view from river

above left to right elevation and wetlands, FEMA, waterfront

below left to right urban design, existing conditions, land use, transportation

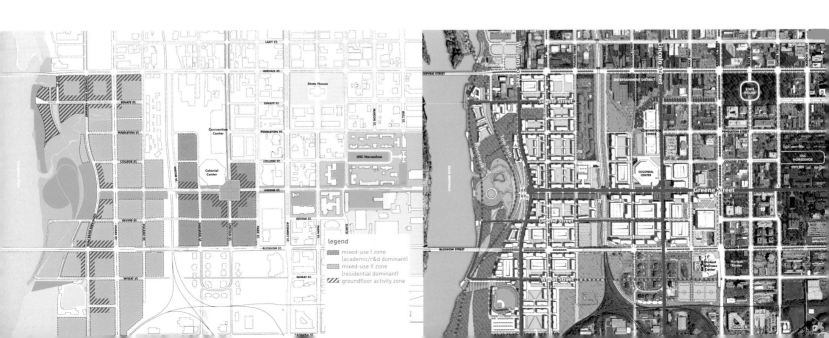

legend

mixed-use I zone (academic/r&d dominant)

mixed-use II zone (residential dominant)

groundfloor activity zone

legend

▨ mixed-use/retail/restaurant

▨ mixed-use/office/retail

▨ mixed-use/residential/retail

△ pedestrian access

▲ parking/service access

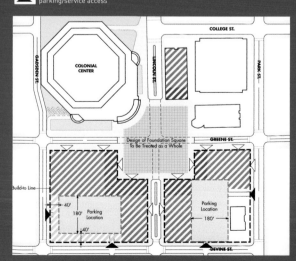

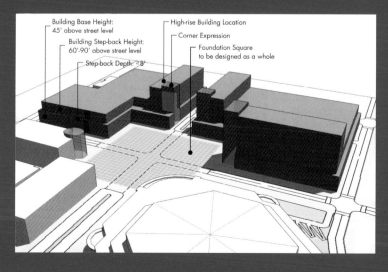

top Greene Street corridor

opposite left first floor use guidelines

opposite right building envelope guidelines

above Greene Street existing

left Greene Street after implementation

top and right Foundation Square with and without tree canopy

below stormwater concept

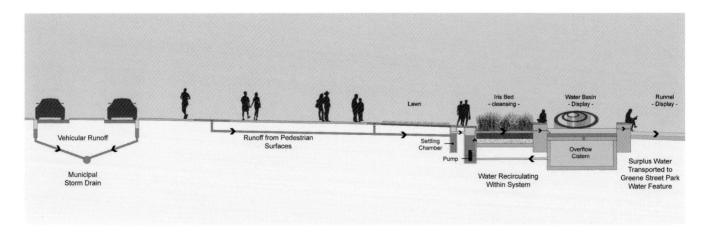

Vehicular Runoff

Municipal
Storm Drain

Runoff from Pedestrian
Surfaces

Lawn

Settling
Chamber

Pump

Water Recirculating
Within System

Iris Bed
- cleansing -

Water Basin
- Display -

Overflow
Cistern

Runnel
- Display -

Surplus Water
Transported to
Greene Street Park
Water Feature

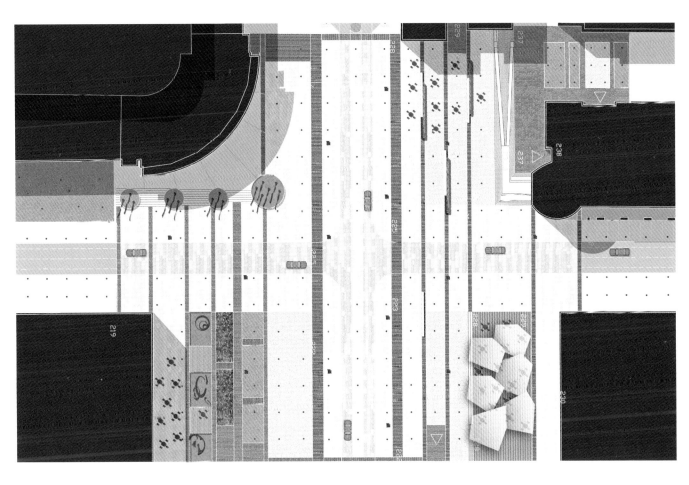

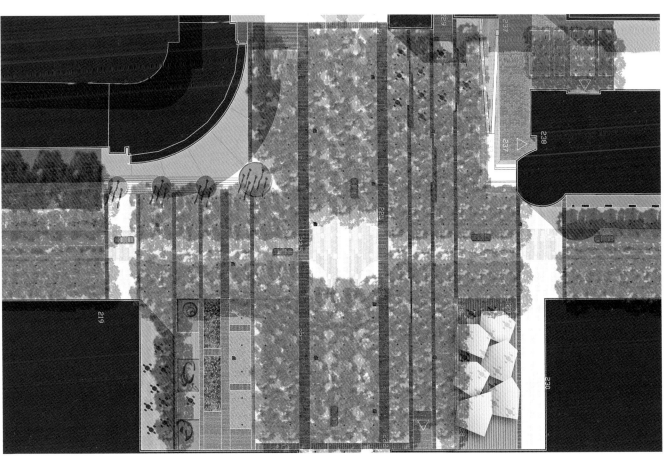

Rensselaer Polytechnic Institute, Troy, New York

Rensselaer Polytechnic Institute's (RPI) East Campus Master Plan is a framework for residential, student-life, and athletic development of the eastern portion of the campus, which currently consists of open fields and unconnected buildings.

The first phase of the East Campus Olympic Village will include the renovated Houston Field House, home of the Institute's championship Division One Hockey team, a new 7,500-seat stadium, and a new 1,500-seat basketball arena. The second phase will include a fifty-meter pool and a 60,000-square-foot indoor track-and-field facility. These buildings will all be arrayed around the Georgian Terrace, a pedestrian-dedicated open piazza that on major game days will become the social center of the RPI campus. Meant to be a place of meeting and interaction at all hours and in all seasons, the Terrace will take full advantage of the Institute's dramatic hilltop setting, with views of the Hudson River Valley spreading out beyond a double row of high-canopy ginkgo trees.

The master plan brings order and flow to pedestrian movement through a series of east/west running pedestrian spines. Because of the dramatic sloping topography of the East Campus, a series of north/south running terraces provide the flat areas necessary for sport facilities, such as fields for track and field, soccer, and football. The challenging topographic restraints are folded into the design by a series of arching, precast seatwalls that use the grade change to provide spectator seating.

More than just a locus of sports and recreation activity, the fully developed East Campus will serve as an important pedestrian link between existing graduate-student housing farther to the east and the main campus. It will serve as a tangible example of the Institute's renewed commitment to a more broadened student experience—emphasizing the arts as well as the sciences, and nourishment of the body and spirit as well as the mind.

top left aerial view of completed Athletic Events Center

above stadium concourse; and varsity strength and conditioning facility

top right Georgian Terrace

right stadium section

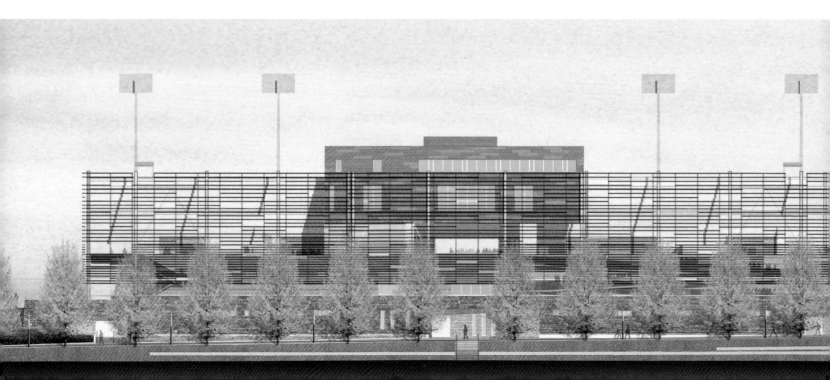

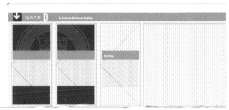

① Elevation - Typical Closed Gate at Field
Scale: 1/4" = 1'-0"

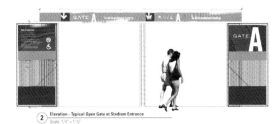

② Elevation - Typical Open Gate at Stadium Entrance
Scale: 1/4" = 1'-0"

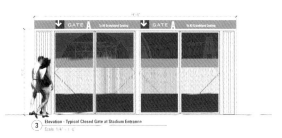

③ Elevation - Typical Closed Gate at Stadium Entrance
Scale: 1/4" = 1'-0"

fabricated aluminum cabinet
painted with applied vinyl graphics

↓ GATE **D** To General Admission Seating

④ Typical Layout Gate ID
Scale: 1" = 1'-0"

aluminum panel painted
with applied vinyl graphics

Rules & Regulations

No smoking in the stadium.
No glass containers of any kind.
All bags, backpacks and purses.
No unmbrellas.
No artificial noise makers or air horns.
The Athletic Department reserves the right
to ask guests to move or remove banners with
the throwing of objects from the stands
is strictly prohibited.
Fans violating any of the above rules
are subject to removal from stadium.

⑤ Context Elevation
Scale: 3/32" = 1'-0"

⑥ Typical Layout - Gate Door Panel
Scale: 1" = 1'-0"

top left entry promenade

above environmental graphics

below elevation with Georgian Terrace in foreground

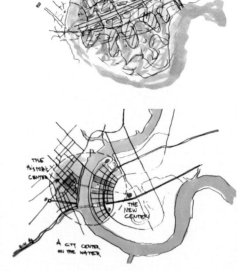

Ho Chi Minh City, Vietnam

Ho Chi Minh City, the historic Vietnamese city formerly known as Saigon, has long been a dynamic center of human habitation. Today, the historic downtown features grand public boulevards, narrow tree-lined streets, and throngs of citizens and tourists on motorbikes and on foot. Rapid urbanization is now placing significant development pressure on this urban fabric, particularly in the city's historic District 1, which sits on the western bank of the Saigon River.

Concerns that the city could not easily integrate the demands of these twenty-first-century developments have led to a planning process for a new urban district on a peninsula of land on the opposite or east bank of the Saigon River. Nearly surrounded by the sweep of the river, this peninsula is known as Thu Thiem.

The transformation of Thu Thiem represents a momentous opportunity for the people of Ho Chi Minh City and a major national initiative for the economic development of Vietnam. A number of strategic actions are now coalescing to make development of Thu Thiem feasible, including the construction of a tunnel underneath the Saigon River that will connect to a new international airport east of Thu Thiem; a new Thu Thiem bridge that connects the peninsula to existing residential areas in the north and employment centers in the south; municipal proposals for water, sewer, and electrical power upgrades; and relocation of the adjacent river ports to points farther south along the Saigon River.

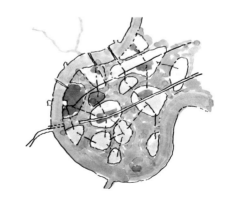

In 2003, Sasaki Associates won first prize in an open international competition for the Thu Thiem New Urban Area. As an urban, mixed-use district with over six million square meters of new development, Thu Thiem is designed in harmony with its remarkable natural setting and is poised to emerge as an environmentally sustainable, economically vibrant twenty-first-century city center for Ho Chi Minh City and Vietnam—indeed, potentially for all of Southeastern Asia.

top left model of peninsula

above schematic sketches

right urban design concept

Crescent Park
retail edges
central plaza
landmark building
view corridors
urban axes
urban edges
high towers
medium towers
low towers
mini towers
public parks
resorts/recreation/education
wetlands

The design emphasizes residential areas in close proximity to water; a new, mixed use CBD of commercial and office high-rises; cultural, tourism and institutional uses; pedestrian-oriented streets and boulevards; and an extensive network of public spaces and waterfront parks. Over the course of twenty years, Thu Thiem will become home to 200,000 citizens and attract an employment population of 350,000. An extensive system of underground, light-rail, water-based, and bus transportation is proposed to serve a broad area of the new district.

The existing waterways and canals, low lying lands, distinctive upland areas, and opportunistic native vegetation at Thu Thiem form a unique ecological identity specific to South Vietnam. The Thu Thiem plan integrates this natural landscape system into an urban delta incorporating the "wet" conditions as part of the urban development, rather than obliterating such a natural feature. Certain land areas will be slightly raised above flood plain level for development, while those areas below flood level will be kept "green" as stormwater-management assets. In particular, the southern (and lowest) part of the site will be the focus of a restored mangrove forest that will purify the air and water, control erosion, and protect the canal banks.

Within Thu Thiem, new urban canals, lakes, and reshaped natural canals will become ecological corridors, able to absorb typical and extreme tidal changes, seasonal flooding, and 50- and 100-year flood events. Thu Thiem is designed as an open system with no locks or dams to control the flow of water through the peninsula. As water from the Saigon River infiltrates the peninsula, moving north to south through Thu Thiem's canals and lakes, the water will be filtered by natural means before rejoining the river along the peninsula's southern edge. The city is also proposing a new wastewater treatment facility at Thu Thiem to mitigate direct stormwater and wastewater runoff into the canals and river. As a designed ecological environment, the Thu Thiem peninsula will benefit the ecology of greater Ho Chi Minh City and will also encourage new and sustainable strategies for planning and developing other land areas within the city.

top left night view of Thu Thiem from District 1

right top transit plan

right water circulation

far right master plan

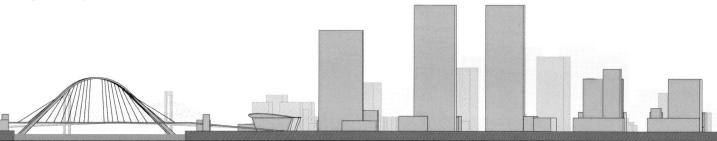

legend

1. new city center
2. residential district
3. public institution district
4. urban village
5. commercial center
6. convention center
7. arena
8. museum
9. sports center
10. university
11. cultural center/ information center
12. neighborhood center
13. central plaza
14. riverfront promenade
15. riverfront crescent park
16. city park
17. aquatic park
18. entertainment
19. resort hotel
20. botanical garden
21. Delta Research Institute
22. marina
23. preserved wetland
24. observation tower
25. amphitheater
26. historic structure
27. subway station

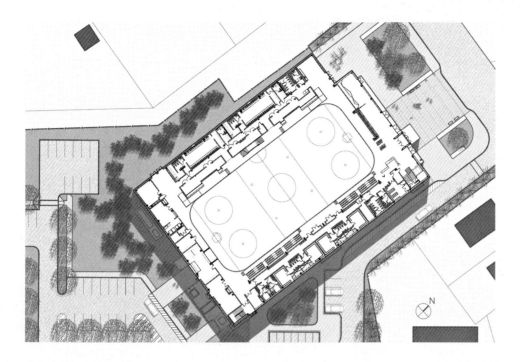

Trinity College, Hartford, Connecticut

The new Koeppel Community Sports Center enhances both the college and its urban surroundings by transforming an off-campus section of the neighborhood into a shared recreational-sports facility. As a symbol of the partnership between Trinity and the community, the building provides a collegiate ice-hockey rink for the varsity sports programs at the college and community recreation space for the city of Hartford. In its first winter season, neighborhood use was over 1,000 children per week.

The unique exterior is a simple, pre-engineered building clad with custom-designed metal façades along the two street edges. Strategically placed windows frame views, bring in sunlight, and add warm wood accents. Inside, the 55,000-square-foot building has an open layout. From the lobby, the 90' x 200' ice sheet, seating for 1,150 spectators, community lounge, snack bar, public lockers, and skate changing area are all within view. The upper level, which overlooks the entire east side of the rink and provides views to the neighborhood, features another lounge and four community rooms for meetings, functions, fitness, and gatherings. The lobby and arena are bathed in natural light and bright, warm colors.

top left first floor and site

above building details

top right entrance façade

right community rink use

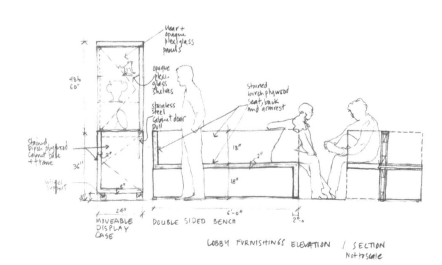

LOBBY FURNISHINGS ELEVATION / SECTION
Not to scale

top views of lobby

bottom left ergonomic study

right window detail

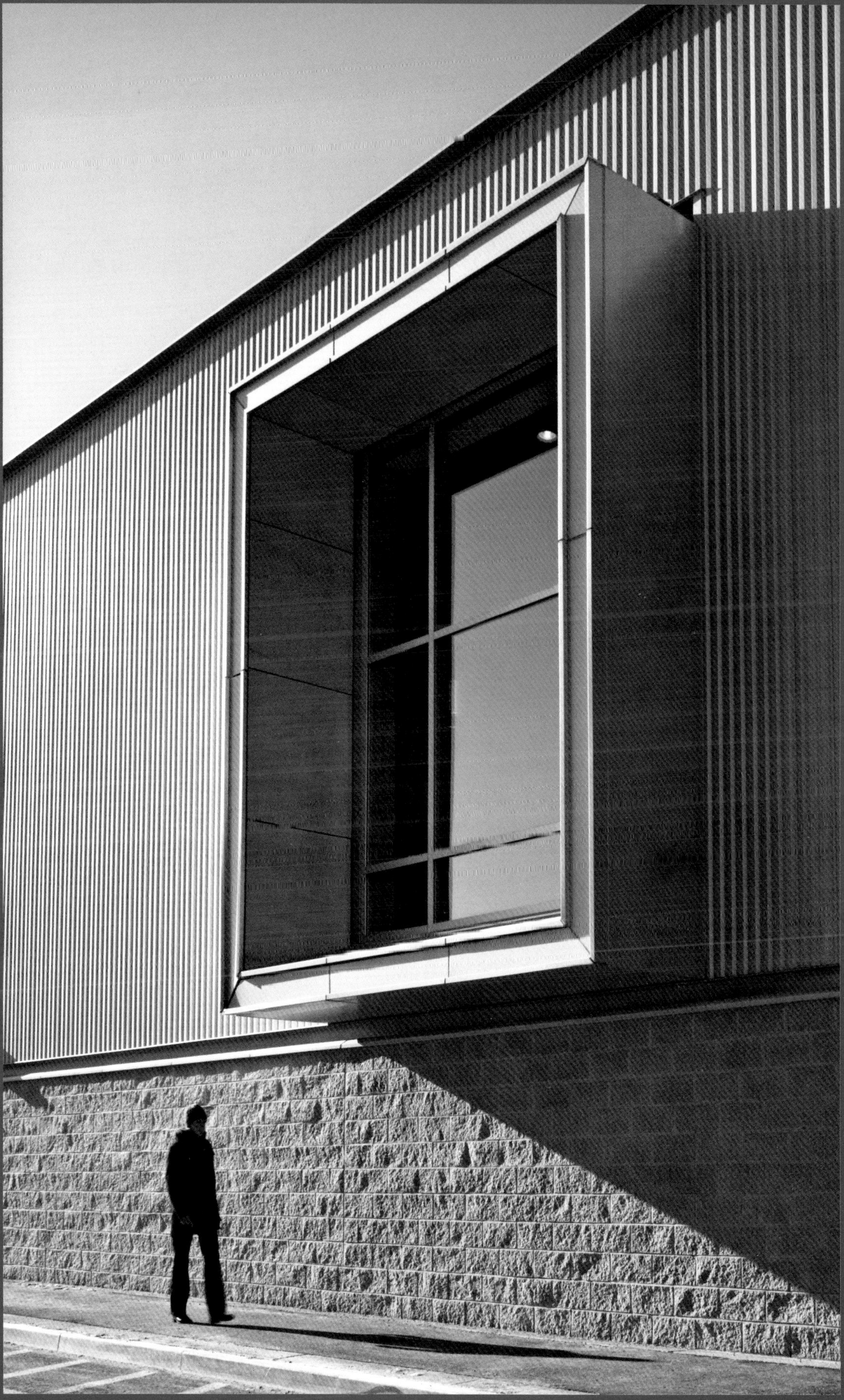

Kunming, China

Known as China's "Eternal Spring City," Kunming has a temperate climate year-round, and picturesque scenery. Although it is already known as a significant destination for visitors to experience the rich cultural history and natural beauty of Yunnan Province, the city is also an emerging economic center of Southwestern China. It is the gateway to China for members of the Association of Southeast Asian Nations (ASEAN) such as Thailand and Vietnam. This dynamic growth is leading Kunming to quickly evolve from a quiet, provincial capital into an international destination for business and tourism.

Working with Shui On Land, Sasaki helped to identify approximately 520 hectares of land, which would reconnect the core of the city to the shores of Dianchi Lake. The urban-design strategy seeks to transform this previously neglected waterfront into the new "living room" of Kunming, composed of cultural and entertainment venues, pedestrian-oriented streets with ground level retail and restaurants, a collection of offices geared toward creative industry, multiple schools, and a variety of unique residential neighborhoods with dramatic views of the lake.

Caohai North Shore is designed as a sustainable new community which can become a model for ecologically restorative development in the region. One of the key elements of the plan is to restore a portion of the lake (currently one of the most polluted bodies of water in China) via strategies which identify locations for new wastewater treatment plants, dredge existing sediment to reduce current phosphorus and nitrogen loads, construct additional wetlands to filter stormwater from the community, and re-introduce native vegetation and wildlife.

top left regional context

top right master plan

bottom left lake clean-up strategies

bottom right urban design concept

following pages Daguan Park lighting plan and master plan

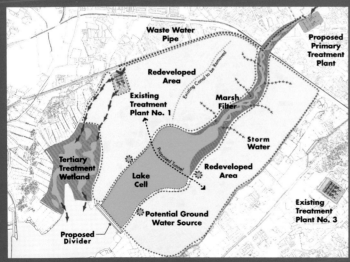

Waste Water Pipe

Proposed Primary Treatment Plant

Redeveloped Area

Existing Treatment Plant No. 1

Marsh Filter

Storm Water

Redeveloped Area

Tertiary Treatment Wetland

Lake Cell

Proposed Tunnel

Existing Canal to be removed

Potential Ground Water Source

Existing Treatment Plant No. 3

Proposed Divider

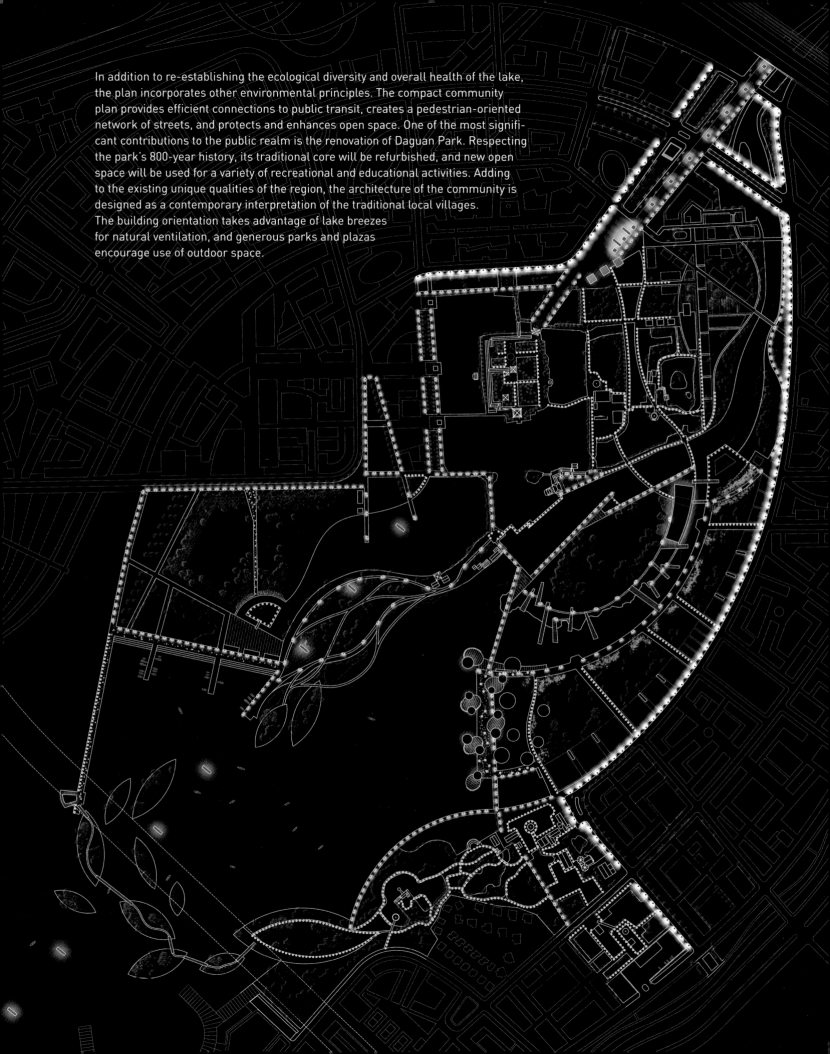

In addition to re-establishing the ecological diversity and overall health of the lake, the plan incorporates other environmental principles. The compact community plan provides efficient connections to public transit, creates a pedestrian-oriented network of streets, and protects and enhances open space. One of the most significant contributions to the public realm is the renovation of Daguan Park. Respecting the park's 800-year history, its traditional core will be refurbished, and new open space will be used for a variety of recreational and educational activities. Adding to the existing unique qualities of the region, the architecture of the community is designed as a contemporary interpretation of the traditional local villages. The building orientation takes advantage of lake breezes for natural ventilation, and generous parks and plazas encourage use of outdoor space.

Lijiang, China

The Lashihai Basin is one of the most distinctive places in China, with a unique landscape composed of wetlands, alpine forests, meadows, and agricultural lands. The lake at the center of the basin is an important seasonal habitat for migratory birds, eight of which are on the endangered-species list. The villages around the lake have co-existed in this fragile setting for generations. When the adjacent historic town of Lijiang was certified as a cultural heritage site in 1997, Lashihai faced unprecedented development pressure. These external forces upon this very sensitive landscape have brought the basin to a tipping point. In an effort to create a master plan to guide Lashihai's future growth, Sasaki teamed with Shui On Land and the Yunnan provincial government to create an environmentally and economically sustainable framework for the region. Without a strategy to create enforceable development guidelines, the characteristics that make Lashihai one of the "last great places on earth" may be lost forever.

Creating a comprehensive land-management strategy for the entire 9,400-hectare basin was the key component of the planning and design process. The plan sought to integrate aesthetic, social, cultural, and economic objectives, as well as long-term strategies to promote ecological conservation and restoration. Working with Shui On, Sasaki identified a limited amount of carefully sited land for new development, which will not upset the delicate ecological and cultural balance of the basin, thus preserving the unique environmental and traditional heritage. The new development will be a mix of uses such as hotels and spas, residential communities, cultural attractions, and educational facilities, ensuring that the area will attract low-impact tourism. Development areas are sited to minimize impact to existing villages and agricultural land, and buildings are organized to echo the fabric of traditional settlements based upon patterns of a unique architectural vernacular.

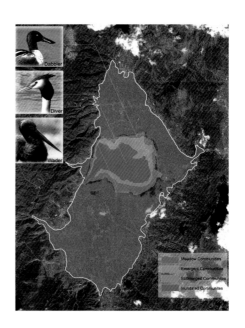

top left existing conditions

above habitat study

A

B

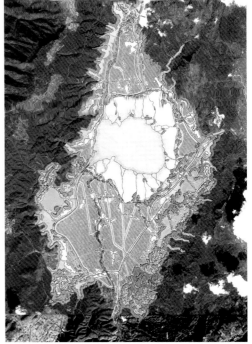

top eastern hillside

above reservoir enlargement and associated loss of wetlands and native fauna (A) contrasted with the preferred naturally fluctuating water system (B) that preserves wetlands and fauna.

above master plan

top left visitor center

left southern hillside

top right village center

right western waterfront

The Village at Centennial Square

San Francisco State University, San Francisco, California

True to its name, this is a village within a city. It is a resolutely urban complex that houses almost 800 students and yet has a sense of transparency and porosity—the entire university community is free to pass through it and enjoy its public open space and courtyards, as well as areas of private rest, study, and conversation. It forms the crucial function of mediating between the academic core of the university to the east and an existing student residential precinct to the west.

The Village's main gateway is a grand set of stairs from the west. Users pass through a monumental portal and enter a great courtyard, a raised plaza over structured parking below that is landscaped with native plants and flowers. Along the southern edge, massing is limited to two stories to let abundant sunlight into the courtyards, which is of special importance to residents of this often cool and foggy area of the city. Toward the north, the massing becomes higher.

From the exterior, the Village reads not as a single monolith but as multiple buildings defined by a consistent palette of stucco punctuated by projecting bays of corrugated-metal panels and aluminum storefront windows. Logical and contextual systems of streets, courtyards, and sidewalks define both the perimeter and interior, and promote easy navigation within the village. Vertical circulation points—stairs and elevators—are clearly identified by strong accent colors. Stacks of two-level student lounges at prominent building corners read at night or through the coastal fog as lighted beacons, welcoming centers of community activity. Within the complex, a variety of ground-floor retail spaces cater to residents' needs. At the project's northeast corner, a new Student Service Building is strategically located to provide convenient, one-stop business transactions for both the resident campus community and SFSU's large commuter student population.

o SERIES OF TOWERS — very efficient.

BUT

VERY DEADLY SPATIALLY.

o I'h LIKE to explore "bridging" a series of towers w/ smaller scale pieces.

@grade

or

above grade

top left and right courtyards

top main gateway

above early schematic sketches

The mixed-use Village at Centennial Square was designed and constructed in less than two years for a budget of approximately $150 per square foot.

left main gateway

top left entry courtyard

middle and bottom right site plan and section

top right campus context plan

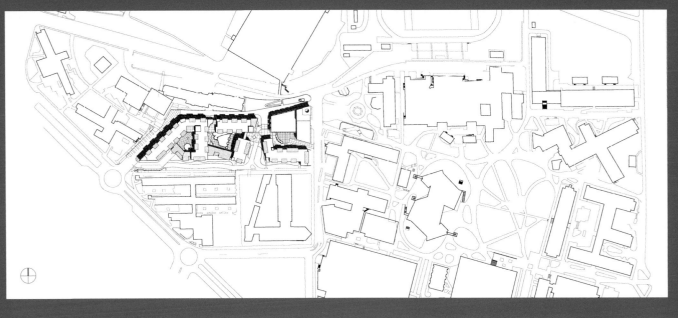

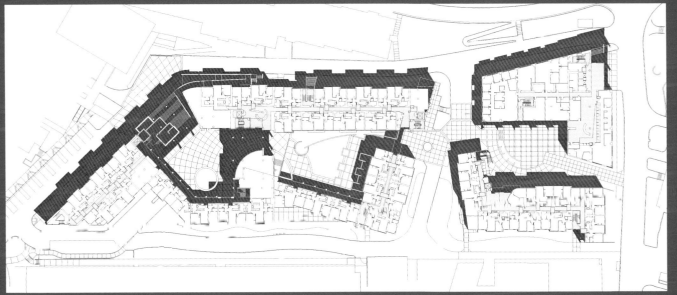

Philips Solid-State Lighting Solutions

Burlington, Massachusetts

Philips Solid-State Lighting Solutions is a pioneer in diverse applications of energy-saving LED technology. The company's new headquarters in Burlington, Massachusetts serves several functions: a showroom conceived as a "canvas" for displaying the firm's innovative lighting systems, an administrative headquarters, and a laboratory for testing and research.

The color palette and furnishings are meant to be a backdrop for the company's portfolio of work—creative lighting. A key goal was spatial flexibility—movable walls and floating ceiling "clouds" allow multiple configurations to be set up and evaluated, both by clients and Philips employees, to show how Philips' products can transform space through light. All of the lighting applications are controlled by computer and can be changed multiple times throughout the day as needed. LED lighting was used extensively throughout, with the idea that the entire office and adjacent showroom and laboratory will be completely LED as technology allows.

The offices are evenly divided between administrative and laboratory space. However, a split in the ambience between these two functions would be not only jarring but antithetical to the spirit of the company. The design is non-hierarchical in that the perimeter is reserved more for shared spaces and there are few private offices; most employees work in six-person "pods" that can be customized visually through light. Common areas include "war rooms" wherein designers and engineers can leave drawings, models and other remnants of the creative process over several days. "Portals" are transition spaces that allow further exploration of the limits of lighting design; a central café encourages casual employee interaction and socializing. The Philips headquarters seeks to break down the barrier between creative and administrative functions, preferring to cast the entire 200-plus head-quarters employees as innovators and participants in the company's mission. The space reflects a corporate ethos of creativity, inclusiveness and environmental responsibility.

top left conference room

above and top right reception area

right 'portal' under different light conditions

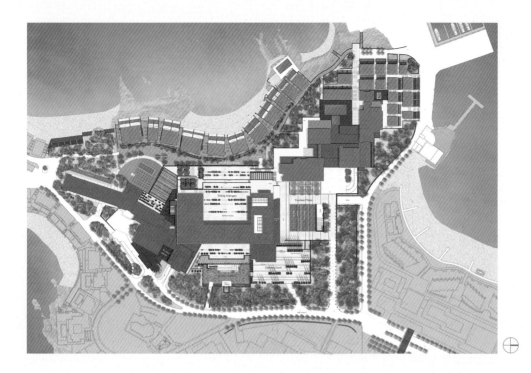

Grand Resort Lagonissi

Lagonissi, Greece

The Attica coast south of Athens includes ruins of ancient temples, but also convenient access to the Athens International Airport. Because of this strategic combination, the Lagonissi peninsula in Attica has been the site of a hotel for decades. Several years ago, believing the site was not living up to its full potential, the Greek government asked for proposals from developers. The mandate was to expand the hotel facilities and add luxury housing and a conference center, but nonetheless keep the entire peninsula, as well as its stunning views and hidden coves, accessible to the public. Helios Hotels, a Greek luxury-hotel chain, was designated the developer and is redeveloping the peninsula based on a master plan and landscape design by Sasaki. Sasaki's work also includes the design of the new boutique hotel, recommended renovations to the existing hotel, a new conference center, and luxury housing.

The new conference center occupies the highest point at the center of the peninsula on a rocky escarpment. U-shaped in plan, the building seems to rise gently from this landscape and is sheathed in native limestone. A large, open terrace with a view toward the south and west has foliage mounted on tracks to allow for quick readaptation, depending on the function—it can serve as a casual porch or an "outdoor ballroom" for a major event. The building's largest openings are framed with limestone porticos that add a sense of monumentality while defining major entry points to the complex. A system of metal panels adjusts to shade the interior, and their patterns also add syncopation and variety to the façade. Strategically placed at key points, translucent alabaster panels glow from within at night. An adjacent grotto and submerged chapel allow for weddings of virtually any size, from a dozen intimates to 2,000 guests. A "green shawl" (a band of Mediterranean trees) designed by Sasaki landscape architects, surrounds the entire complex.

top left conference center and hotel site plan

top right hotel swimming pool

above existing conditions

right master plan

below sketch of villa

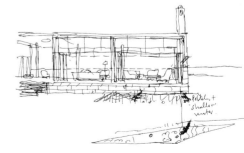

legend

1. reception
2. tennis center/parking garage
3. public beach entertainment complex
4. public beach
5. swimming pool complex
6. spa-fitness club
7. Captains Restaurant
8. New Ouzeri Restaurant
9. Veghera Bar
10. residential village
11. coffee place
12. reception/retail complex
13. spa
14. Grand Hall Conference Center
15. chapel
16. Grand Hall Fountain and Skating Rink
17. Sunset Hotel
18. chapel
19. marina promenade
20. Polynesian Restaurant
21. Porto Rotondo Beach
22. Porto Rotondo Apartments
23. heliport

The entire peninsula will cor
and accessibility, while celeb
traditions and preserving the

ain the feeling of openness
rating Greek architectural
stunning natural setting.

The boutique hotel, to be marketed under Helios's "Kiwi" brand, picks up some of the same materials and massing but has a softer and more intimate feel; for example, it has wood window shades instead of metal. The stepped massing allows for small, private courtyards and pools—and the kind of privacy hotel guests in this price range demand. Rich eastern Mediterranean foliage abounds throughout. The entire peninsula will contain a feeling of openness and accessibility, while also celebrating Greek architectural traditions and preserving the stunning natural setting.

left Conference Center landscape architecture including sections at drop-off court, terrace and wedding chapel

above and below façade studies for Conference Center showing alternative configurations of active shade devices

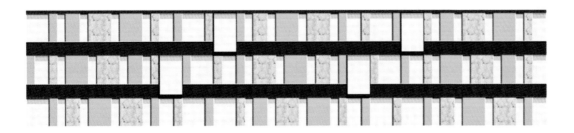

Lulu Island Vision Plan

Abu Dhabi, United Arab Emirates

"Lulu" is an Arabic word for "pearls". Before oil was discovered in the late 1950's, pearls were the industry that sustained Abu Dhabi, capital of the United Arab Emirates. Lulu Island is located strategically between the center of the city of Abu Dhabi and the Persian Gulf. The island is unique in that it is close to the city—separated by a small channel—but affords a long stretch of beachfront directly on the Gulf.

Abu Dhabi envisions Lulu Island as a low-rise, open island with world-class resorts and meeting facilities, as well as a mix of residential, commercial and office development. The island is considered a shared resource, part of the wealth of the nation. It is therefore meant to be open and inviting to all, not a sequestered oasis limited to a few. It is estimated that buildings will cover only about a quarter of the island, the remainder being composed of parks, walkable streets, waterways and cultural landscapes.

For millennia, nature has shaped Abu Dhabi into a series of bands aligned by the direction of the prevailing winds. This forms the basic idea of the design of the island—"Bands of Development." A central grand canal will bisect the island from its northeast to its southwest, with a series of smaller canals woven throughout. The highest density development is closest to the city, gradually decreasing as one cuts across the "Bands of Development" that follow roughly the same east/west path across the island. Clustered around a pedestrian bridge, which is the main access from the city, are destination buildings—shopping centers, hotels, a performing-arts center, museums and other cultural amenities. Each neighborhood is given a distinct quality and is served by community facilities like schools and mosques. An aerial view of the island shows land becoming more open and less developed as one moves away from the city and toward the Gulf. The landscape becomes greener and more softly defined, with angles giving way to curves, hardscapes and buildings giving way to lush vegetation. Finally, a broad, beautiful beach fronts the sea, where pearls were once harvested, and now forms a splendid gateway, open and inviting to all of Abu Dhabi.

top left model view northeast

above existing conditions

top right seafront promenade

right marina neighborhood

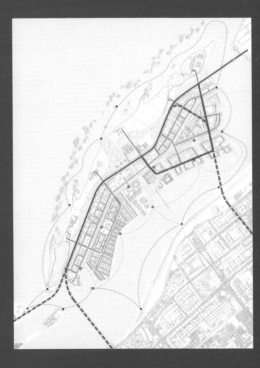

top right gardens and children's museum

far left master plan

center left landscape concept

near left circulation concept

following pages resort hotel fronting on Persian Gulf

A broad and beautiful beach
pearls were once harvested,
gateway, open and inviting t

ronting the sea, where
now forms a splendid
all of Abu Dhabi.

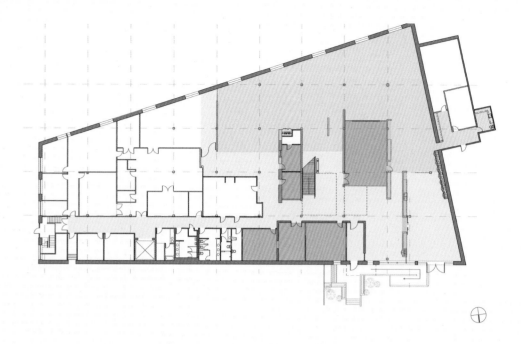

Newton, Massachusetts

This headquarters renovation was part of an overall rebranding and revisioning effort for Continuum, a design-strategy and industrial-design firm. Creating a space that "felt like Continuum" was less about aesthetic choices and more about developing an approach that would allow for maximum flexibility and collaboration for staff, projects, and clients, and would further establish a connection between people, process, and output. Continuum, which also has offices in Seoul and Milan, is credited with creating iconic consumer products like the Reebok "pump" sneaker and a prototype for a $100 laptop computer that would bring the Internet to third-world children. The firm boasts more than 186 awards and 300 design patents.

As a company that employs professionals from multiple disciplines who are involved in projects from the very small to the very large, Continuum requires flexibility on a daily basis. An open office "desking" system allows for communication and the easy movement of staff from one work area to another, as needed. Team rooms distributed throughout the space allow for project teams to have a common area in varied size groups. These rooms serve not only as meeting space, but as places to store and display project-related work. Minimal fixed walls and abundant natural light from added central skylights allow for work space anywhere within the building.

These same factors contribute also to collaboration, which is central to what Continuum is all about. The desking system and limited walls allow for easy communication. There are no boundaries between groups. Both the team rooms and more informal group work spaces are places in which ideas are displayed and shared, not only between project staff, but also with the entire group and with clients. The central, skylit space opens up what was once two separate floors and fosters a strong connection with a grand, communicating staircase. The space is expansive and loft-like, and allows occupants to have a clear sense of activity both upstairs and downstairs. This becomes the heart of Continuum.

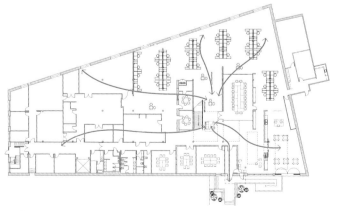

top left first floor

top central skylit space

right schematic concept

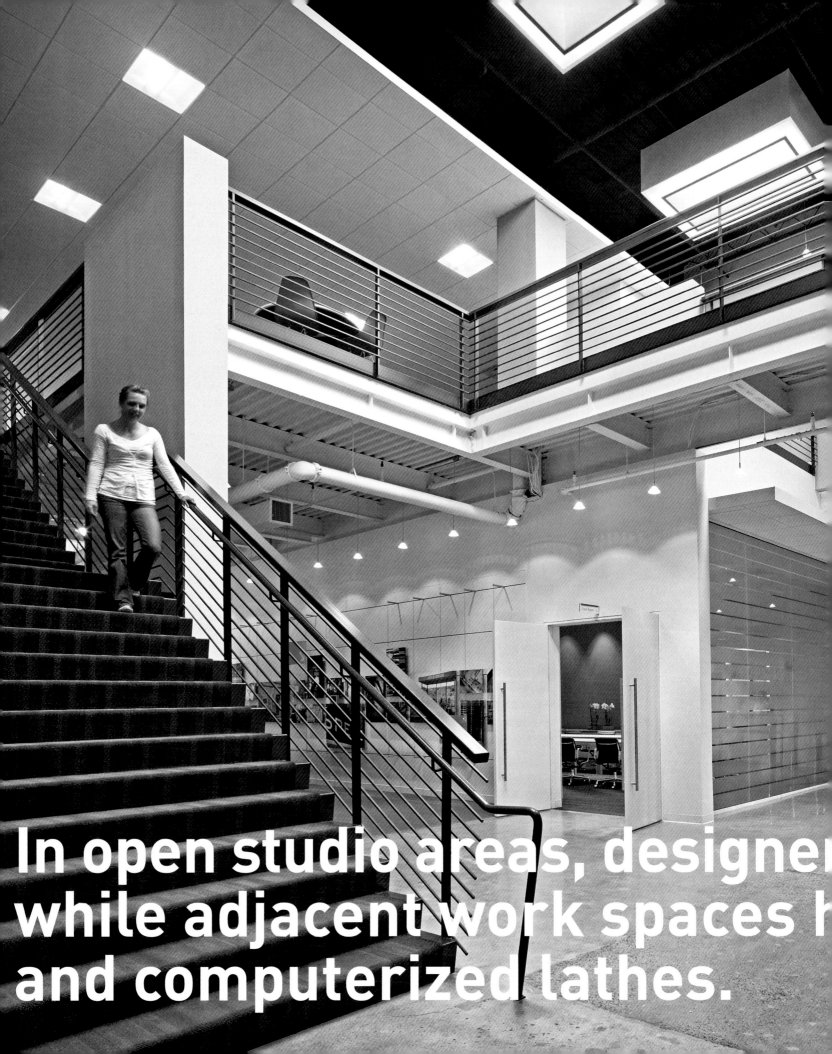

In open studio areas, designer
while adjacent work spaces h
and computerized lathes.

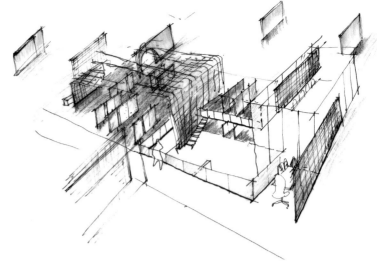

It is from this space that the entirety of the Continuum story can begin to be told. It provides the start of a "tour route" for potential clients so that they can experience the creative process of the group, examine prototypes produced in the shop, and consider work in progress in the team spaces. It is the main gathering space for all staff meetings, and it offers the opportunity for industry-critical events to be held in a space that showcases what Continuum is all about.

above sketch showing reconfiguration of interior spaces

left reception area

s busily wor
um with the

Hongxing Oceanfront Community

Dalian, China

Situated on a series of peninsulas reaching into the sea, Dalian is known for its scenic oceanfront setting of steep cliffs, hidden coves, and secluded beaches. It is also a growing city, quickly becoming a center for technology and multi-national business in northeastern China. This economic boom is contributing to Dalian's rapid population growth, which is attracting an influx of both foreign and domestic entrepreneurs seeking to contribute to the region's success. The 200-hectare site selected for this new community embodies the spirit of the unique Dalian landscape. Consisting of three major valleys that reach from the sea back into the mountains, oceanfront cliffs, and a protected cove adjacent to Dalian's "new development zone," the property is not only beautiful but offers an opportunity to create a live/work community that protects and restores the site's unique ecological systems.

The dramatic natural qualities of the site provided the inspiration for the master plan, which began by considering existing open-space systems and identifying ecological connections to create important linkages among various landscape communities. Learning from the traditions of existing coastal villages around Dalian, the plan located development on south-facing slopes. This move maximizes solar orientation to help reduce energy consumption while also protecting north-facing slopes from development. By terracing low- and medium-density residential units on the hillside, the team was able to minimize topographical impacts and maximize distant views to water. Northern slopes, which are primarily coniferous forests, provide a year-round habitat for a variety of native plants and wildlife. Their conservation preserves this unique ecological setting, contributes to the health of the watershed, and ensures that the view from the neighborhoods on the southern slopes is of a pristine landscape uninterrupted by development. At the valley floor, the riparian corridors leading to the sea are restored, creating a system of neighborhood parks that are used both for community recreation and treatment of stormwater runoff. Seasonal drainage corridors on the southern slopes are also protected, creating pedestrian links to the valley park system.

top left riparian corridor and recreation valley

above concept diagram

right master plan

Museum

Shopping Center

Cinema

Promenade

Plaza

Marina

Hotel

Boat House

Public Beach

Lookout

Recreation/Sports Center

Recreation
Mountain Trails

School Complex

Recreation
Mountain Trails

Lookout

Coastal Road
Bike Trail

Dining Complex

Ocean View
Platform

Lookout

Amphitheater

Lookout
Ocean View Platform

Community Club House

Lookout

Recreation
Mountain Trails

Hotel

The flat lands on the northern part of the site are located in a protected cove adjacent to existing high-density developments in this new district of Dalian. Concentrating additional density in this area allows for more residents to take advantage of nearby public transit while also creating a distinct sense of place on the waterfront. Linear landscape and pedestrian links reach from adjacent residential developments offsite directly into the heart of this mixed-use district. Lined with retail, restaurants, hotels, and other public accommodations, the cove waterfront will be a vibrant downtown with an active street life. The cove area serves not only as the center of the new community in Hongxing, but also as a destination for the entire district. Its generous system of waterfront promenades, public parks, and plazas create a venue for outdoor celebrations, festivals, and other gatherings. Iconic cultural buildings such as a museum, theater, and environmental learning center are strategically located along the waterfront promenade.

A new coastal road links the density of the cove waterfront to the three distinct valley neighborhoods. As part of the larger scenic-drive network already established throughout the city, public connections to the waterfront remain uninterrupted. Pedestrian and bike paths along the corridors ensure contiguous access along the entire coastline and also provide links into the valley neighborhoods. Additional public facilities such as a sailing school, swimming pools, beach access, cafés, and scenic overlooks that take advantage of the dramatic coastline views provide an identity for each valley neighborhood and ensure that each has a presence on the waterfront.

top left valley pier

above site context

top right and bottom waterfront plaza

At the valley floor, the riparian
are restored, creating a syste
that are used both for commu
and treatment of stormwater

corridors leading to the
m of neighborh
nity recrea
runoff.

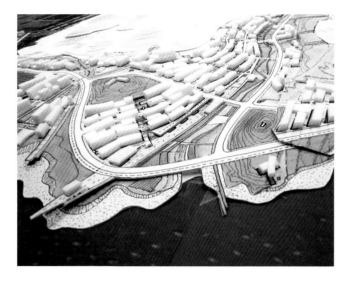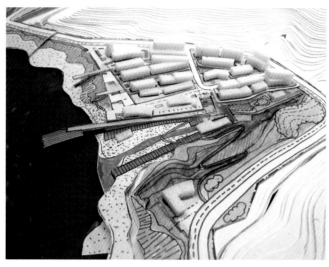
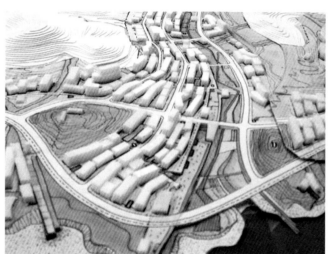

above study model concepts showing valley area development

below section through valley

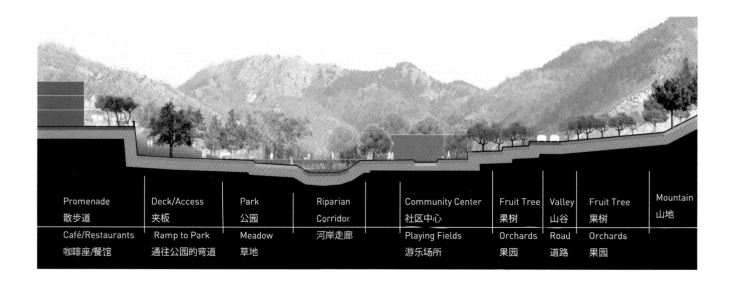

Promenade 散步道	Deck/Access 夹板	Park 公园	Riparian Corridor	Community Center 社区中心	Fruit Tree 果树	Valley 山谷	Fruit Tree 果树	Mountain 山地
Café/Restaurants 咖啡座/餐馆	Ramp to Park 通往公园的弯道	Meadow 草地	河岸走廊	Playing Fields 游乐场所	Orchards 果园	Road 道路	Orchards 果园	

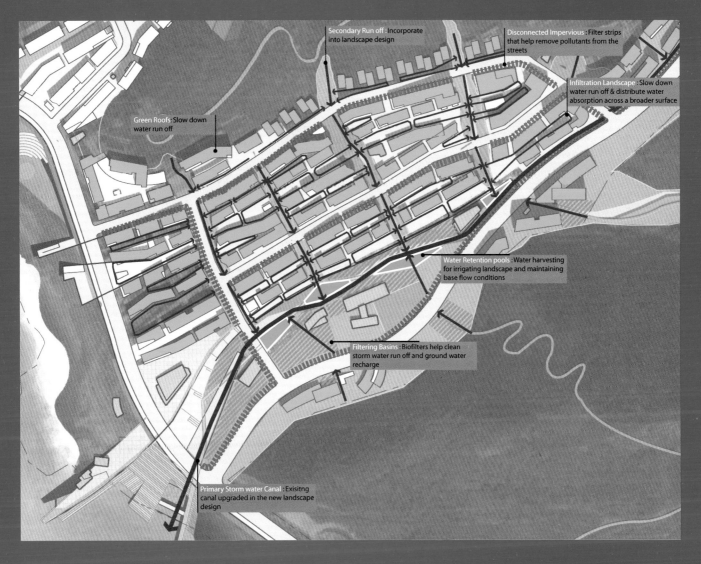

Secondary Run off : Incorporate into landscape design

Disconnected Impervious : Filter strips that help remove pollutants from the streets

Green Roofs : Slow down water run off

Infiltration Landscape : Slow down water run off & distribute water absorption across a broader surface

Water Retention pools : Water harvesting for irrigating landscape and maintaining base flow conditions

Filtering Basins : Biofilters help clean storm water run off and ground water recharge

Primary Storm water Canal : Exisitng canal upgraded in the new landscape design

top and bottom   storm water strategy

STORM WATER MANAGEMENT STRATEGIES

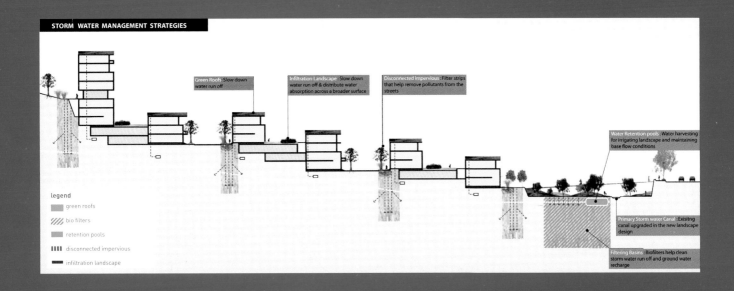

Green Roofs : Slow down water run off

Infiltration Landscape : Slow down water run off & distribute water absorption across a broader surface

Disconnected Impervious : Filter strips that help remove pollutants from the streets

Water Retention pools : Water harvesting for irrigating landscape and maintaining base flow conditions

Primary Storm water Canal : Exisitng canal upgraded in the new landscape design

Filtering Basins : Biofilters help clean storm water run off and ground water recharge

legend

green roofs

bio filters

retention pools

disconnected impervious

infiltration landscape

Sasaki Associates Offices

Watertown, Massachusetts and San Francisco, California

Sasaki Associates has designed its own offices as reflections of the firm's ethos of collaboration, egalitarianism and human diversity. Both complexes are designed not only to stringent LEED® certification ratings, but also as working laboratories for the best in sustainable design and advocacy.

Sasaki's offices in Watertown, Massachusetts, are located at Chase Mills, a large, former mill building located along the Charles River. The buildings are of varied ages and materials, the oldest dating to the nineteenth century. The spaces are open and democratic. Stunning views of the river are not reserved for principals, but are used as shared spaces which include the firm library and the Upper and Lower Overlooks. Throughout the complex there is a sense of openness, light and air. Multiple spaces are given over to tables and seating areas that invite and encourage spontaneous encounters among people in the firm's various design disciplines. At all times, the beautiful natural setting is a powerful reminder to staff of their responsibilities as designers to larger societal ideals.

The San Francisco office is in a more urban setting, yet retains similar thinking. Housed in the landmark former I. Magnin department store building, it is situated close to Union Square. All individual workstations are organized around studio spaces, circulation purposefully designed to engage the studios. One must pass through a project area when moving around the office. The main conference room serves as the heart of the office. It is easily the most dynamic space in the office, leaving a lasting first impression. The studios are designed to further the quality of the work through collaboration and dialogue. Workstations are designed to promote teamwork while providing all the necessary tools, technology, and workspace for the individual. As in Watertown, traditional partitioned cubicles and enclosed offices were abandoned in favor of wide, open workspaces. The resulting "democracy of space" is intended to facilitate interaction, foster the creation of project teams, and allow movement and mobility.

these pages Watertown studio

top left main entrance

top right parking garden

following pages San Francisco studio

Both complexes are designed
certification ratings, but also
the best in sustainable design

not only to stringent LEED®
as working laboratories for
and advocacy.

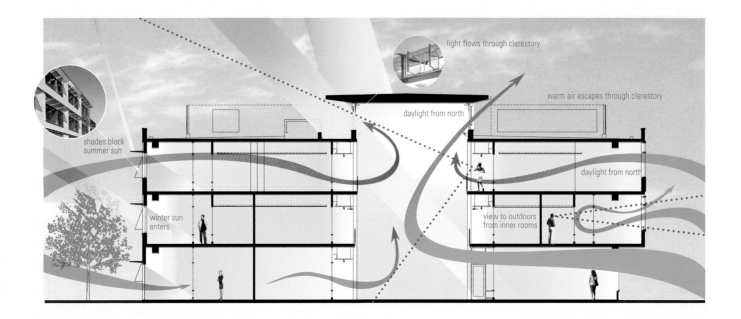

light flows through clerestory

warm air escapes through clerestory

daylight from north

daylight from north

shades block summer sun

winter sun enters

view to outdoors from inner rooms

Student Resource Building

University of California, Santa Barbara, Santa Barbara, California

The Student Resource Building (SRB) houses a diverse group of student-related organizations and offices. Because of its student-centered program, the building was paid for largely out of student fees.

The entire building arrays around a central glazed space called the Forum. The Forum is the marketplace, the center of activity for students, and is expressed on the exterior of the building as a shaded glass volume. The organization draws students to each floor of the building, reinforcing the interaction among staff, faculty, and students. The space is traversed by a glass bridge and also features clerestory windows and large glazed walls at either end that frame dramatic campus vistas. The Multi-Purpose Room is an oval-shaped volume that has an angled roof and is also expressed visually on the building's exterior.

The building has an environmentally sustainable design and is currently certified LEED® Silver, although the university is pursuing a Gold certification. The project's location both reinforces the master-plan principles and orients the building mass in an ideal configuration for daylighting, climate control, and natural ventilation. The selected site has an east/ west orientation optimal for environmental conditions.

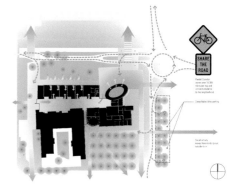

top left light and air flow

above site circulation

right interior wood screens filter light and create privacy zones

From an urban standpoint, the SRB is also appropriately situated on the border between the campus and the Isla Vista neighborhood, a funky urban oasis long known for coffee shops, used bookstores, one-of-a-kind retailers, and a rich, ethnic mix of residents. The neighborhood houses forty percent of the students at UCSB. Its location makes the SRB not just a campus gateway but a multi-generational building. A Child Care Center is located on the south portion of the site to serve students who are parents. The south-facing orientation of the building courtyard maximizes sunlight for the outdoor play areas and buffers the center from the noise and activity of the SRB. The Child Care Center is treated as a garden pavilion. The masonry-clad east façade leading to the entry is treated as an espaliered garden wall framing the grove of trees.

left and above views of the Forum

The Forum is the marketplac students, and is expressed or as a shaded glass volume.

e, the center of activity for
the exterior of the building

top left shaded southern façade

top right technology lab,

far right terrace

left oval multi-purpose room

right, top to bottom floors 1–3

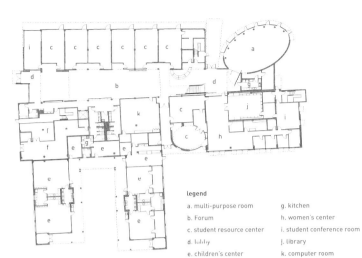

legend

a. multi-purpose room
b. Forum
c. student resource center
d. lobby
e. children's center
f. mechanical/electrical
g. kitchen
h. women's center
i. student conference room
j. library
k. computer room

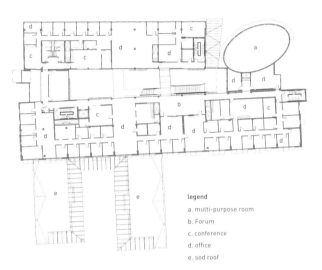

legend

a. multi-purpose room
b. Forum
c. conference
d. office
e. sod roof

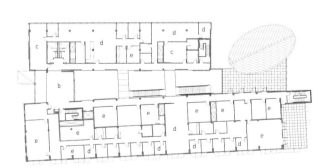

legend

a. multi-purpose room
b. Forum
c. conference
d. office
e. seminar/tutorial

University of Pennsylvania Swimming Facilities
Philadelphia, Pennsylvania

Crossings New Community Master Plan
Delhi, India

Hangzhou Creative Community
Hangzhou, China

Mangrove Tree Resort
Hainan Island, China

Biogen Idec Inc. Dining
Cambridge, Massachusetts

TJX Family Memorial Garden
Framingham, Massachusetts

Jing'an Art Park
Shanghai, China

Magic Beans
Wellesley, Massachusetts

Mayeux Ranch
Saint Gabriel, Louisiana

Johns Hopkins Ralph S. O'Connor Recreation Center
Baltimore, Maryland

Qinhuangdao Waterfront Urban Design Plan
Qinhuangdao, China

Kunming University City
Kunming, China

Waterway Square
The Woodlands, Texas

Cultural Park
Shanghai, China

New University
Dubai, United Arab Emirates

sasaki
GREEN

Sustainability is deeply ingrained in the culture and history of Sasaki Associates. Founding the firm in the early 1950s, while chairman of the Landscape Architecture department at Harvard University, Hideo Sasaki was prescient in his thinking about the designer's impact on the environment. In his work, he insisted on non-invasive and regenerative design interventions, achieving notable success in projects in coastal South Carolina in the late 1950s and early 1960s. Such environmental sensitivity might seem like common sense to us now, but at the time it was revolutionary. Moreover, it set the stage for the formation of an interdisciplinary practice that to this day provides a powerful vehicle for addressing the myriad challenges facing our environment, economy, and society. Our practice integrates the work of each of our disciplines on a common course to achieve sustainable solutions. Sasaki's work addresses all aspects of the built environment—from the earliest stages with master plans for new and existing communities to the complete design of buildings and landscapes. Firm professionals are encouraged to think beyond the boundaries of their discipline to explore areas outside their traditional professional areas of expertise. We continually evaluate our work to understand its effects and to achieve more innovative solutions. Our work is built on the following principles:

Integrate Environments

"Nature is to work together with the economy," a directive of Hideo Sasaki that recognizes the basis of sustainable planning and design by integrating concerns for the social, economic and environmental realms. Express this commitment in plans and designs that reflect community goals, engage stakeholders, work with nature and perpetuate community heritage.

left Through the Penn Connects Plan, the University of Pennsylvania is integrating its environments by: reclaiming newly purchased land creating green recreation and park space that integrates with a new enhanced green space plan for the current campus; connecting the university and the City of Philadelphia both physically and economically with mixed-use development on key connecting streets; and creating social sustainability by strengthening the relationship between the university and city populations.

Promote Transportation Options

Motivate individuals' commitment to walking, bicycling, and public transit by ensuring convenient alternative transit and a quality outdoor urban experience. Create a mix of uses and locate destination points to provide a safe and attractive civic realm. Think first of the pedestrian experience while realizing effective transportation systems that rely on human-powered and energy efficient systems.

right The site for the University of California, Santa Barbara Student Resource Building is designed to encourage and support a variety of non-single occupant vehicles by providing: bike paths; right of ways and storage; surfaces friendly to skate boards, scooters, etc.; convenient routes for public transportation; and by directing single-occupant vehicle traffic to the edges of campus.

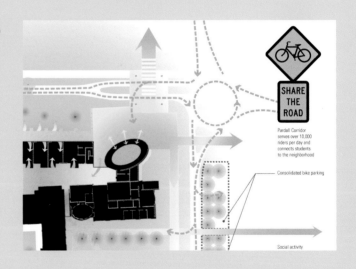

Manage Materials for a Healthy Earth

Employ materials management practices that promote environmental health and contribute to the economy through diversification of manufacturing and disposal practices. Design for longevity and materials reuse, and specify non-toxic materials. Select products that are locally extracted, harvested, and manufactured, fortifying the local economy and the firm's commitment to design that embraces local cultures.

left Also at the Student Resource Building, carefully chosen materials create a rich environment that is sustainable. Interior finish materials were minimized because the design incorporated an exposed structural concrete frame. Flooring consists of rapidly renewable rubber and recycled (post-industrial) nylon carpet tiles. Internal walls are finished with low VOC paints and recycled (post-consumer) nylon, fabric-wrapped panels.

Enhance Water Resources

Limit the need for inter-basin or inter-watershed transfers and plan for efficient water consumption and critical watershed protection strategies. Prevent toxins from entering the water supply and, through redevelopment of contaminated sites, restore polluted water resources.

right The Southworks design allows for 91% of the site's watershed to directly infiltrate into the soil, thereby bypassing Chicago's combined sewer system and returning directly to the lake. As part of the stormwater-management plan, "finger parks" serve as large scale biofiltration and infiltration areas. In a joint city/state initiative, clean dredge material is brought to the site from downstate Illinois in a program known as "Mud to Parks", which will enrich the site's current soil profile and capacity to sustain new landscape strategies. Refinements to the stormwater plan include pervious pavements at all alleys and parking lanes, the use of rain gardens in roadway medians, and the storage and reuse of rainwater from the larger roof-catchment areas. The site is treated 55% by water-quality treatment structures and 30% by naturalized infiltration water-quality treatment basins.

Design for Renewable Energy Systems and a Clean Atmosphere

Promote human health and comfort. Reduce the reliance on non-renewable energy systems through conservation, emphasis on natural energy sources such as sun and wind, and the integrated use of renewable clean fuels.

left The primary expression of the Drexel Recreation Center Expansion is its faceted glass module giving scale and interest to the long façades, directing views to the city, and reducing light incidence on the glass. Because of the large amount of glazing, Ecotect, an energy and daylighting software, was employed as a design and analytical tool to study the impact of the shading inherent in the design and areas for improvement with respect to thermal comfort, glare, and mechanical loads. Daylight is maximized for the reduction of artificial light and solar heat gain in the winter. The design strategy included strategically placed overhangs and faceting, the shading properties of Panelite, a series of extruded acrylic tubes acting as an internal shading device between the layers of the insulated glass unit, and high-performance translucent glass which reduces the cooling loads of the south façade by 50% and the east façade by 30% compared with conventional glass walls.

Champion Natural Habitats

Enhance habitat diversity through open space preservation and the selection of native vegetation. Redevelop sites to regenerate natural habitats.

right Industry ruined the original marshland that existed along the Charleston Waterfront. The restoration of the salt marsh offers habitat, cleanses pollutants, and buffers the land from the force of coastal storms. The area has been mitigated, and a unique robust river habitat now flourishes, supporting the marine ecology and wildlife that had fled or was dying before the restoration. To preserve the site history, pilings from previous wooden industrial structures were retained, providing landing spots that enhance the habitat for local birds.

Practice
Integrating sustainability into our work

SpaceGREEN
Architecture, Interior & Graphic Design

SiteGREEN
Eco-Technologies & Landscape Architecture

PlanningGREEN
Planning & Urban Design

Operations
Leading by example

GreenRED
Researching

GreenLAB
Testing

GreenDAY
Educating

GreenNEWS
Communicating

GreenOrganization

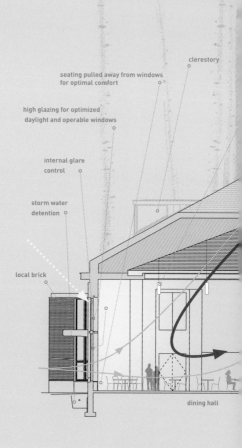

clerestory

seating pulled away from windows for optimal comfort

high glazing for optimized daylight and operable windows

internal glare control

storm water detention

local brick

dining hall

Sasaki's Watertown, Massachusetts office is located in a former industrial mill building along the banks of the Charles River. This adjacent riparian environment is a powerful daily reminder of our responsibility as designers to larger environmental concerns. The San Francisco office is located in a rejuvenated building in San Francisco's Union Square neighborhood. Both locations reflect the values of the firm: use of existing buildings and sites, commitment to public transportation and the public realm, and appreciation of human diversity and social equity.

Sustainability informs the firm's daily operations, from employee benefits to motivate sustainable practices, to selection of office locations on public transportation routes, to the environment of the workplace itself. Both of our offices are LEED® certified and are treated as working laboratories for testing green design and practices. Beyond the walls of its offices, Sasaki professionals are engaged in the teaching design at colleges and universities, with emphasis on incorporating sustainable principles and practices.

SasakiGREEN is a firm-wide vehicle to achieve our vision of planning and design excellence with sustainability as a critical factor. The group ensures that Sasaki will strive to understand the immediate and long-term impacts of our work by being a leader in the green design field.

To achieve this goal of leadership, SasakiGREEN focuses on **Practice** and **Operations**. Most professionals within the firm serve on one of the many SasakiGREEN committees. The Practice groups focus intensely on increasing the levels of sustainability in our projects; the Operations groups seek to apply the latest sustainable design thinking within our own walls, which will in turn inform our work for clients.

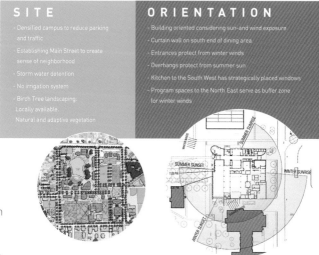

SITE
- Densified campus to reduce parking and traffic
- Establishing Main Street to create sense of neighborhood
- Storm water detention
- No irrigation system
- Birch Tree landscaping. Locally available. Natural and adaptive vegetation

ORIENTATION
- Building oriented considering sun and wind exposure
- Curtain wall on south end of dining area
- Entrances protect from winter winds
- Overhangs protect from summer sun
- Kitchen to the South West has strategically placed windows
- Program spaces to the North East serve as buffer zone for winter winds

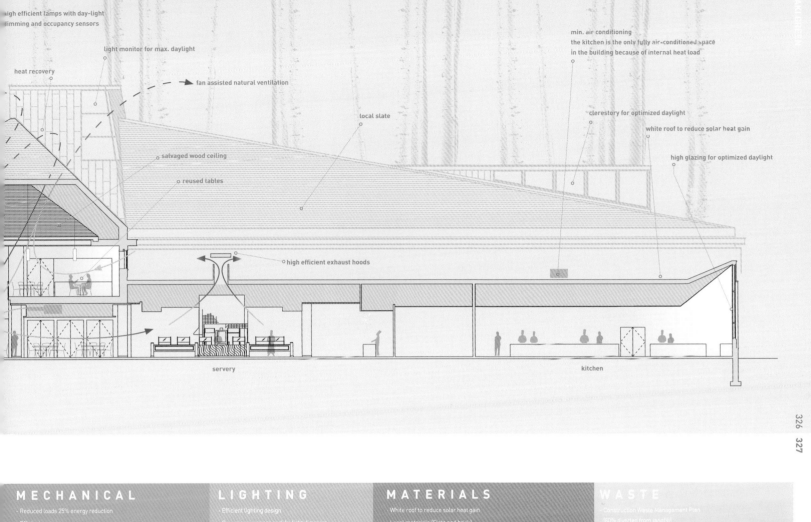

high efficient lamps with day-light dimming and occupancy sensors

light monitor for max. daylight

heat recovery

fan assisted natural ventilation

salvaged wood ceiling

reused tables

local slate

high efficient exhaust hoods

servery

kitchen

min. air conditioning
the kitchen is the only fully air-conditioned space
in the building because of internal heat load

clerestory for optimized daylight

white roof to reduce solar heat gain

high glazing for optimized daylight

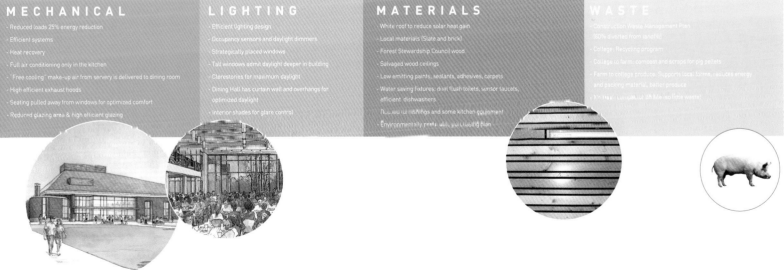

MECHANICAL

- Reduced loads 25% energy reduction
- Efficient systems
- Heat recovery
- Full air conditioning only in the kitchen
- "Free cooling" make-up air from servery is delivered to dining room
- High efficient exhaust hoods
- Seating pulled away from windows for optimized comfort
- Reduced glazing area & high efficient glazing

LIGHTING

- Efficient lighting design
- Occupancy sensors and daylight dimmers
- Strategically placed windows
- Tall windows admit daylight deeper in building
- Clerestories for maximum daylight
- Dining Hall has curtain wall and overhangs for optimized daylight
- Interior shades for glare control

MATERIALS

- White roof to reduce solar heat gain
- Local materials (Slate and brick)
- Forest Stewardship Council wood
- Salvaged wood ceilings
- Low emitting paints, sealants, adhesives, carpets
- Water saving fixtures: dual flush toilets, sensor faucets, efficient dishwashers
- Reused furnishings and some kitchen equipment
- Environmentally responsible purchasing plan

WASTE

- Construction Waste Management Plan (80% diverted from landfill)
- College Recycling program
- College to farm: compost and scraps for pig pellets
- Farm to college produce. Supports local farms, reduces energy and packing material, better produce
- Minimally compostable on-site so little waste!

above Bates College Dining Commons demonstrates an overall sustainable approach from master plan to implementation that is the result of the design and resources of SasakiGREEN.

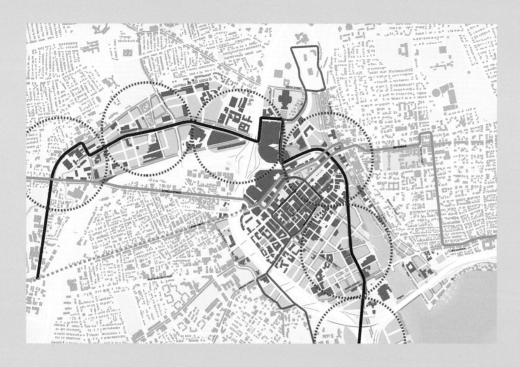

GreenPractice

The SasakiGREEN practice is arrayed into three broad categories as a means of honing specialization and encouraging the cross-pollination of knowledge. PlanningGREEN, SpaceGREEN, and SiteGREEN provide resources and tools, specific to their disciplines, including seminars and field trips to educate our staff and provide research assistance to project teams.

PlanningGREEN focuses on our **planning and urban design** practice. As evidenced by the early work of Sasaki at key coastal locations, some of the most dramatic environmental benefits can be attained at the very early stages of a project. The siting of buildings, the incorporation of transit and other key infrastructure, the use of infill and brownfield sites are all critical decisions made at the planning stage, with profound and lasting effects on the project even decades into the future.

SpaceGREEN focuses on our **architecture, interior design,** and **graphic design** practices. This is among the most information intensive of our sustainable work because of the continued emergence of the various LEED® categories and other processes of documentation and advancement. Multiple times in any given week, Sasaki offices are host to vendor demonstrations. Groups often venture out of the office for field trips where innovative and proven sustainability strategies have been implemented.

SiteGREEN focuses on our **eco-technologies and landscape architecture** practices. SiteGREEN deals with such critical subjects as drainage, rainwater management, irrigation, and other natural systems. Sasaki's early and prescient success in restoring coastal ecosystems has allowed us to build up decades of experience and problem-solving approaches now applied to a variety of projects.

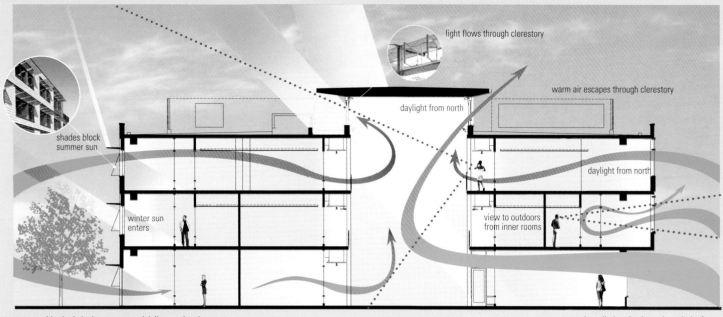

sunlight enters forum in the winter   overhang shades forum in the summer

light flows through clerestory

warm air escapes through clerestory

daylight from north

shades block summer sun

winter sun enters

daylight from north

view to outdoors from inner rooms

trees provide shade in the summer and deliver cooler air

natural ventilation circulates through the forum

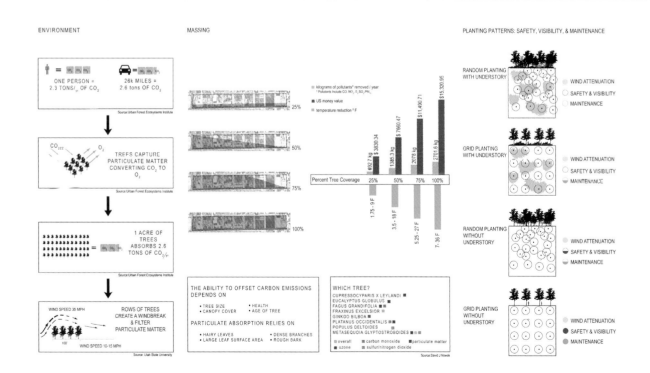

ENVIRONMENT

ONE PERSON = 2.3 TONS/yr OF CO₂
26k MILES = 2.6 tons OF CO₂
Source: Urban Forest Ecosystems Institute

TREES CAPTURE PARTICULATE MATTER CONVERTING CO₂ TO O₂
Source: Urban Forest Ecosystems Institute

1 ACRE OF TREES ABSORBS 2.6 TONS OF CO₂/yr
Source: Urban Forest Ecosystems Institute

WIND SPEED 35 MPH
ROWS OF TREES CREATE A WINDBREAK & FILTER PARTICULATE MATTER
WIND SPEED 10-15 MPH
Source: Utah State University

THE ABILITY TO OFFSET CARBON EMISSIONS DEPENDS ON
• TREE SIZE   • HEALTH
• CANOPY COVER   • AGE OF TREE

PARTICULATE ABSORPTION RELIES ON
• HAIRY LEAVES   • DENSE BRANCHES
• LARGE LEAF SURFACE AREA • ROUGH BARK

MASSING

25%
50%
75%
100%

WHICH TREE?
CUPRESSOCYPARIS X LEYLANDI
EUCALYPTUS GLOBULUS
FAGUS GRANDIFOLIA
FRAXINUS EXCELSIOR
GINKGO BILBOA
PLATANUS OCCIDENTALIS
POPULUS DELTOIDES
METASEQUOIA GLYPTOSTROBOIDES
overall   carbon monoxide   particulate matter
ozone   sulfur/nitrogen dioxide
Source: David J Nowak

kilograms of pollutants* removed / year
*Pollutants include CO, NO₂, O₃, SO₂, PM₁₀
US money value
temperature reduction °F

Percent Tree Coverage	25%	50%	75%	100%
	692.7 kg	1385.3 kg	2078 kg	2701.6 kg
	$3830.34	$7060.47	$11,490.71	$15,320.95
	1.75 - 9 F	3.5 -18 F	5.25 - 27 F	7 - 36 F

PLANTING PATTERNS: SAFETY, VISIBILITY, & MAINTENANCE

RANDOM PLANTING WITH UNDERSTORY
WIND ATTENUATION
SAFETY & VISIBILITY
MAINTENANCE

GRID PLANTING WITH UNDERSTORY
WIND ATTENUATION
SAFETY & VISIBILITY
MAINTENANCE

RANDOM PLANTING WITHOUT UNDERSTORY
WIND ATTENUATION
SAFETY & VISIBILITY
MAINTENANCE

GRID PLANTING WITHOUT UNDERSTORY
WIND ATTENUATION
SAFETY & VISIBILITY
MAINTENANCE

top left Providence 2020 public transit strategy

middle left 601 Congress green roof

bottom left Loyola College playing fields landfill regeneration

top University of California Santa Barbara, Student Resource Building passive design approach

above Port of Los Angeles tree study

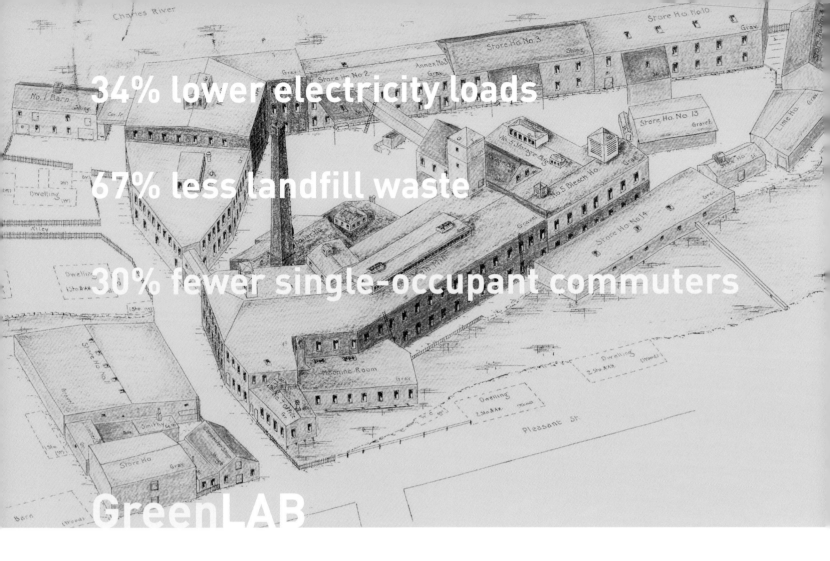

34% lower electricity loads

67% less landfill waste

30% fewer single-occupant commuters

GreenLAB

Sasaki formed its GreenLAB in 2003 as a means of using our workplaces as laboratories for green design. The aim is to test and experiment with various energy-saving and sustainability strategies. Some of the results have been dramatic. For example, in Watertown we installed energy-efficient fluorescent bulbs with new ballasts and photocell technology designed to reduce light output as natural light enters the space. This resulted in a 34% reduction in electricity costs, such a marked decrease that the regional power utility sent investigators to our site to ensure that the meters were working properly.

The GreenLAB was instrumental in helping Sasaki earn LEED® certification for both of its offices. Chase Mills, along the Charles River just outside of Boston, dating from 1834, is now the oldest Gold LEED® E.B. (Existing Building) certified structure in the United States. Because of the building's age and proximity to the river, the certification process took almost two years and involved inspection and documentation of multiple aspects of the building's operations. Sasaki's San Francisco office, located in the old I. Magnin Building just off of Union Square, is LEED® C.I. (Corporate Interiors) certified.

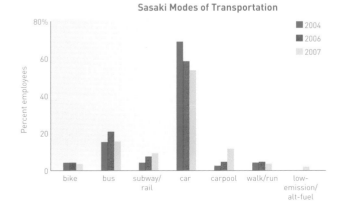

Sasaki Modes of Transportation

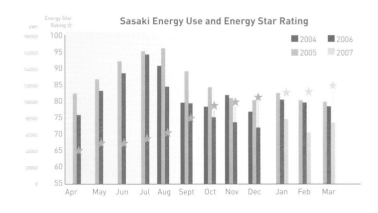

Sasaki Energy Use and Energy Star Rating

Site Installed porous paving options • Reduced water use for landscape irrigation Building Reduced electricity loads by 34% • Installed photo-sensing ballasts • Conducted a lighting comfort survey • Installed and monitor interior light-shelves • Monitored human comfort Water Testing water-saving fixtures • Purifying drinking water on-site Purchasing Selected organic fair trade coffee • Purchased reusable porcelain plates, glass tumblers, and cutlery • Testing new green building material • Choose organic caterers • Offer Green dry-cleaning • Print soy inks on recycled papers Waste Reduced landfill waste by 67% • Reuse construction materials Transportation Reduced single occupant commuting by 30% • Reserve parking spaces for low-emission vehicles • Subsidize mass transit tickets • Provide full facilities for bicyclists

LEED-EB   LEED-CI

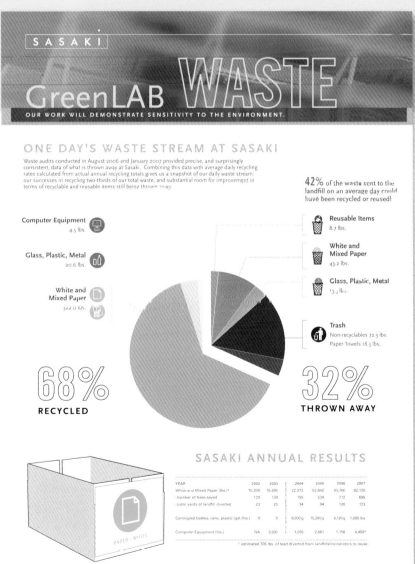

SASAKI

GreenLAB WASTE
OUR WORK WILL DEMONSTRATE SENSITIVITY TO THE ENVIRONMENT.

ONE DAY'S WASTE STREAM AT SASAKI

Waste audits conducted in August 2006 and January 2007 provided precise, and surprisingly consistent, data of what is thrown away at Sasaki. Combining this data with average daily recycling rates calculated from actual annual recycling totals gives us a snapshot of our daily waste stream: our successes in recycling two-thirds of our total waste, and substantial room for improvement in terms of recyclable and reusable items still being thrown away.

42% of the waste sent to the landfill on an average day could have been recycled or reused!

Computer Equipment
4.5 lbs.

Glass, Plastic, Metal
20.6 lbs.

White and Mixed Paper
322.0 lbs.

Reusable Items
8.7 lbs.

White and Mixed Paper
43.2 lbs.

Glass, Plastic, Metal
13.3 lbs.

Trash
Non-recyclables 72.3 lbs.
Paper Towels 18.3 lbs.

68%
RECYCLED

32%
THROWN AWAY

PAPER - WHITE

SASAKI ANNUAL RESULTS

YEAR	2002	2003	2004	2005	2006	2007
White and Mixed Paper (lbs.)*	15,200	16,295	22,972	62,842	83,766	82,126
number of trees saved	129	139	195	534	712	698
cubic yards of landfill diverted	23	25	34	94	126	123
Comingled bottles, cans, plastic (gal./lbs.)	0	0	9,000g	15,200g	6,120g	1,695 lbs
Computer Equipment (lbs.)	NA	3,031	1,010	2,681	1,158	4,409*

* estimated 705 lbs. of lead diverted from landfills/incinerators to reuse.

Chase Mills original design

biking Sasaki commuter

pervious parking surface test plots

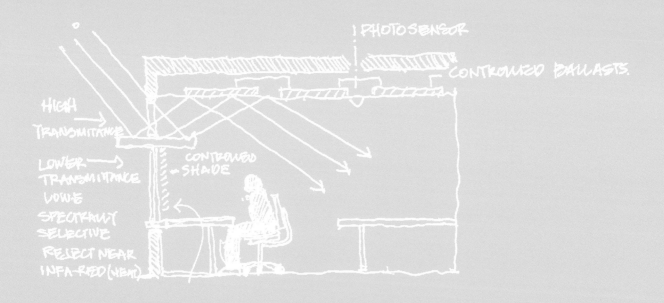

HIGH TRANSMITTANCE

LOWER TRANSMITTANCE LOW-E SPECTRALLY SELECTIVE REJECT NEAR INFA-RED (HEAT)

CONTROLLED SHADE

PHOTOSENSOR

CONTROLLED BALLASTS.

GreenRED

True to its roots in the academic world, Sasaki places high value on research, investigation, and testing of ideas.

GreenRED (**R**esearch, **E**ducation, **D**evelopment) grants encourage research by individuals or groups within Sasaki to investigate promising sustainable design initiatives. The research is intended to further the professional's and Sasaki's leadership in a particular facet of sustainable design. RED grants include:

At **Port of Los Angeles (POLA)**, the research involved potential use of titanium dioxide panels, a new technology that, when exposed to ambient daylight, breaks down air pollutants.

Using computer modeling, day-lighting software, light meters and monitoring of human comfort, studied the effects of **light shelves**, both at Sasaki offices and at client sites.

Researching alternative, lower input turf species, their cultural and management requirements, and commercial availability for the **Ohio State University (OSU)** River of Trees.

At **Southworks,** a former Chicago steel plant fronting Lake Michigan, efficacy of a mass tree planting that will immediately "green" the site as it is built out over the next ten to fifteen years, assessing whether such reforestation can mediate effects of past pollution, improve public perception of the site and have a broader application at other urban brownfield sites.

top light shelf study

above light shelf

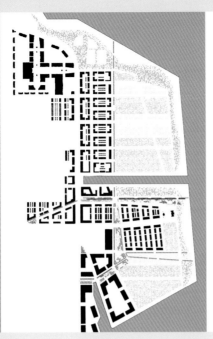
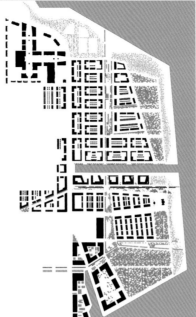
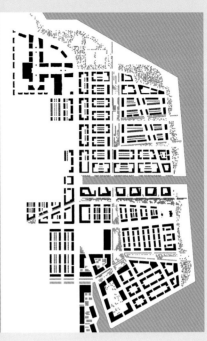

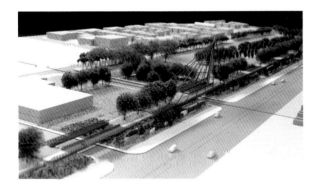

top Southworks reforestation plan for development phases 1–4

above, below and right use of titanium dioxide panels along the buffer wall at Port of Los Angeles

Factors influencing photocatalysis

temperature
wind
light intensity and wavelength
relative humidity
concentration of pollutants
speed of traffic

Reactants

photocatalyst TiO_2 + particulates, benzene, formaldehyde, sulfur monoxide and dioxide, nitrogen monoxide and dioxide, carbon monoxide =

toxic chemicals and carcinogens

Products

trace amounts of:
water soluble nitrates and nitrites
sulfuric/bivalent acids
carbon monoxide or dioxide
water-soluble organic substrates
inorganic oxidized compounds

Hot summer days with low relative humidity and no wind would provide optimal conditions for reducing air pollution. This type of scenario often coincides with high levels of smog.

The products of the reaction are gases or simple organic/inorganic compounds that may be washed away by rain or water. Any acidic products are absorbed or neutralized by the alkaline substrate in the concrete.

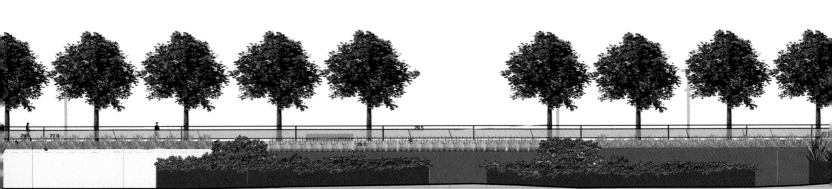

GreenDAY/GreenNEWS

ALL WEEK! MAY 16TH - 20TH

Alternative Transportation
Carpool, Walk, Run, Bike, Train, Bus, Skip and Kayak to
be eligible for GreenDAY prizes.

Clothing and Household Goods Donation *(Accounting)*
Give your belongings a new life instead of sending them
to the landfill. Bring them to the Accounting area all week
for the Vietnam Veteran's Association of America.

Light Bulb Exchange! *(Lower Overlook)*
Exchange your incandescents in your task lights for
compact fluorescents to save energy.

MONDAY, MAY 16TH
**Richard Jackson - State Public Health Officer -
California Department of Public Health** *(Crit rm 12⁰⁰-1⁰⁰)*
View his presentation on Health and Design given
at GreenBuild 2004

TUESDAY, MAY 17TH
Yoga for the Work Place *(Great Space 12⁰⁰-12³⁰)*
FREE! Debbie Cohen of Core Yoga will be leading an office
session. Learn how to energize, unwind and de-stress the
periodically throughout the course of the work day.

WEDNESDAY, MAY 18TH
Blood Drive *(Front Parking Lot 10⁰⁰-3⁰⁰)*
For more information see sign outside of HR.

THURSDAY, MAY 19TH
GreenDAY Riverwalk *(Meet in Great Space 12⁰⁰-1⁰⁰)*

GreenDAY is an annual, day-long event for Sasaki staff to participate in wide-ranging
presentations, discussions, seminars and other activities. Usually held in May, the event
is the culmination of a week of presentations by national leaders in sustainable design.

GreenDAY is envisioned as an opportunity to reinforce and learn new information related
to sustainability across all our disciplines. While the format of GreenDAY has changed over
the years, the mission remains to highlight sustainable design and to foster its integration
into our work.

Employees embrace the opportunity to work with colleagues outside their current projects.
The day is similar to a mini-conference with a keynote speaker followed by learning
workshops. Some years have included a mini-trade show with vendors of innovative
sustainable products.

Recent keynote speakers were Susan Szenasy, editor of *Metropolis* magazine, and Ray
Anderson, leader of global carpet giant Interface. "You have design power," said Szenasy
in her opening plenary at Sasaki's GreenDAY 2006 "You're designing buildings as large as
500,000 square feet, and that's a huge buying block. I live in a 400-square-foot apartment.
I have no power. You have power."

GreenNEWS is a quarterly publication that serves as a source of information for the firm's
employees. Produced digitally, each issue features a cross section of the offices' sustainable projects and celebrates the accomplishments of staff, such as LEED® certification,
speaking engagements, and project news. GreenNEWS is an educational tool, information
exchange, and record of Sasaki's activities.

GREENDAY VENDORS

Site	Interiors	Architecture
A.J. Harris, Graham Gurry	Dauphin Chair	Agriboard Industr
Grid Tech, Arthur Erhardt	Hag Chair (Ritz Associates)	American Hydrote
Hancor, Guy Canto	Shetka Stone	Carona Internatic
Ideal Concrete Block Co.	Salshade	Eco lighting-FMS:
Lantz of New England	Shaw Tile	Metro Architectur
LeBaron Foundry	Auburn Enterprises	(Arc Structures, N
North American Green	Eurostone	Newton Distributir
Pavestone Co	Nano Technology	rep for Excel Hanc
Pettinelli Associates	Mondo Rubber	Rheinzink America
Unilock Inc	Seventh Generation	Sherwin Williams -
Weston Solutions	Concious Flooring	Urell - Rep for Totc
Filtera	Conklin Office Furniture	Vistawall Architec
Rainbird	Longleaf Lumber	Waterless Urinals
Perma-till	Mirra Chair/Kira Panel	
Omni-lite	(Hermann Miller)	
New England Wildflower Society		

HARVARD U
homeneny gym
sustainable fac

HEALTHY DESIGN
enDAY 2005
THE ENVIRONMENT.

FRIDAY, MAY 20TH. GREENDAY!

8³⁰ - 9   Breakfast *(Tent)*

9 - 10   Opening Plenary *(Tent)*
Pliny Fisk Co-director, Center for Maximum Potential Building Systems
Design for Life - A Maximum Potential Perspective

10¹⁵ -11⁴⁵   Morning Session 1 *(Tent)*
Gail Vittori Co-Director, Center for Maximum Potential Building Systems
Evolving a Healthy Building Agenda

Morning Session 2 *(Great Space)*
Tony Cortese President, Second Nature and Co-founder, Campus Sustainability Day
Transforming Planning and Design to Create a Healthy, Just and Sustainable Society

11⁴⁵-2¹⁵   Resource Fair *(Office)*

12 -1   Lunch Buffet

2¹⁵-3⁴⁵   Afternoon Session 1 *(Tent)*
John Porretto President, Sustainable Building Solutions, Inc.
Former Executive Vice President and COO of the University of Texas Health Science Center
Sustainability - Informing the Debate from Lessons Learned

Afternoon Session 2 *(Great Space)*
Peter Del Tredici Senior Research Scientist, Arnold Arboretum
Sustainability Starts with the Soil

4-5³⁰   Closing Plenary & Panel Discussion *(Tent)*
All Session Speakers with Pliny Fisk as Moderator

second floor

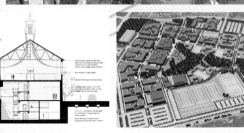

GreenDAY 2007
OUR WORK WILL DEMONSTRATE SENSITIVITY TO THE ENVIRONMENT.

GreenDAY began in 2003 as a way to recognize Sasaki's commitment to sustainable design across all of our disciplines. The day was also envisioned as an opportunity to reinforce and learn new information related to sustainability. While the format of GreenDAY has changed over the years, the mission of the day remains to highlight sustainable design and foster its integration into our work.

WEDNESDAY, MAY 23ʳᵈ GREENDAY KEYNOTE   3:45 PM–6:00 PM

3:45–5:00   **GreenDAY Keynote by Ray Anderson, Founder and Chairman of Interface, Inc.**

Ray Anderson will give this year's GreenDAY keynote address. The design and manufacturing business communities recognize Mr. Anderson as one of the world's most environmentally progressive leaders on sustainable commerce. His globally positioned company's core business is sustainable carpets and fabrics. While Interface is noted in its industry for high quality design and innovation, it is distinguished as a leader in the green business movement. Following Susan Szenasy's challenge during GreenDAY 2006 to engage manufacturers, Sasaki has invited Mr. Anderson to speak about the future of sustainable products and collaboration with designers.

5:00–6:00   **Reception**

THURSDAY, MAY 24ᵗʰ GREENDAY 2007   8:00 AM–5:30 PM

GreenDAY workshops will provide the opportunity for Sasaki staff to further their understanding of a specific sustainable design topic. Consulting advisors will facilitate the workshops, introducing the topics in detail and leading design exercises focused on our ongoing work at the University of Pennsylvania. The workshop will culminate in presentations and discussions highlighting the results of day.

8:00–8:30   Breakfast at Sasaki

8:30–9:00   GreenDAY Introduction and Project Briefing

9:00–3:45   Workshop With Working Lunch

4:00–5:00   Presentations

5:00–5:20   Panel Discussion

5:20–5:30   Closing Remarks

WORKSHOP	ADVISOR
Microclimate Analysis	Duncan Phillips, *RWDI* Bill Waechter, *RWDI*
Renewable Energy Master Planning	Mark Crowdis, *Think Energy*
Sustainability and Campus Planning	Cindy Pollock Shea, *UNC-CH* Tony Cortese, *2ⁿᵈ Nature*
Building Siting and Orientation	Chris Schaffner, *The Green Engineer*
Sustainable Lighting	Mark Loeffler, *Atelier Ten* Samantha LaFleur, *Atelier Ten*
The Sustainability vs. Design Debate	Lindsay James, *InterfaceFLOR*
Permaculture Techniques	Jono Neiger, *Regenerative Design*
Innovative Wastewater Alternatives	Pio Lombardo, *Lombardo Associates*

DESIGN EXERCISE: UNIVERSITY OF PENNSYLVANIA

Penn Connects, the Campus Development Planning study for the University of Pennsylvania, was submitted by Sasaki Associates in June 2006. The focus of the study was the unprecedented opportunity to transform the Penn campus in response to the acquisition of the 24-acre postal property along the Schuylkill River. This campus expansion of contiguous land will enable the University to establish a major physical presence along the Schuylkill River, evaluate current building and open space use, and establish new connections with the surrounding communities.

GreenDAY 2007 presents the opportunity to evaluate this campus expansion from the perspective of eight different sustainable strategies ranging in scale from campus policy to materials selection. The overall goals of the day are to provide an enriching educational experience for Sasaki and to generate ideas that will guide sustainable growth at the University of Pennsylvania.

Newsletter 1 (top-left)

AMBYSTOMA MACULATUM

THE SPOTTED SALAMANDER

SiteGreen recently launched their new meeting series format. Read "Merging Habitats" on pg. 4 about the SiteGreen fall series, titled "Habitat", and how these planning considerations are being integrated into the team's approach for the Quarterpath project in Williamsburg, VA.

in this issue

SASAKI GREEN VISION — 1
NEWS BRIEFS — 2
OAKLAND 12TH STREET RECONSTRUCTION — 3
MERGING HABITATS — 4
GREEN SPOTLIGHT — 5
TECH CORNER — 5
CONSULTANTS CORNER — 5
GREEN MONSTER — 6
GREEN GROUP UPDATES — 6-7
CALENDAR — 8
RESOURCES — 8

SASAKI GREEN VISION

BY ALAN RESNICK

When a client asks, "How many green projects have you designed?", instead of noting where, when and why, our answer will be, "All of our projects are designed to be environmentally responsible." When a client asks "How much more will it cost to include sustainable design principles?", instead of quoting cost premiums for green design, we will respond by advising our clients as to how much it will cost not to include our recommendations — from operational costs to reduced job performance and absenteeism, not to mention the secondary impacts on the environment.

It's time for a change of mindset. Choosing to pursue green initiatives on certain projects means we are choosing not to on others. Why? As long as we think there is a choice to avoid environmentally responsible design, we are continuing to hold on to the past and not looking toward the future.

Should we be planning campuses and communities that encourage people to use their cars unnecessarily? Should we be designing buildings that consume more fossil fuel than necessary, with marginal light and poor air quality? Of course not. Our job is to create spaces that enhance quality of life, human performance and comfort, all of which should not be considered a premium cost. So, how can we convince our clients that the long-term effects of poor development decisions are far greater than the initial costs associated with an environmentally responsible design? Two thoughts.

First, we will establish a new sustainable baseline for design, nothing overly aggressive or exotic, but a solid, environmentally responsible standard, "Sasaki's Green Line." This "Green Line" would be based on the LEED certification criteria

CONTINUED ON PG. 4

Newsletter 2 (top-right)

DIANCHI TIAN DI RETAIL AT CAOHAI NORTH SHORE

in this issue

CAOHAI NORTH SHORE 1
NEWS BRIEFS 2
GREEN MONSTER 2
QUEEN'S UNIVERSITY: The Impact of Policy, Planning & Design 3
GreenRED: INVESTING IN INNOVATION 4
CONSULTANTS CORNER . . . 4
SPECIES OF THE QUARTER . . 5
TECH TALK 5
GREEN GROUP UPDATES . . . 6
GREEN LAB 6
GREEN SPOTLIGHT 7
CALENDAR 8
RESOURCES 8

WINTER EMERGENCE!

Crawling out of a stream on a freezing January day might not sound romantic, but love is in the air this month for a group of insects known as winter stoneflies. This quiet time of the year begins the winter stoneflies' annual mating period and marks the slow return of longer days.

WINTER STONEFLY, ALLOCAPNIA

CAOHAI NORTH SHORE

In April 2005, Sasaki was appointed by Shui On Land to complete a master plan for a 538 hectare (1,330 acre) site on the shores of Dianchi Lake in Kunming, China. Envisioned as a high quality mixed-use new waterfront district for the city, the program for the development includes retail, cultural amenities, entertainment facilities, and a diversity of residential units. The centerpiece of the development is historic Daguan Park, one of the most visited attractions in the city of 6 million because of it's beautiful views and access to the lakefront.

Upon the Sasaki team's first visit to the site, however, it became apparent that the depth of the problem went far beyond the typical urban design issues. A short boat trip intended to view the site from the water led to deeper questions related to the water quality of the lake.

Initial research during the site analysis phase led to the discovery that Dianchi is in fact one of the most polluted lakes in China, if not the world. This new information raised a serious question for Shui On: develop the site with the lake as a purely visual amenity, or focus on strategies to clean the lake and contribute to the overall quality of life in the city? For Shui On, the decision was clear. They had built their reputation with projects that did not simply seek an easy solution, but rather with projects that define a new standard in Asia.

The Caohai North Shore project, however, quickly became a lesson in long term city building and regional sustainability issues, with implications reaching far beyond the 538-hectare site. Based on Sasaki's recommendation, Shui On hired Smart & Associates of Cary, North Carolina to begin

CONTINUED ON PAGE 5

Newsletter 3 (bottom-left)

in this issue

WALKING WITH THOREAU — 1
NEWS BRIEFS — 2
TECH TALK — 2
BUILDING LESS, DOWNTOWN — 3
GREEN GROUP UPDATES — 4
UC SANTA BARBARA — 5
GREEN SPOTLIGHT — 7
CONSULTANT CORNER — 7
GREEN MONSTER — 6
SPECIES OF THE QUARTER — 6
CALENDAR — 8
RESOURCES — 8

THOREAU'S PATH ON BRISTER'S HILL

The forest walk invites visitors to explore the details of the landscape.

In the small, overlooked, natural object, he discovered the universal; in the ordinary he found the sacred, and praised it.

don't forget! GreenDay is on May 19th

WALKING WITH THOREAU

Thoreau's Path on Brister's Hill is located on land in Concord, Massachusetts acquired by the Walden Woods Project to stop suburban development. It is an 18.6 -acre parcel of land in the center of the 2,680 acre historic Walden Woods. The site conditions, altered by sand mining operation, provide a unique opportunity to interpret the succession of plants within a sand plain environment, the native ecosystem of Walden Woods.

The existing plant community ranges from early successional lichens and mosses, to a pioneer woodland dominated by White Birch and Pitch Pine, to a later stage Oak Hickory forest. The landscape design balanced the natural succession of native plants with restoration of areas extensively damaged by off-road vehicles. An ongoing program of landscape restoration and invasive plant removal was also instituted.

The interpretive exhibits are arranged along a simple loop path with granite and bronze elements featuring quotations that focus on Thoreau's thinking, observations and writing. The path is organized around five important contributions of Thoreau, each with a stopping point along the path:

Entry Meadow- as Conservationist
Brister's Orchard- as Social Reformer and Commentator
Sand Plain- as Teacher and Observer
Forest Succession- as Scientist
Reflection Circle-Thoreau's Philosophy, including its spiritual dimensions, and his influence on others.

To create an environment of discovery, visitors are encouraged to explore. Visitors are not led from place to place or provided detailed descriptions of what they are seeing. Instead, Thoreau's quotes, carved into stones and set into the earth, lead people through the site. Landscape features that are illustrative of Thoreau's observations

CONTINUED ON PG. 3

Newsletter 4 (bottom-right)

looking south across the courtyard of the proposed center expansion

IN THIS ISSUE

The University of Arizona Student Recreation Center Expansion 1
From the Editors 2
Residence Halls at the College of William and Mary earn LEED certification 4
Species of The Quarter 6
Green Monster 6
Dealing with Contradictions in Exurban Boston-Hopkinton, MA 7
News Briefs 8
Green Group Updates 9
Green Spotlight: Information Services 10
Consultants Corner 11
LEED lessons 11
Resources 12
Calendar 12

THE UNIVERSITY OF ARIZONA STUDENT RECREATION CENTER EXPANSION

In September of 2006, Sasaki was selected as the design architect for the University of Arizona's Student Recreation Center Expansion (teamed with MJ Engineering and Arup). This project represents the University's first project seeking LEED Certification. Our team's integrated approach to sustainable design was fundamental to our selection.

Before a single concept for the building had been tested, a series of project goals were articulated to frame future design decisions. These goals evoke sustainable principles:

- Develop a strong indoor & outdoor environment
- Capitalize on the use of daylight
- Utilize aesthetics to promote and foster fitness and health
- Integrate outdoor space (programmed and non programmed)
- Be responsible stewards of the student's money (this being a student fee funded project).

Furthermore, our desire to create a project that represents an authentic expression of the local Sonoran Desert continued to the project approach.

Initially, the expansion program contained a large Fitness Room, a Multi-Activity Court (MAC) Gymnasium, Multi-purpose Classrooms, a Climbing Wall, and space for the Outdoor Adventures program. However, as is typical in this construction market, budget concessions forced us to

continued on page 3

Top-left newsletter

SASAKI

WWW.SASAKIGREEN.COM

GreenNEWS

THE LATEST GREEN NEWS | PROJECTS | PRODUCTS

fall 2006

PERVIOUS PAVING OPTIONS STUDIED FOR THE PRESIDIO OF SAN FRANCISCO.

in this issue

PRESIDIO PERVIOUS PAVEMENT STUDY............1

NEWS BRIEFS................2

GREEN SPOTLIGHT...........2

LEED-NC AT THE PLANNING LEVEL................3

GREEN GROUP UPDATES.........4

PHOTOVOLTAICS AT UCSB....5

TECH TALK...............6

GREEN MONSTER............6

CONSULTANTS CORNER.....7

SPECIES OF THE QUARTER..7

CALENDAR................8

RESOURCES..............8

TURTLE HIGHLIGHT

Snapping turtles right in Sasaki's front yard. Learn more on page 7.

PRESIDIO PERVIOUS PAVEMENT STUDY

As one of the nation's youngest national parks, the Presidio of San Francisco, CA, provides a unique opportunity to renew the National Park traditions of conservation, stewardship, recreation, and scenic beauty with 21st century technology. The Presidio has a strong commitment to sustainable design and management outlined in the park's guiding document, the Presidio Trust Management Plan (2002, authored in part by Sasaki). One of it's goals is to decrease the quantity of impervious surfaces within the park through the use of pervious paving. Sasaki was asked to research the application of different types of pervious pavements in both pedestrian and parking areas.

The report is divided into three sections:

• Section 1 presents a general summary of urban hydrology and pervious pavement systems, and reviews the environmental and economic benefits of pervious pavements.

• Section 2 presents data sheets on nine types of pervious pavements (porous aggregate, soft porous surfaces, porous turf, plastic geocells, decking and boardwalks, open celled paving grids, open jointed paving blocks, porous concrete, and porous asphalt), comparing their properties and characteristics and identifying possible exclusions and appropriate vehicular and/or pedestrian applications.

• Section 3 addresses the specific application of the systems in the Presidio, given an area's use and underlying soil (which range in permeability from dune sands to intertidal clay deposits).

CONTINUED ON PAGE 2

1

Top-right newsletter

SASAKI

WWW.SASAKIGREEN.COM

GreenNEWS

THE LATEST GREEN NEWS | PROJECTS | PRODUCTS

spring 2007

southworks lakefront park

IN THIS ISSUE

Southworks: Reclaiming a Post-Industrial Landscape.....................1

News Briefs.....................2

Green Monster: LEED-EB.....................2

Monitor Group: Interiors Reflect Local Landscape.....................4

Tech Talk: TiO.....................4

A Classic Gets a Green Refurbishment.....................5

Species of the Quarter: The Yellow Warbler.....................5

Green Group Updates.....................6

From the Editors: Survey Results.....................7

Green Spotlight: Green Terrace Competition.....................7

Calendar.....................8

Resources.....................8

SOUTHWORKS:
Reclaiming a Post-Industrial Landscape

For more than a century, the 400-acre steel factory known as "Southworks" supplied the structural steel that helped build many of Chicago's landmark skyscrapers. Located along the shoreline of Lake Michigan on Chicago's Far South Side, Southworks operated as a small city itself, employing over 20,000 people at its peak, many of whom lived in the stable working class neighborhoods nearby. With the decline of the domestic steel industry, Southworks was downsized in the 1970s and 1980s and eventually closed by US Steel in 1992. A few years later, the plant and its infrastructure were demolished except for exterior three enormous "ore" walls and an adjacent barge slip stretching into

Lake Michigan, each over 2,200 feet in length.

In late 2004, Sasaki Associates, in collaboration with SOM, was hired by a private development consortium to prepare a mixed-use master plan for the site. The team created a plan for a vibrant new lakefront community, with mixed residential and commercial uses, a clear street network as an extension of the neighborhood grid, generous public spaces, and a new lakefront park. The master plan centers on ideas of connectivity: connecting the existing residential neighborhoods to the west that have long been cut off from the lakefront to the east by the Southworks site; and connecting existing parks to the north with those to the south through a new 100-acre lakefront park. When completed, the park will be one of

continued on page 3

Printed on 100% post consumer paper and manufactured with 100% non-polluting wind generated energy.

1

Bottom-left newsletter

SASAKI

GreenDay 2005

GreenNEWS

THE LATEST GREEN NEWS | PROJECTS | PRODUCTS

summer 2005

in this issue

A BROADER VIEW OF SUSTAINABILITY.....................1

NEWS BRIEFS.....................2

GREENDAY 2005 RECAP.....................2

SUSTAINABILITY-INFORMING THE DEBATE FROM LESSONS LEARNED.....................3

SASAKI GREEN SPOTLIGHT.....................3

SUSTAINABILITY STARTS WITH THE SOIL.....................4

EVOLVING A HEALTHY BUILDING AGENDA.....................4

WHY SUSTAINABILITY AND WHY NOW?.....................5

VENDOR FAIR.....................6

FROM THE EDITORS.....................6

GREEN MONSTER.....................7

GREEN GROUP UPDATES.....................7

CALENDAR.....................8

RESOURCES.....................8

A BROADER VIEW OF SUSTAINABILITY

Pliny Fisk·Center for Maximum Potential Building Systems (CMPBS)

Pliny Fisk develops and implements cutting-edge green architecture and sustainable development in Austin, TX at the Center for Maximum Potential Building Systems, an organization which he founded in 1975. Based on his enthusiasm, success and the relevance of his work to Sasaki, Mr. Fisk was chosen to deliver the opening plenary session for GreenDay 2005.

With broad content and deep understanding, Pliny Fisk blazed through an abridged, but energized discussion on innovative sustainable theories and practices. He discussed the unique concepts of carbon balancing, saltwater usability, innovative foundation technology, coal recycling and natural wastewater treatment processes. Many of these concepts

GREEN·ABOUT EVERYTHING!

Careful thought was given to all aspects of GreenDay 2005's planning, from food choices and packaging to transportation and signage, to ensure that the event was as environmentally sensitive as possible.

have been implemented either at the CMPBS facility in Austin or through his involvement in developments throughout the world.

Mr. Fisk's message was broad-reaching and presented to the participants a challenge: that we each ask ourselves, "What is my responsibility?" As we approach our work, Mr. Fisk suggests that we consider all the options and possibilities in our practice, and to reach beyond the status quo and pioneer new horizons in sustainability in our work.

JASON LOISELLE

1

Bottom-right newsletter

SASAKI

WWW.SASAKIGREEN.COM

GreenDAY 2007

GreenNEWS

THE LATEST GREEN NEWS | PROJECTS | PRODUCTS

summer 2007

looking at greenday from above

IN THIS ISSUE

Anderson Urges 'New Industrial Revolution'.....................1

From the Editors.....................2

Pre-GreenDAY Events.....................3

GreenDAY Workshops.....................4-8

News Briefs.....................10

Green Monster.....................10

Green Group Updates.....................11

Pre-GreenDAY Continues.....................11

Calendar.....................12

Resources.....................12

ANDERSON URGES 'NEW INDUSTRIAL REVOLUTION'

The regional drawl, the neat grey pinstripe, the courtly manner all suggest a dapper southern businessman in the traditional mold. And yet Ray Anderson is anything but traditional—he's a self-described "Radical Industrialist" who wants to reinvent the American corporation following a model of environmental sustainability. Delivering the keynote address to Sasaki's GreenDAY 2007 on May 23, Anderson combined a preacher's passion with a CEO's practicality and vision.

"We want to be the prototypical company of the 21st Century," leaders of a new Industrial Revolution modeled after nature," said Anderson, founder and CEO of Atlanta based Interface Inc., one of the world's largest carpet manufacturers.

For a man who heads a billion-dollar corporation, and who the day before had been profiled in the New York Times, Anderson was remarkably low-key and approachable. His warm demeanor clearly charmed his hosts at the event, which consisted of virtually every employee of Sasaki in Watertown, several Sasaki employees from San Francisco, and numerous clients and consultants.

Anderson dates his self-described conversion "from predator to protector" to 1994, when he was suddenly confronted by a group of designers and asked to express his company's environmental policy.

"I could not come up with anything except, 'We obey the law,'" Anderson recounted. He then stumbled upon Paul Hawken's book The Ecology of Commerce, and it changed his life. More than a

continued on page 2

1

I am inspired by the opportunity I have to recognize and protect the planet's natural resources.

Mark Reaves
Eco-Technologies

The waterfront environments in which we work continually amaze me. They offer rich and inherent opportunities for sustainable design; and they can have a lasting impact on cities and the people to whom they ultimately belong.

Gina Ford
Landscape Architecture

At Sasaki, we have the opportunity to research and apply ecological and sustainable ideas at every scale and in every discipline, working across cultures and places around the world.

Dennis Pieprz
Urban Design

To me, the idea of sustainability gets exciting when we think about the "big picture," going beyond picking the right product to looking at a group's culture, identity, work ethic, and values. That can inform our best building and environmental solutions and create something that will endure and is truly sustainable.

Victor Vizgaitis
Architecture/Interior Design

As urban planners, we are instrumental at the very early stage of the process. The challenges while practicing green design go beyond the workplace and really confront the way we live and think about our planet's resources.

Nishant Lall
Urban Design

On my second day at Sasaki, I spent an hour picking through the company's trash with rubber gloves. An interesting introduction to sustainability! I'm constantly applying what I've learned here to make up for lost time.

Gretchen Mendoza
Graphic Design

I fold sustainability into my children's daily education. They know we should walk more, drive less, use paper bags instead of plastic. My younger daughter doesn't want to take yogurt to daycare anymore because they don't recycle!

Dou Zhang
Landscape Architecture

We share a personal value in greening our practice, and in so doing, elevating the conversation with our clients, consultants, and peers.

Vitas Viskanta
Architecture

I'm proud of becoming the first LEED® accredited professional in Sasaki's San Francisco office, as well as working on three LEED® projects (Sasaki's own space in San Francisco, UC Merced, and UCSB SRB). I'm inspired by the idea that sustainable design is good design, and by working in an environment that feels healthy.

Evan Jacob
Architecture

The exciting thing about practicing sustainability is that it brings everyone to the same table. There's a great energy about it.

Beth Foster
Planning

Children can teach you a lot about the small wonders of the natural world—everything is new to them.

Peter Hedlund
Landscape Architecture

Within our urban planning discipline, every line we draw has a sustainable impact, especially when considering most of our sites are greater than 100 hectares. Design has been an incubator of sustainable theories. However, a project needs creative and strategic action by its users to truly become a sustainable project.

Riki Nishimura
Urban Design

My perspective on sustainability starts with the environment, specifically with puzzling through how to develop land that hosts sensitive ecosystems or is contaminated. Brownfield development is, of course, critical to the other two components of sustainability—social and economic.

Willa Kuh
Planning

Good design today requires an awareness that extends beyond our individual design disciplines. A holistic approach to design encompasses not just the environmental impact of the places we create, but the social, economic, and emotional qualities as well. Successful interior spaces cannot exist as isolated events, but must be direct extensions of the outside world.

Christine Dunn
Interior Design

Working internationally, it is critical that we address issues of resource availability and sustainability at all levels. Our projects in Asia and the Middle East, in particular, present unique challenges and compel us to create innovative and sustainable systems related to water, energy, and infrastructure. As urban planners and designers working in the global arena, it is our responsibility to guide our clients toward equitable and thoughtful solutions that will support a healthy planet.

Mitch Glass
Landscape Architecture/Planning

Visionary sustainable design means having the courage to break old habits and the will and creativity to re-think ways of doing things.

Anna Monnelly
Architecture

Sustainability is not simply defined by specifying green materials and processes; it is a comprehensive approach to context, addressing both cultural and environmental issues in subtle and enhanced ways. As urban designers, we must constantly confront these issues as part of our work.

Sejal Agrawal
Urban Design

Designing university recreational facilities is approaching sustainability from a wide perspective—students increasingly want to see architecture that is "healthy" for the planet—and thus aligned with their own increasingly health-conscious lifestyles. For an institution to invest in sustainable design is a clear message that it supports students and shares their values.

David Dymecki
Architecture

I like the challenge of trying to convince developers to go green. I argue there are cost savings over time, and it can help position the project advantageously in the marketplace.

Alan Ward
Landscape Architecture/Urban Design

Basic sustainable practices have become green mantras, but the challenge is constantly to do it better. I am fortunate that many of my clients share similar sustainable goals, thus providing opportunities to maximize the potential of our projects. I am also professionally invigorated by the challenge of persuading clients to explore, expand, and implement these goals.

Joanna Fong
Landscape Architecture

I am wondering about how to do more with less. Every day I ask myself: How can I lead a life and inspire the people I work with and for, to embrace a future that involves less stuff and more time? Less quantity and more quality?

Janne Corneil
Urban Design

Every member of the team—the architects, consultants, clients—must be committed to the idea of sustainability if a building project is to succeed environmentally. As architects, we must demystify the notion of sustainability as a design commodity and work with our clients to realize that sustainable design is simply good, logical design. The basic ideas that underpin sustainable architecture have been around for centuries.

Pablo Savid-Buteler
Architecture

In Asia, I am constantly exposed to the most damaged environments on the planet. But I see a real commitment by many of our clients there to be leaders in sustainable design. Their great passion and genuine interest inspires me to continue to seek solutions that can repair the ecological problems they, and we, face.

Michael Grove
Landscape Architecture/Planning

Growing up in England after World War II was a daily exercise in sustainability; everything was reused and scarcity made us frugal.

Philip Parsons
Strategic Planning

My proudest accomplishment has been working on a civic and statewide scale to make Massachusetts the greenest state in the union.

Marcus Springer
Architecture

We are at a pivotal moment when we must make a major cultural shift toward sustainability. Colleges and universities have historically been at the forefront of such moments. We design buildings and campuses that can have profound impacts on the ways students view their relationship to the natural world. They then go out into the world demanding higher standards of the places in which they live and work.

Meredith Elbaum
Director of Sustainable Design

In the big picture, I'm concerned about the world my kids—and their kids—will live in. I also feel that sustainability is a great lens through which to view and pull different disciplines—beyond just Sasaki—into the planning and design process.

Peter Brigham
Planning

In my home community, Waltham, MA, I help administer the Massachusetts Wetlands Protection Act. Learning how these systems work is both inspiring and humbling. We engineers and designers can learn a great deal from Mother Nature's portfolio of work.

Bill Doyle
Eco-Technologies

Sustainability isn't just designing green buildings. Investing in urban and regional transit systems furthers social sustainability, providing mobility to existing residents as well as making it possible for new generations to live in dense and vibrant urban centers. A $100 million public investment can yield a billion-dollars-plus in construction and other private investment in our cities.

Jason Hellendrung
Landscape Architecture

Every opportunity we have to shape the built environment is an opportunity to remind people which way the wind blows, where the sun rises and how the world works. The future is a place where we remember what we have forgotten: We are just a part of the whole.

Nick Brooks
Architecture

I've been involved with promoting and developing the concepts of sustainability over the past fifteen years, especially in water usage, stormwater management, and other crucial practices—water is elemental. It relates to everything we do on this planet.

Steve Benz
Eco-Technologies

There's such a demand for green knowledge by young people especially. One of my proudest accomplishments is creating an interior design class at the Boston Architectural College entitled "Thinking Green."

Terry Harris
Interior Design

sasaki
strategies

Sasaki Strategies has generated a new mindset within Sasaki, and its work has influenced much of the planning illustrated in this volume. The group works as a think tank experimenting with alternative approaches to planning and focusing on ways to integrate the multiple skills, perspectives, and concerns that contribute to effective planning and design. Sasaki Strategies challenges traditional methodologies through new decision support systems, and by bringing new skills to the table, such as economic analysis and educational planning, integrating problem solving that might previously have been left to a subconsultant, or ignored. With Sasaki Strategies, the social, economic, and environmental aspects of projects are examined in interplay with each other, supporting a comprehensive vision of sustainability.

At its most ambitious, Sasaki
how the work of planning is u

While Sasaki Strategies represents a new and important focus for planning at Sasaki, it is very much an interpretation of Hideo Sasaki's conviction in founding the firm that successful planning and design depend on the seamless integration of multiple disciplines.

Sasaki Strategies relies on the power of new technologies to take that integration to a new level, and is driven by the mantra that design is more than design.

Just as new software has revolutionized what is possible in design, and has released an explosion of new talent, technology has encouraged Sasaki to explore new approaches to planning, and in turn those new approaches have sparked the need for new technological tools. Sasaki Strategies has been developing those tools and has become a leader in the design of analytical tools and visualization techniques. At its most ambitious, Sasaki Strategies aims to reinvent how the work of planning is undertaken. There are multiple components to this effort, and visualization is often central.

Perhaps the most significant component is the blending of program, design, and finance. Traditionally, these elements are tackled separately and sequentially; first the program mix is determined, then a design is developed, then financial analysis is completed. The tools used for each of these stages are distinct, and the tasks demand a different mindset, and a different set of talents. In an ideal world, each of these elements is shaped by the other two, and they proceed concurrently and iteratively. The planner may have specialized skills, but his or her work is fully informed by an easy understanding of the other elements that will shape the success of the project.

Strategies aims to reinvent
ndertaken.

Sasaki has spent several years developing unique tools to support this approach. One result is SmartPlan, a tool where a site design is actively linked to a spreadsheet, and changes in program—such as housing type, or mix of uses—are immediately linked to, for example, calculation of parking demand, carbon footprint, fiscal impact, or return on investment. A 3-D model driven by these considerations can instantly be generated, and the design can then be modified based on a review of the model. Design changes are then immediately reflected in calculations of program, fiscal analysis, and so forth. Changes can be made at the last minute and can generate an illustrative plan or a PowerPoint show. This not only encourages a team approach, engaging Sasaki's client more fully in the planning process, but also takes much of the drudgery out of planning, leaving more time for creative and innovative approaches.

Another component is Sasaki Strategies' focus on scenario planning, allowing for more complex financial analysis than is usually possible in a planning exercise, and revealing sensitivities that shape capital investment and operating budgets for clients, making possible the implementation of master plans that might otherwise have sat on a shelf. Dynamic graphic visualization of alternative financial trajectories quickly opens up new possibilities.

A third component is the development of custom visualization tools to communicate the intersecting components of complex decisions. Better communication tools lead to better decisions and help clients understand the relationships between competing forces.

The tools and approach developed by Sasaki Strategies are influenced by MIT's Michael Schrage, and his book *Serious Play*. They illustrate an approach to problem-solving that is free of boundaries, experimental, non-linear, and iterative. Sasaki's plans incorporate this vision of how planning should be undertaken.

2008

**Sasaki Associates, 77 Geary Street Offices;
San Francisco, California**
Merit Award, Best Sustainable Commercial/Industrial
Project, Gold Nugget Awards Program

**University of California, Riverside, Glen Mor Housing;
Riverside, California**
Merit Award, Best Apartment Project Four or More
Stories, Gold Nugget Awards Program

**United States Military Academy Arvin Cadet Physical
Development Center; West Point, New York**
Honor Award, Chief of Engineers Design and Environ-
mental Awards Program, U.S. Army Corps of Engineers

Continuum; Newton, Massachusetts
Award for Design, Boston Society of Architects

**Fort Ticonderoga Garrison Grounds Master Plan;
Ticonderoga, New York**
Honor Award for Landscape Analysis and Planning,
Boston Society of Landscape Architects

798 Arts District Plan; Beijing, China
Merit Award for Planning and Analysis, Boston Society
of Landscape Architects

**Erie Canalway National Heritage Corridor Preservation
and Management Plan; Syracuse, New York**
Daniel Burnham Award for a Comprehensive Plan,
American Planning Association

**University of California Santa Barbara Student
Resource Building; Santa Barbara, California**
Merit Award, International Interior Design Association
Northern California Chapter

Merit Award, Best Specialty Project, Gold Nugget
Awards Program

2007

Sasaki Associates
Firm Award, American Society of Landscape Architects

Charleston Waterfront Park; Charleston, South Carolina
Landmark Award, American Society of Landscape
Architects

**University of Pennsylvania Vision Plan; Philadelphia,
Pennsylvania**
Honor Award, Analysis and Planning, American Society
of Landscape Architects

Merit Award, Landscape Analysis and Planning, Boston
Society of Landscape Architects

Honor Award for Planning on an Established Campus,
Society of College and University Planning and the
American Institute of Architects' Committee on
Architecture for Education

Innovista Master Plan; Columbia, South Carolina
Honor Award, Landscape Analysis and Planning,
Boston Society of Landscape Architects

Charter Award, Congress for the New Urbanism

Mixed-Use Design Commendation, International
Making Cities Livable Organization

University of Balamand Master Plan; Tripoli, Lebanon
Honor Award, Analysis and Planning, American Society of
Landscape Architects

**University of California Santa Barbara Student
Resource Building; Santa Barbara, California**
Merit Award, American Institute of Architects Orange
County Chapter

Southworks; Chicago, Illinois
Sustainable Design Award, American Institute of
Architects Chicago Chapter

**College of William and Mary Jamestown Residence
Halls; Williamsburg, Virginia**
Design Achievement for Architecture, American
Institute of Architects Hampton Roads, Virginia Chapter

**Trinity College Koeppel Community Sports Center;
Hartford, Connecticut**
Citation, Boston Society of Architects Higher
Educational Facilities Awards

**Walden Woods, Brister's Hill and Thoreau's Path;
Concord, Massachusetts**
Merit Award, Communications, Boston Society of
Landscape Architects

**Port of Los Angeles, Wilmington Waterfront
Development; Los Angeles, California**
Citation, Excellence in Urban Design, American Insti-
tute of Architects San Francisco Chapter

Honor Award, American Society of Landscape Architects Northern California Chapter

**Utah State University, Manon Caine Russell and
Kathryn Caine Wanlass Performance Hall; Logan, Utah**
Citation, Excellence in Architecture, American Institute
of Architects San Francisco Chapter

Merit Award, American Institute of Architects New
England Regional Council

Coconut Grove Waterfront; Coconut Grove, Florida
Orchid Award, The Urban Environment League

**Cleveland State University Recreation Center;
Cleveland, Ohio**
Award of Excellence, New Construction, Cleveland
Engineering Society

Continuum; Newton, Massachusetts
Large Renovation of the Year Award, CoreNet Global
New England Chapter

**Harvard University Hemenway Gymnasium Renovation;
Cambridge, Massachusetts**
Outstanding Indoor Sports Facility, National
Intramural-Recreational Sports Association

**University of California Santa Barbara Student Recre-
ation Center Expansion; Santa Barbara, California**
Facility of Merit Award, *Athletic Business* Magazine

2006

Caohai North Shore Master Plan; Kunming PRC
Design Excellence Award for Master Planning,
Shui On Land Limited

Channel Center; Boston, Massachusetts
Citation for Adaptive Reuse and New Construction,
American Institute of Architects Boston and New York
Chapters Housing Design Awards

**Sasaki Associates; Watertown, Massachusetts and
San Francisco, California**
"Top Twenty Architectural Firms to Work for in the United
States", ZweigWhite

**Oklahoma City Federal Building; Oklahoma City,
Oklahoma**
Ross Barney + Jankowski Architects; Sasaki Associates,
Landscape Architects

Citation Award for Excellence in Federal Design,
U.S. General Services Administration/Public
Buildings Service

**Morgan State University Student Center;
Baltimore, Maryland**
Citation Award for Excellence in Design, American
Institute of Architects Maryland Chapter

**San Diego Historic Waterfront Plan; San Diego,
California**
Orchid for Urban Design Awards, San Diego
Architectural Foundation Orchids & Onions Awards

**University of California, Davis Segundo Commons;
Davis, California**
Merit Award, Best Public/Special Use Facility,
Gold Nugget Awards Program

Merit Award, Best Specialty Project, Gold Nugget
Awards Program

Best New Concept, *Food Management* Magazine Awards

Facility Design Project of the Month, *Food Management*
Magazine Awards

**Yosemite National Park, Design and Construction
of Yosemite Lodge, Expansion of Camp 4, & Relocation of
Northside Drive; Yosemite, California**
First Prize, Central Section of the California Chapter
American Planning Association Awards

**Harvard University Hemenway Gymnasium;
Cambridge, Massachusetts**
Facility of Merit Award, *Athletic Business* Magazine

**Sasaki Associates, 77 Geary Street Offices;
San Francisco, California**
"Design Is ..." Award, Shaw Contract Group

**Sasaki Associates; Watertown, Massachusetts and
San Francisco, California**
"Best Workplaces for Commuters", Environmental
Protection Agency

**Utah State University, Manon Caine Russell and
Kathryn Caine Wanlass Performance Hall; Logan, Utah**
Honor Award, American Institute of Architects
Utah Chapter

Erie Canalway National Heritage Corridor
Preservation and Management Plan; New York
Outstanding Planning Project, Comprehensive
Planning for a Regionally Based Plan, American
Planning Association New York Upstate Chapter

Ohio State University Medical Center and College of
Health Sciences Master Plan; Columbus, Ohio
Merit Award for Urban Design and Planning, American
Institute of Architects Ohio Chapter

University of South Carolina Innovista Master Plan;
Columbia, South Carolina
Honor Award for Excellence in Campus Planning,
Boston Society of Architects/Society for College and
University Planning Campus Planning Awards

University of Pennsylvania Vision Plan; Philadelphia,
Pennsylvania
Honor Award for Excellence in Campus Planning,
Boston Society of Architects/Society for College and
University Planning Campus Planning Awards

University of California, Berkeley Landscape
Heritage Plan; Berkeley, California
Citation for Excellence in Campus Planning, Boston
Society of Architects/Society for College and University
Planning Campus Planning Awards

The Presidio Trust Management Plan;
San Francisco, California
Award of Excellence, Urban Land Institute

Sasaki Associates: 50
Award of Excellence, Special Events Piece, Society for
Marketing Professional Services San Francisco Bay Area
Chapter, Founder's Awards

Best of Show, Society for Marketing Professional Services
San Francisco Bay Area Chapter, Founder's Awards

Caohai North Shore Conceptual Master Plan;
Kunming, Yunnan, China
BusinessWeek/Architectural Record China Awards
Planning Category

2008 Beijing Olympics, Olympic Green; Beijing, China
BusinessWeek/Architectural Record China Awards
Green Projects Category

Honor Award, Boston Society of Landscape Architects

Indianapolis Riverfront; Indianapolis, Indiana
Award of Excellence, Boston Society of Landscape
Architects

Providence 2020 Vision Plan; Providence, Rhode Island
Excellence Award, American Society of Landscape
Architects

Merit Award, Boston Society of Landscape Architects

Charter Award, Congress for the New Urbanism

Au Bon Pain; Pembroke, Massachusetts
Superior Achievement in Design and Imaging,
Fast Casual Category, Retail Traffic Magazine

Merit Award, the Center for Design and Business,
ReBrand 100

601 Congress Street Green Roof; Boston, Massachusetts
Green Roof Award of Excellence, Intensive Commercial
Category, Green Roofs for Healthy Cities

2005

Renaissance Plaza; White Plains, New York
First Place, Main Street Award Competition,
New York Conference of Mayors

Addison Circle Park; Addison, Texas
Honor Award, Boston Society of Landscape Architects

University of North Texas, Dallas Master Plan;
Dallas, Texas
Excellence in Planning Award, Society of College and
University Planning and the American Institute of
Architects' Committee on Architecture for Education

California State Polytechnic University, Pomona
Residential Suites, Pomona, California
Merit Award in Apartment-Rental Category,
Builder's Choice Design and Planning Awards

Merit Award, American Institute of Architects Orange
County Chapter

Merit Award, Gold Nugget Awards Program,
Best Mid-Rise Apartment Project (4 to 6 stories)

Merit Award for Campus Housing, Residential Architect

University of Nevada, Reno Comprehensive Campus
Master Plan; Reno, Nevada
Campus Master Planning Citation, American School &
University's Architectural Awards

University of California, Berkeley Landscape Heritage
Plan; Berkeley, California
Merit Award, American Society of Landscape Architects
Northern California Chapter

University of California, Berkeley Landscape Heritage
Plan Website; Berkeley, California
People's Voice, Webby Award

University of California, Santa Barbara Recreation
Center Expansion; Santa Barbara, California
Public Institutional Category, Goleta Valley Beautiful
Award

Cabot Corporation; Boston, Massachusetts
The Center for Design and Business – ReBrand 100

Los Angeles Southwest College Facilities Master
Plan; Los Angeles
Merit Award, Category of Master Planning, Community
College Facility Coalition Design Awards

2004

Sasaki Associates Company Website
Best in Show, Society for Marketing Professional
Services San Francisco Chapter

Best Website, Society for Marketing Professional
Services San Francisco Chapter

Texas A&M University Master Plan;
College Station, Texas
Campus Planning Award, Boston Society of Architects/
Society for College and University Planning Campus
Planning Awards

San Francisco State University, The Village at
Centennial Square; San Francisco, California
Merit Award for Campus Housing, Residential Architect

Chambers Creek Master Site Plan; Tacoma, Washington
with Arai/Jackson Architects and Planners and
Berger/Abam Engineers Inc.

Current Topic Award: Parks and Public Lands

American Planning Association, National Planning
Awards

The Presidio Trust Management Plan;
San Francisco, California
Outstanding Planning Award For Implementation,
American Planning Association, National Planning
Awards

University of Balamand Master Plan; Tripoli, Lebanon
Campus Planning Award, Boston Society of Architects/
Society for College and University Planning Campus
Planning Awards

Fitcorp at 600 Technology Square; Cambridge,
Massachusetts
Recreation Management's Innovative Architecture and
Design Award

Southwood; Tallahassee, Florida
Merit Award, Planning Category, Boston Society of
Landscape Architects

2003

Detroit Riverfront Civic Center Promenade;
Detroit, Michigan
In association with Albert Kahn Associates

Honor Award in Urban Design, American Institute of
Architects Detroit Chapter

The Pinehills; Plymouth, Massachusetts
Gold Award, Best Innovative Land Planning Design,
Builders Association of Greater Boston

Gold Award for Best Master Planned Community in the
United States, National Association of Home Builders

Aphrodite Hills Resort; Paphos, Cyprus
Award for Best New Integrated Leisure Resort in
Europe, INVGolf European GOLF Investment and Real
Estate Conference

San Francisco State University, Village at Centennial
Square; San Francisco, California
Excellence in Design Award, American Institute
of Architects San Francisco Chapter, Best of the
Bay Awards

University of California, Berkeley New Century Plan;
Berkeley, California
Urban Design Award, American Institute of Architects
San Francisco Chapter, Best of the Bay Awards

Central Indianapolis Waterfront; Indianapolis, Indiana
Merit Award in Landscape Architecture, Monumental
Affair Awards

Central Indianapolis Riverfront - Upper Canal;
Indianapolis, Indiana
Excellence on the Waterfront Honor Award,
The Waterfront Center

Massachusetts Institute of Technology,
Al and Barrie Zesiger Sports and Fitness Center;
Cambridge, Massachusetts
Facility of Merit, *Athletic Business*

Wheeling Heritage Port; Wheeling, West Virginia
Honor Award for Waterfront Design, Boston Society
of Landscape Architects

Excellence on the Waterfront Honor Award,
The Waterfront Center

Route 87 Visual Design Study - Taylor Street Bridge/
Urban Interchange; San Jose, California
Award of Excellence, Portland Cement Association

Sweet Briar College Master Plan; Sweet Briar, Virginia
Merit Award for Planning, Boston Society of
Landscape Architects

Bethlehem Southside District; Bethlehem, Pennsylvania
Merit Award for Planning, Boston Society of
Landscape Architects

Schuylkill Gateway; Philadelphia, Pennsylvania
Institute Honor Award for Regional and Urban Design,
American Institute of Architects

South Fork Lodge; Swan Valley, Idaho
Project of the Year, National Association of Home Builders

Honorary Mention, Responsible Development Awards,
Mountain Living Magazine

Grand Award, Best Public/Private Specialty Use
Facility, Annual Gold Nugget Awards, Pacific Coast
Builders Conference

The Presidio Trust Management Plan;
San Francisco, California
First Place Award, Planning Implementation –
Large Jurisdiction, American Planning Association
California Chapter

Outstanding Planning Document, The Association
of Environmental Planners

Merit Award for Planning and Analysis, American
Society of Landscape Architects

Gold and Silver Awards, Showcase of Print Excellence,
Printing Industry of Northern California

Award for Comprehensive Planning, Large Jurisdiction,
Northern Section American Planning Association

Presidents National Environmental Excellence Award,
National Association of Environmental Professionals

Honor Award, California Association of Environmental
Professionals

2002

Loyola College in Maryland Fitness and Aquatic Center;
Baltimore, Maryland
Outstanding Indoor Sports Facility, National
Intramural-Recreational Sports Association

Merrimack College Sakowich Campus Center;
N. Andover, Massachusetts
Excellence in Construction Award, Associated Builders
and Contractors

Indianapolis Capital City Landing; Indianapolis, Indiana
Community Choice Award, Monumental Affair Awards

The Pinehills; Plymouth, Massachusetts
Grand Award, Builders' Choice Awards

Rice University Jamali Plaza; Houston, Texas
Brick Paving Design Award, Brick Industry Association

University of Scranton Mulberry Street Housing;
Scranton, Pennsylvania
Merit Award, Boston Society of Architects Housing Awards

Oregon State University Valley Library; Corvallis, Oregon
with SRG Partnership

Honorable Mention - Excellence in Masonry,
Rehab/Restoration

Mason Contractors Association of America Awards in
the International Excellence in Masonry Awards

University of South Florida Master Plan; Tampa,
Florida
Excellence in Planning Award, Society of College and
University Planning and the American Institute of
Architects' Committee on Architecture for Education

University of Scranton Master Plan; Scranton,
Pennsylvania
Excellence in Planning Award, Society of College and
University Planning and the American Institute of
Architects' Committee on Architecture for Education

2001

Loyola College in Maryland Fitness and Aquatic Center;
Baltimore, Maryland
Facility of Merit, *Athletic Business*

Oklahoma City National Memorial; Oklahoma City,
Oklahoma
Honor Award for Architecture, Boston Society
of Architects

Merrimack College Sakowich Campus Center;
N. Andover, Massachusetts
Honor Award for Architecture, Boston Society
of Architects

Narragansett Landing; Narragansett, Rhode Island
Excellence on the Waterfront Honor Award, The
Waterfront Center

San Francisco State University, The Village at
Centennial Square; San Francisco, California
Award of Merit; American Institute of Architects
Orange County Chapter

Grand Award—Best Apartment Project (Five stories
or more), Merit Award—Best Infill, Redevelopment and
Rehab Project, 2001 PCBC Gold Nugget Awards

University of California, Santa Barbara Recreation
Center; Santa Barbara, California
National Intramural-Recreational Sports Association
Outstanding Sports Facility

St. Olaf College Buntrock Commons; Northfield,
Minnesota
Excellence in Architecture, American Institute of
Architects New England Regional Council

University System of Georgia Master Plan Template;
Atlanta, Georgia
Excellence in Planning Award, Society of College and
University Planning and the American Institute of
Architects' Committee on Architecture for Education

Loyola College Fitness and Aquatic Center;
Baltimore, Maryland
Award of Excellence, Associated Builders and
Contractors, Inc.

Guangzhou Pearl River Urban Design Plan;
Guandong, China
Citation for Sustainable Planning, Boston Society of
Architects Sustainable Design Awards

Oklahoma City National Memorial; Oklahoma City,
Oklahoma
Honor Award for Memorial Design, Boston Society of
Landscape Architects

Merit Award, American Society of Landscape Architects

2000

California State University, Monterey Bay Master Plan;
Seaside, California
Merit Award, American Society of Landscape Architects

University of Colorado at Boulder, Humanities Building
and Woodbury Hall; Boulder, Colorado
Award for Highest Achievement in Design Excellence,
American Institute of Architects Denver Chapter

DART Transitway; Dallas, Texas
Merit Award, American Society of Landscape Architects

Southwood; Tallahassee, Florida
Merit Award, American Society of Landscape Architects

Central Indianapolis Riverfront Development;
Indianapolis, Indiana
Outstanding Concrete Achievement Award,
Indiana Ready Mixed Concrete Association

Alaska Native Heritage Center, Anchorage, Alaska
Merit Award for Excellence in Architecture,
American Institute of Architects Alaska Chapter

Project Credits

Utah State Performance Hall
Logan, Utah

Client: Utah State University

Completion Date: 2006

Consultants:

Gould Evans Associates – Associate Architect
Spectrum Engineers – Mechanical Engineer
Artec Consultants – Acoustical Consultant
Reaveley Engineering – Structural Engineer
Cache Landmark Engineering – Civil Engineer
Horton Lees Brogden Lighting Design – Lighting
Jacobsen Construction – Contractor

Photographer: Robert Benson

NTNU Strategy Plan
Trondheim, Norway

Client: Norwegian Institute of Science and Technology

Completion date: 2006

Monitor
New York, New York

Client: Monitor

Completion date: 2008

Consultants:

R.G. Vanderweil Engineers, Inc. – Mechanical/Electrical/Plumbing Engineer
Simpson Gumpertz & Heger Inc. – Structural Engineer
LAM Partners, Inc. – Lighting Design
Schimer Engineering Corporation – Code Consultant
Turner Interiors – Contractor

Photographer: Robert Benson

Monitor
San Francisco, California

Client: Monitor

Completion date: 2006

Consultants:

Glumac International – Mechanical/Electrical Engineer
BCCI – Contractor

Photographer: Robert Benson

University of Balamand
Tripoli, Lebanon

Client: University of Balamand

Completion Date: 2004 (master plan); Implementation is ongoing.

Potomac School Master Plan and Landscape
McLean, Virginia

Client: Potomac School

Completion date: 2007

Consultants:
JFW, Inc. – Project Manager
Cox Graae + Spack Architects (CGS) – Architect
VIKA – Civil Engineer
Coakley & Williams Construction – General Contractor

Photographer: Craig Kuhner

Wildcat Activity Center
Chico, California

Client: California State University

Completion Date: 2009

Consultants:

Flack + Kurtz – Mechanical/Electrical/Plumbing/Technology Engineer
Rutherford & Chekene – Structural Engineer
Sandis – Civil Engineer
Entre Prises – Climbing Wall Design
JF Otto – Contractor
Hughes Associates, Inc. – Code Consultant
Aquatic Design Group – Pool Design
TopFlight Specs – Specifications Writer
TRC Companies, Inc. – Environmental Engineer
Wallace Kuhl – Soils Engineer

Illustrator: Art Zendarski

Cal Poly Residential Suites Phase I
Pomona, California

Client: California State Polytechnic University, Pomona

Completion date: 2004

Consultants:

C & B Consulting Engineers – Mechanical Engineer
KPFF Consulting Engineers – Structural Engineer
Huitt-Zollars Inc. – Civil Engineer
Davis Langdon – Cost Estimator
Infrastructure Design Associates – Technology Consultant
Charles M. Salter Associates – Acoustical Consultant
John McCaffrey, AIA, CCS – Specifications
Edge Development – Contractor

Photographers: Greg Hursley, David Wakely

Henry C. Lee Institute of Forensic Science
West Haven, Connecticut

Client: University of New Haven

Completion date: 2010

Consultants:

R. G. Vanderweil Engineers, Inc. – Mechanical/Electrical/Plumbing Engineer
Foley Buhl and Roberts – Structural Engineer
Haley & Aldrich, Inc. – Geotechnical Engineer
Design Island Associates, Inc. – Exhibit Designer
ACT Associates, Inc. – Audio Visual Consultant
Cavanaugh Tocci Associates, Inc. – Acoustical Consultant
LAM Partners, Inc. – Lighting Design

Mark Kalin – Specifications
Petra Construction Corporation – Construction Manager

Sacred Heart University
Fairfield, Connecticut

Client: Sacred Heart University

Completion date: 2002 (master plan); 2009 (chapel); 2013 (humanities building and library)

Consultants:

Chapel

Cosentini Associates – Mechanical/Electrical/Plumbing Engineer
LeMessurier Consultants – Structural Engineer
Acoustic Dimensions – Acoustical Engineer
Horton Lees Brogden Lighting Design – Lighting Consultant
Schirmer Engineering Corporation – Code Consultant
Potente Studios – Liturgical Consultant
Centro Aletti, Father Marko I. Rupnik – Liturgical Artist
Casavant Fréres – Organ Builder
Chime Masters – Bell Maker
Petra Construction Corporation – Construction Manager
Rose -Tiso – Surveying
Richard White – Specifications

Humanities Building and Library

Cosentini Associates, Inc. – Mechanical/Electrical/Plumbing Engineer
LeMessurier Consultants – Structural Engineer
Schimer Engineering Corporation – Code Consultant
Rose -Tiso – Surveying

The Commons
Baltimore, Maryland

Client: Morgan State University

Completion Date: 2007 (student center); 2008 (library)

Consultants:

Student Center

Cochran, Stephenson & Donkervoet – Associate Architect
Henry Adams, Inc. – Mechanical Engineer
Allen & Schariff Corp. – Electrical Engineer
ReStl Designers Inc. – Structural Engineer
A. Morton Thomas and Associates, Inc. – Civil Engineer
Froehlin & Robertson, Inc. – Environmental
Birchfield Jacobs Foodsystems – Food Service
Hess Construction Company – Contractor

Photographer: Robert Benson

Library

Design Collective, Inc. – Executive Architect
Henry Adams, Inc. – Mechanical/Electrical Engineer
KES Engineering – Plumbing Engineer
Hope Furrer Associates – Structural Engineer
Froehlin & Robertson, Inc. – Geotechnical Engineer
Site Resources – Civil Engineer
Hanscomb – Cost Estimator

Jay Lucker – Library Programmer

FON Architects – Associate Architect

Hess Construction Company – Contractor

Photographer: Robert Benson

Model Builder: GPI Models

Miller Nichols Library and Interactive Learning Center
Kansas City, Missouri

Client: University of Missouri, Kansas City

Completion Date: 2008

Consultants:

Peckham Guyton Albers & Viets – Architect of Record

BGR Consulting Engineers, Inc. – Mechanical/Electrical Engineer

SK Design Group, Inc. – Civil Engineer

Walter P. Moore – Structural Engineer

J.E. Dunn Construction – Preconstruction Services

Segundo Commons
Davis, California

Client: University of California, Davis

Completion Date: 2005

Consultants:

GLUMAC International – Mechanical/Electrical Engineer

Rutherford & Chekene – Structural Engineer

Cunningham Engineers – Civil Engineer

Hanscomb Associates – Cost Estimator

Webb Design – Food Service Consultant

Dennis J Amoroso – Contractor

Howard S. Wright – Contractor

Tree Associates – Arborist

Decker Landscaping, Inc. – Landscape Contractor

Photographers: Tim Rue, David Wakely, Greg Hursley

West Campus Lands
Calgary, Canada

Client: University of Calgary

Completion Date: 2007

Consultants:

Kasian Architecture, Interior Design, and Planning Ltd. – Local Architect

Morrison Hershfield, Ltd. – Transportation Planner

U3 Ventures – Develoment Advisor

GWL Realty Advisors – Market Research

Illustrator: Anderson Illustration Associates

Photographer: Ewan Nicholson

St. Edward's University Landscape
Austin, Texas

Client: St. Edward's University

Completion Date: 2003 – Ongoing

Consultants

RVi – Local Landscape Architect

Baker - Aicklen and Associates Inc. – Local Civil Engineer

Photographer: Craig Kuhner

Glen Mor Student Apartments
Riverside, California

Client: University of California Riverside

Completion Date: 2007

Consultants:

Khalifeh & Associates – Mechanical Engineer

Gausman & Moore – Electrical Engineer

Ricca Newmark – Food Service Consultant

KPFF Consulting Engineers – Civil Engineer

Saiful/Bourquet – Structural Engineer

Davis Langdon – Cost Estimator

George Tiedemann – Specifications

Rosen, Goldbert & Der – Acoustical Consultant

Sweeney & Associates – Irrigation

Guise & Associates – Sports Turf Consultant

E-Structure – Structural Peer Review

ProWest Constructors – Contractor

Photographer: Tim Griffith

Graduate School of Management
Davis, California

Client: University of California, Davis

Completion Date: 2009

Consultants:

Timmons Design Engineers – Mechanical/Electrical/Plumbing Engineer

Intech Mechanical – Mechanical Contractor

Royal Electric – Electrical Contractor

Rutherford & Chekene – Structural Engineer

Sandis – Civil Engineer

Sundt Construction – Contractor and Cost Estimator

3-D Renderer: Digital Imaging Studio

Grumbacher Sports and Fitness Center
York, Pennsylvania

Client: York College of Pennsylvania

Completion Date: 2006

Consultants:

Cosentini Associates, Inc. – Mechanical/Electrical/Plumbing/Fire Protection Engineer

LeMessurier Consultants – Structural Engineer

Steven R. McHugh – Specifications

D. Schweppe Lighting Design – Lighting Consultant

Schirmer Engineering – Building Code and Life-Safety Consultant

Cavanaugh Tocci Associates, Inc. – Acoustical and Sound System Consultant

Kinsley Construction – General Contractor

Photographers: Robert Benson, Bob Lenz

Stony Brook Recreation Center
Stony Brook, New York

Client: Stony Brook University

Completion Date: 2010

Consultants:

Highland Associates – Mechanical/Electrical/Fire Protection/Structural Engineer

Hirani Engineering and Land Surveying – Civil/Geotechnical Engineer and Survey

FD+CC – Cost Estimator

Steven R. McHugh – Specifications

Arizona Student Recreation Center Expansion
Tucson, Arizona

Client: University of Arizona

Completion Date: 2009

Consultants:

M3 – Architect/Mechanical/Electrical/Structural/Civil Engineer

ARUP – Sustainability/Mechanical Engineer

Wheat Scharf Associates – Landscape Architect

Compusult – Cost Estimator

Sundt Construction – Construction Manager

UC Santa Barbara Recreation Center Expansion
Santa Barbara, California

Client: University of California, Santa Barbara

Completion Date: 2005

Consultants:

Glumac International – Mechanical/Electrical/Fire Engineer

Rutherford & Chekene – Structural/Civil Engineer

George Tiedemann – Specifications

Hanscomb Faithful Gould – Cost Estimator

Entre Prises – Climbing Wall Design

Viola Constructors Inc. – Contractor

Photographers: Misha Bruk, Patrick Carney, Robert Benson

Valparaiso Student Union
Valparaiso, Indiana

Client: Valparaiso University

Completion Date: 2008

Consultants:

Design Organization Inc. – Architect of Record

KJWW – Mechanical/Electrical/Plumbing/Structural Engineer

Bonar – Civil Engineer

Ricca Newmark – Food Service Consultant

M.A. Mortenson – Contractor

Purdue West Lafayette Master Plan
West Lafayette, Indiana

Client: Purdue University

Completion Date: 2008

Consultants:

Scholer Corporation – Architect

Residence and Student Life on Rose Hill Campus
Bronx, New York

Client: Fordham University

Completion Date: 2009

Consultants:

Cosentini Associates, Inc. – Mechanical/Electrical/
Plumbing Engineer

LeMessurier Consultants – Structural Engineer

Leonard H. Strandberg and Associates – Civil Engineer

Horton Lees Brogden Lighting Design – Lighting

Mueser Rutledge Consulting Engineers – Geotechnical
Engineer

Badey & Watson Surveying & Engineering P.C. –
Surveyor

Schirmer Engineering – Code Consultant

Luthin Associates Inc. – Energy Management Consultant

Gotham Construction Company LLC – Construction Manager

Joseph Edward Gallo Recreation and Wellness Center
Merced, California

Client: University of California, Merced

Completion Date: 2006

Consultants:

Taylor Engineering – Mechanical/Plumbing Engineer

KPFF Consulting Engineers – Structural Engineer

The Engineering Enterprise – Electrical Engineer

Sandis – Civil Engineer

Davis Langdon – Cost Estimator

George Tiedemann – Specifications

Howard S. Wright – Contractor

Photographer: Tim Griffith

The American University in Cairo

Photographer: Dave Desroches

Illustrator: Michael McCann

Cleveland State University Recreation Center

Photographer: Robert Benson

Hemenway Gymnasium

Photographer: Robert Benson

Walden Woods Project

Photographer: Robert Benson

Regenerative Cities

Charleston Waterfront Park
Charleston, South Carolina

Client: City of Charleston

Completion date: 1990

Consultants:

Holladay, Coleman & Associates – Electrical Engineer

LAW Engineering and Environmental Services, Inc. –
Structural Engineer

Edward Pinckney Associates, Inc. – Local Landscape
Architect

Ruscon Construction Company, Inc. – Contractor

Photographers: Craig Kuhner, Landslides

Penn Connects: A Vision for the Future
Philadelphia, Pennsylvania

Client: University of Pennsylvania

Completion Date: 2006

Illustrators: Michael McCann, Archpartners

Dallas Area Rapid Transitway
Dallas, Texas

Client: Dallas Area Rapid Transit Authority

Completion Date: 1996

Consultants:

Campos Engineers – Electrical Engineer

Berryhill-Loyd – Structural Engineer

Arrendondo & Brunz; Huitt-Zollars, Inc. – Civil
Engineer

Branston – Lighting Design

HJM – Architecture

Ogelsby – Architecture

Goldberg – Artist

Photographers: Craig Kuhner, Greg Hursley

Charlotte Light Rail Transit
Charlotte, North Carolina

Client: Charlotte Area Transit System

Completion date: 2007

Consultants:

Parsons Transportation Group – Prime Consultant

King Guinn – Structural Engineer

ARUP – Structural Engineer

McCracken & Lopez – Mechanical/Electrical/
Plumbing Engineer

D. Schweppe Lighting Design, Inc. – Lighting

STV Ralph Whitehead – Construction Manager

Archer-Western – Contractor

798 Arts District Vision Plan
Beijing, China

Client: Urbis Development

Completion Date: 2006

Illustrator: Frank Li

Drexel Recreation Center
Philadelphia, Pennsylvania

Client: Drexel University

Completion date: 2009

Consultants:

EwingCole – Mechanical/Electrical/Plumbing/Fire
Protection Engineer and Cost Estimator

Pennoni Associates – Civil/Geotechnical Engineer

RJC Designs, Inc. – Audio-Visual Consultant

Cavanaugh Tocci Associates, Inc. – Acoustical Consultant

Turner Construction Company – Construction Manager

East Baltimore Neighborhood Plan
Baltimore, Maryland

Client: East Baltimore Development, Inc.

Completion date: 2007

Consultants:

ArchPlan Philipsen – Local Architect and Urban
Planner

Planning and Design Research Group – Local Planner
and Infrastructure

Real Estate Strategies – Market Analyst

RK&K – Transportation Engineer

Detroit Civic Center Riverfront Promenade
Detroit, Michigan

Client: City of Detroit

Completion date: 2001

Consultants:

Albert Kahn Collaborative – Architect of Record

NTH Consultants, Ltd. – Geotechnical Engineer

Tucker Young Jackson Tull, Inc. – Civil/Structural/
Electrical Engineer

Photographer: Christopher Lark

The Wilmington Waterfront
Los Angeles, California

Client: Port of Los Angeles

Completion Date: 2007 (Master Plan); 2009 (Harry
Bridges Buffer Area); 2013 (Waterfront Park)

Consultants:

ah'be landscape architects – Local Landscape Architect

Arup – Bridge Engineer

Brookwater – Irrigation Consultant

Davis Langdon – Cost Consulting

Earth Mechanics, Inc. – Geotechnical Engineer

Economic & Planning Systems, Inc. – Market Analysis

Edgett Williams Consulting Group – Elevator Consultant

Fine Arts Services, Inc. – Public Art Consultant

Historic Resources Group – Historic Resources Assess-
ment

Horton Lees Brogden – Lighting Design Lighting/
Electrical Consultant

Hughes Associates – Code Consultant

Kaku Associates, Inc. – Transportation/Traffic Planner

Katherine Padilla & Associates – Public Outreach

Moffatt + Nichol – Civil Engineer, Marine Engineer, Cost
Estimator

Rico Associates – Specifications

Rutherford & Chekene – Structural Engineer

Stephen Glassman – Artist

STO Design Group – Water Feature Design

Tech/Knowledge, Inc. – Security

IMAD Taylor & Gaines – Structural, Mechanical/Electrical/Plumbing Engineer

Wagner Engineering & Surveying Inc. – Tentative Tract Map/Surveying

Auraria Higher Education Center Campus Plan
Denver, Colorado

Client: Auraria Higher Education Center

Completion date: 2007

Consultants:
studioINSIGHT – Prime Consultant/Landscape Architect
U3 Ventures – Public-Private Partnerships

Illustrator: Anderson Illustration Associates

Central Indianapolis Waterfront
Indianapolis, Indiana

Client: U.S. Army Corps of Engineers, in association with the City of Indianapolis and the White River State Park Board

Completion Date: 1997

Consultants:
The Design Consortium – Landscape Architect
RATIO Architects – Landscape Architect and Irrigation
Ann Beha Architects – Historic Preservation
CSO Architects and Engineers – Mechanical/Electrical Engineer
FRP – Structural Engineer and Cost Estimator
ATEC Associates, Inc. – Geotechnical/Hydrology/Wetlands
Fink Roberts & Petrie, Inc. – Civil Engineer
Pflum, Klausmeier & Gehrum – Transportation
RUST Environmental & Infrastructure – Environmental Consultant
MSE Engineering – Survey
Wallace Roberts & Todd – Construction Documents
Wilhelm – Contractor
Paul I. Cripe – Construction Phase Services
RQAW Engineering – Construction Phase Services
Dann Pecar Newman & Kleiman – Attorney

Photographers: Craig Kuhner, Landslides, Jim Barnett

Loyola Intercollegiate Athletic Complex

Baltimore, Maryland

Client: Loyola College in Maryland

Completion Date: 2009

Consultants:
Gipe Associates, Inc. – Mechanical/Electrical/Plumbing Engineer
Hope Furrer Associates, Inc. – Structural Engineer
Steven R. McHugh – Specifications
Diversified Engineering, Inc. – Site Mechanical/Electrical/Plumbing Engineer

VPC Incorporated – Video Production Consultant

RCI Sound Systems – Audio-Visual Consultant

Koffel Associates, Inc. – Code Consultant

The Whiting-Turner Contractors – Construction Manager

Providence 2020

Providence, Rhode Island

Client: City of Providence, RI

Completion Date: 2006

Consultants:
Barbara Sokoloff Associates, Inc. – Local Planner
Vanasse Hangen Brustlin – Transportation Consultant
ZHA, Inc. – Economic/Market Research

Illustrator: Michael McCann

Savannah East Riverfront Public Spaces
Savannah, Georgia

Client: Savannah East Riverfront Landing LLC

Completion date: 2010

601 Congress Street Roof Garden
Boston, Massachusetts

Client: Financial services company

Completion Date: 2004

Consultants:
Skidmore, Owings & Merrill, L.L.P. – Project Architect
ValleyCrest Landscape Development – Landscape Contractor

Photographers: ValleyCrest Landscape Development

Harbor Point
Stamford, Connecticut

Client: Antares Real Estate

Completion Date: Phase 1 – 2009

Consultants:
Cooper, Robertson & Partners – Co-Master Planner
Perkins Eastman – Architect
EDI Architecture – Architect
DeSimone Consulting Engineers – Structural Engineer
Milone & MacBroom, Inc. – Civil Engineer
Langan Engineers – Geotechnical Engineer
Loureiro Engineering Associates – Environmental Engineer
EarthTech – Traffic Engineer

Cincinnati Riverfront Park

Cincinnati, Ohio

Client: Cincinnati Park Board

Completion Date: 2010

Consultants:
KZF Design, Inc. – Architect
Kolar Design – Graphic Design

BHE Environmental, Inc. – Environmental Consultant

Hargreaves Associates – Landscape Architect

Megen Construction Company – Contractor

Southworks
Chicago, Illinois

Client: Southworks Development, LLC

Completion Date: ongoing

Consultants:
Skidmore, Owings & Merrill, LLC – Co-Master Planner and Architect
Antunovich Associates – Retail Planning and Architect
Spaceco Inc. – Civil Engineer
Conestoga-Rovers – Environmental
STS Consultants – Foundations and Geotechnical
Bell, Boyd & Lloyd – Environmental Attorney
KLOA – Traffic
Kenny Construction – Contractor and Costing
O'Neil Construction – Contractor and Costing
Christopher B. Burke Engineering, LTD. – Civil Engineer
Shaw Environmental & Infrastructure, Inc. – Sustainability (prior to 2006)

City of Baton Rouge Wayfinding

Photographer: Ed Wonsek

Charleston Maritime Center

Photographer: Greg Hursley

Cleveland Gateway

Photographer: Roger Mastroianni

Dorchester Shores Beach Restoration

Photographer: Landslides

Schenley Plaza

Photographer: Craig Kuhner

Wheeling Heritage Port

Photographer: Jim Barnett

New Social Realities

2008 Beijing Olympic Green
Beijing, China

Client: Beijing Municipal Planning Commission

Completion Date: 2002

Tsinghua Planning Institute – Associate Planner and Landscape Architect for the landscape design competition.

Illustrators: Michael McCann, Crystal Imaging

Addison Circle Park
Addison, Texas

Client: Town of Addison

Completion Date: 2004

Consultants:
JFD Group – Construction Manager
Georgia Fountain Company, Inc. – Fountain Design
Irritech Corporation – Irrigation Design
Campos Engineering, Inc. – Mechanical/Electrical/
Plumbing Engineer
Cunningham Architects – Pavilion Architect

Photographers: Craig Kuhner, Paul Chaplo

Agilent Technologies
Beijing China

Client: Agilent Technologies

Completion Date: 2006

Consultants:
Environetics Design Group – Interior Design

Photographer: Zhong Bao Sun/Abao Sunbox Studio

Innovista Master Plan
Columbia, South Carolina

Client: The University of South Carolina, Guignard
Associates, LLC., The River Alliance, The City of
Columbia, South Carolina

Completion Date: 2008

Consultants
Economic Research Associates – Market Research
Analyst
Dr. Donald L. Schunk, Moore School of Business,
University of South Carolina – Research Economist
Hunter Morrison & Associates – Planning Consultant

Illustrator: Dalin Janpathompong

RPI Stadium and Athletic Events Center
Troy, New York

Client: Rensselaer Polytechnic Institute

Completion Date: 2009

Consultants:
Cosentini Associates, Inc. – Mechanical Engineer
LeMessurier Consultants – Structural Engineer
One Lux Studio – Lighting
Acentech – Acoustical / AV Consultant
ARUP – Code Consultant
Steve McHugh – Specifications
Think Energy – Energy Conservation
Faithful & Gould – Cost Consultant
Whiting-Turner Contracting – Construction Manager

Illustrator: Archpartners

Thu Thiem New Urban District
Ho Chi Minh City, Vietnam

Client: City of Ho Chi Minh City and Thu Thiem
Investment and Construction Authority

Completion Date: 2005

Consultants:
Urban Planning Institute of Ho Chi Minh City (UPI) –
Local Liaison

Model Builder: Bohai

Koeppel Community Sports Center
Hartford, Connecticut

Client: Trinity College

Completion Date: 2006

Consultants:
PHCatalyst – Project Manager
Cosentini Associates, Inc. – Mechanical/HVAC/
Plumbing Engineer
Foley, Buhl & Roberts – Structural Engineer
Cavanaugh Tocci Associates, Inc. – Acoustical Engineer
Haley & Aldrich – Geotechnical Engineer
URS Corporation – Survey
D. Schweppe Lighting Design, Inc. – Lighting
Standard Builders – Cost Estimator
Steven R. McHugh – Specifications
MacLaughlin Management Group – Ice Consultant
O&G – Construction Manager

Photographer: Robert Benson

Caohai North Shore, Daguan Park Regeneration
Kunming, China

Client: Shui On Development Ltd.

Completion Date: 2005

Illustrator: Dalin Janpathompong

Lashihai Conceptual Master Plan
Lijiang, China

Client: Shui On Land, Ltd.

Completion Date: 2007

Illustrators: Dalin Janpathompong, Dongik Lee

The Village at Centennial Square
San Francisco, California

Client: San Francisco State University

Completion Date: 2001

Consultants:
C & B Consulting Engineers – Mechanical/Electrical
Engineer
Rolf Jensen & Associates, Inc. – Fire Protection Engineer
KPFF Consulting Engineers – Structural Engineer
Olivia Chen Consultants Inc. – Civil Engineer
Infrastructure Design Associates – Technology
Consultant
Avinante & Associates – Color Consultant
Davis Langdon – Cost Estimator

Photographers: Reid Yalom, Pat Carney, Greg Hursley

Philips Solid-State Lighting Solutions
Burlington, Massachusetts

Client: Philips Solid-State Lighting Solutions

Completion Date: 2008

Consultants:
Focus Lighting, New York, NY – Lighting Consultant
R.G. Vanderweil Engineers – Mechanical/Electrical
Engineer
J. Calnan & Associates – Contractor

Photographer: Robert Benson

Grand Resort Lagonissi
Lagonissi, Greece

Client: Helios Hotels

Completion Date: Phase 1 – 2004; Conference
Center Final Phase – 2009

Consultants:
Grammatopoulos – Panousakis Architects, Ltd. –
Local Architect
MKV Design – Interior Design
Suzy Baz – Kitchen/Food Consultant
Eltaek S.A. – Construction Manager

Lulu Island Vision Plan
Abu Dhabi, United Arab Emirates

Client: Royal International and Sorouh

Completion Date: 2007

Illustrator: Crystal Imaging, Archpartners

Model Builder: Bohai

Continuum
Newton, Massachusetts

Client: Continuum

Completion Date: 2006

Consultants:
LeMessurier Consultants – Structural Engineer
Commodore Builders – Contractor

Photographer: Robert Benson

Hongxing Oceanfront Community
Dalian, China

Client: Dalian Tsanghao Group

Completion Date: 2007

Illustrator: Frank Li

Sasaki Associates Offices
Watertown, Massachusetts and San Francisco, California

Client: Sasaki Associates, Inc.

Completion Date: 2008 (Watertown); 2005 (San Francisco)

Consultants:

Watertown
Wozny/Barbar & Assoc, Inc. – Mechanical/Electrical/
Fire Protection Engineer

Richmond So Engineers, Inc. – Structural Engineer

Office Environments – Technology Consultant

J. Calnan & Associates, Inc. – General Contractor

Studio F.KIA – Custom Steel Stair and Reception Desk
Design and Fabrication

San Francisco

Stantec – Mechanical/Electrical Engineer

Crociani Construction Company – Contractor

Photographer: Robert Benson (San Francisco)

Student Resource Building
Santa Barbara, California

Client: University of California, Santa Barbara

Completion Date: 2007

Consultants:

ARUP – Mechanical/Electrical/Structural/
Technology Engineer

Penfield & Smith – Civil Engineer

Horton Lees Brogden Lighting – Lighting

Davis Langdon – Cost Estimator

George Tiedemann – Specifications

Rogers Quinn – Contractor

Photographers: Robert Benson, Greg Hursley

Doosan 100 Year Park
Photographer: Seung Hoon Yum

Hangzhou Creative Community

Illustrator: Dalin Janpathompong

Mangrove Tree Resort

Photographer: Mangrove Tree/Philip Yu

QinHuangdao

Illustrator: Dalin Janpathompong

Biogen Idec Inc. Dining

Photographer: Robert Benson

TJX Family Memorial Garden

Photographer: Richard Mandelkorn

Jing'an Art Park

Model builder: Bohai

Shanghai Culture Park

Illustrator: Michael McCann

Magic Beans

Photographer: Robert Benson

This book was printed and bound using a variety of sustainable manufacturing processes and materials including the following: soy-based inks, water-based varnish, VOC- and formaldehyde-free glues, and phthalate-free laminations.

The paper used in this book was manufactured by M-Real Biberest and is chlorine-free. M-Real is committed to integrating environmental-management practices into its entire range of business activities, including sustainable forestry practices and the development and promotion of reliable systems for forest certification.

Sasaki Associates and ORO *editions* have made every effort to minimize the overall carbon footprint of this project. As part of this goal, Sasaki Associates and ORO *editions*, in association with Global ReLeaf, have arranged to plant two trees for each and every tree used in the manufacturing of the paper produced for this book. Global ReLeaf is an international campaign run by American Forests, the nation's oldest nonprofit conservation organization. Global ReLeaf is American Forests' education and action program that helps individuals, organizations, agencies, and corporations improve the local and global environment by planting and caring for trees.

Many Sasaki employees—too many to list individually—contributed material and assistance for this monograph project. Within the firm, the specific monograph team included Dennis Pieprz, Tracy Finlayson, James McCown, Matt McKouen, Dana Ragouzeous, Philip Parsons, Terri Gray-Pearce, and Meredith Elbaum.

ORO *editions*

Publishers of Architecture, Art, and Design

Gordon Goff – Publisher

USA West Coast: PO Box 150338, San Rafael, CA 94915
USA East Coast: 33 Hudson Street - Suite 1006, New York, NY 10013
Asia: Block 8, Lorong Bakar Batu #02–04, Singapore 348743

www.oroeditions.com
info@oroeditions.com

Copyright © 2009 by ORO *editions*
ISBN: 978-0-9793801-5-0

Art Direction: Oscar Riera Ojeda and Matt Kanaracus

Design: Matt Kanaracus and Karen LeDuc, Codesign, Oscar Riera Ojeda and Andres Rodriguez Ruiz, ORO *editions*

Project Coordination: Jill Tabler, Kate Anderson, Cindy Poulos, Fanny Settesoldi

Copy Edits: Nirmala Nataraj, Jill Tabler

Rights, Foreign Editions, and Distribution: Gordon Goff

Production: Andres Rodriguez, Oscar Riera Ojeda, and Gordon Goff

Color Separation and Printing: ORO *editions* Pte Ltd and United Graphic Singapore

Covers: Book is bound in Silky Saifu Cloth from World Cloth Japan with multi color foil stamping

End Paper Sheets: IKPP Woodfree 140 gsm

Text Paper: Biberest Furioso 150 gsm matte coated art paper printed 6 colors with soy inks

Printed in China by ORO Group

Distribution

In North America:
Distributed Art Publishers, Inc.
155 Sixth Avenue, Second Floor
New York, NY 10013
USA

In UK and Europe:
John Rule Sales & Marketing
40 Voltaire Road
London, SW4 6DH
United Kingdom

In Asia:
Page One Publishing Private Ltd.
20 Kaki Bukit View
Kaki Bukit Techpark II, 415967
Singapore